The Growing Edge of Gestalt Therapy

Edited by

EDWARD W. L. SMITH, Ph.D.

Associate Professor of Psychology
Associate Director, Laboratory for Psychological Services
Georgia State University

The Citadel Press   Secaucus, N. J.

First paperbound printing, 1977
Copyright© 1976 by Edward W.L. Smith, Ph.D.
All rights reserved
Published by Citadel Press
A division of Lyle Stuart Inc.
120 Enterprise Ave., Secaucus, N.J. 07094
In Canada: George J. McLeod Limited, Toronto
Published by arrangement with Brunner/Mazel Inc., New York
Manufactured in the United States of America
ISBN 0-8065-0606-7

THE GROWING EDGE OF
GESTALT THERAPY

To

LYNDA, DELILAH,

and

HOPALONG CASSIDY

Preface

Gestalt therapists would rather "do it" than "write about it." This has been continued to be the case since the advent of Gestalt therapy, and understandably so. To be involved in the Gestalt therapy process is to experience powerful contact and excitement, meaningful withdrawal and quiet —the very stuff of aliveness.

One result of this action orientation of Gestalt therapists has been a relative neglect of the creation of a complete literature. Until quite recently, this literature was very limited. I believe the recent increase in theoretical writing is extremely important in providing a systematic and coherent record of the thinking of practicing Gestalt therapists.

The Growing Edge of Gestalt Therapy is my contribution to this increasing literature. In this book I have tried to expand our understanding of the historical and theoretical foundations of Gestalt therapy and to make explicit the contributions of other systems or techniques to its continued evolution. I have picked those systems and techniques which I believe are most influential in pushing Gestalt therapy to its "growing edge." The authors whom I have chosen to present their views of these points on the growing edge are all experienced practitioners in the facilitation of human development. I am pleased to have found these therapists and teachers who valued putting their thoughts, views, and experiences into written form.

The idea for *The Growing Edge of Gestalt Therapy* came out of a series of discussions with Dr. James E. Dublin. Jim and I, having been in graduate school together and having interned together, were introduced to Gestalt therapy at about the same time, early in 1970. Both Jim and I had been heavily influenced by the existential phenomenology of Drs. Erwin Straus, Erling Eng, and Dick Griffith during our traineeship at the Lexington, Kentucky, Veterans Administration Hospital and by the therapy position of Dr. Hellmuth Kaiser, which we had picked up second hand during our arduous graduate school days at the University of Kentucky. With this background we had a "readiness" for Gestalt therapy, reflected in our immediate resonating with its tone and our exclamations of "of course!" By 1973 we were noticing the expansion and refinements of Gestalt therapy, as its representatives were influenced by other therapy positions—and so our idea, an edited book on the "growing edge" of the evolving position of Gestalt therapy. Shortly after our initial design of the book and our choosing of potential authors, Jim decided to focus his energies elsewhere, and I inherited the project.

My wish is that this book will stimulate, or pique its readers into further exploration of the Gestalt approach.

EDWARD W. L. SMITH

Atlanta, Georgia
December, 1975

Acknowledgments

Dr. James E. Dublin, I thank you for inspiring me, supporting me, and helping me to plan this book. If we had not started it together, I doubt that I would have undertaken it. Our association for these eleven years has meant a tremendous amount to me.

To all of the book's contributors, thank you. You are, collectively, the substance of the book.

Jeff Zeig, thank you for all of the details which you handled for me —indexes, proofreading, and so forth—while my graduate assistant.

To all of my colleagues at Georgia State University who have encouraged my efforts on the book, thank you.

A special thank you to my partners in private practice, Drs. Earl Brown, Jackie Damgaard, Joen Fagan, Bernhard Kempler, Ann McKain, David Rouzer, Irma Lee Shepherd and George Taylor. You have all been constant in your support and encouragement. And Joen, your help with the logistics of publishing was very important—thank you.

Thanks, too to the following publishers for their permission to quote materials: Barnes & Noble, Inc.; *The Counseling Psychologist;* Doubleday & Company, Inc.; E. P. Dutton & Co., Inc.; George Allen and Unwin, Ltd.; Hutchinson Publishing Group Ltd.; Alfred A. Knopf, Inc.; Oxford University Press; Random House, Inc.; Real People Press; Routledge & Kegan Paul Ltd.; Science and Behavior Books, Inc.; and John Weatherhill, Inc.

And finally, Lynda, thank you for being you. You stay you even as we shift and turn. I have learned much about stability from you.

Contents

Preface—Edward W. L. Smith vii

Acknowledgments ix

Introduction—Miriam Polster xiii

PART I
HISTORICAL BACKGROUND ... 1

1. The Roots of Gestalt Therapy—*Edward W L. Smith* 3

PART II
FURTHER EXPLICATIONS OF GESTALT THERAPY ... 37

2. Gestalt Therapy as an Open-Ended System
   —*Irma Lee Shepherd* 39
3. A Schema of the Gestalt Concept of the Organismic Flow and
   Its Disturbance—*Robert A. Hall* 53
4. The Gestalt Approach as "Right Lobe" Therapy—*Joen Fagan* 58

5. The Trickster-Healer—*Sheldon B. Kopp* 69
6. Great Diagnosticians Call for Great Patients—*Denis O'Donovan* 83

PART III
GESTALT THERAPY AND JUNGIAN PSYCHOLOGY ... 85

7. Analytical Psychology and Gestalt Therapy
   —*Edward C. Whitmont* and *Yoram Kaufmann* 87
8. Jung and Perls: Analytical Psychology and Gestalt
   —*Donald D. Lathrop* 103

PART IV

GESTALT THERAPY INTEGRATED WITH OTHER
TECHNIQUES AND SYSTEMS ... 109

9. Combining Hypnosis with Gestalt Therapy—*Abraham Levitsky*   111
10. Gestalt Therapy, Existential-Gestalt Therapy and/versus
    "Perls-ism"—*James E. Dublin* 124
11. The Gestalt Thematic Approach—*Bruce Derman* 151
12. Gestalt Therapy and the Core Conditions of Communication
    Facilitation: A Synergistic Approach
    —*Charlton S. Stanley* and *Philip G. Cooker* 160

PART V

GESTALT THERAPY AND EASTERN PHILOSOPHY ... 179

13. Gestalt Therapy, Tantric Buddhism and the Way of Zen
    —*George B. Greaves* 181
14. Gestalt Psychotherapy, Zen Buddhism and Transcendental
    Meditation—*James A. Stallone* 202
15. Taoism and Gestalt Therapy—*Charles Gagarin* 212

PART VI

A SUMMING UP ... 219

16. Comments on the New Directions—*Laura Perls* 221

Biographical Sketches of the Contributors 227

Index 235

Introduction

MIRIAM POLSTER, Ph.D.

As is the case with many compelling teachers and innovators, their own personal style is so powerful that it colors their theoretical statements and determines (or so it seems) the style of those who choose to follow their teachings. This has been the case, surely, with Fritz Perls. His manner so permeated what he said and did as a Gestalt therapist that it left many people spellbound and convinced that there was only one way to be a Gestalt therapist. But Fritz was aware that each person, patient as well as therapist, has his or her own wisdom. It was fresh firsthand knowing that Fritz valued above all hand-me-down insights from someone else, however expert. Often in his demonstrations, when someone would ask him how to resolve a troublesome concern, Fritz would respond by telling him to "put Fritz in the chair and ask him," and then, "Now, sit in Fritz's chair and answer."

This book is a worthwhile continuation of that theme. The contributors are men and women who understand and value their own growing edge. They explore their own professional boundaries and extend themselves beyond, into new influences, new relationships. So each of them presents his or her experience, and the collection of their writings becomes a mosaic of approaches and integrations, a multifaceted reflection of learnings from other disciplines animating and enriching their views of Gestalt therapy.

Throughout the various sections of the book there is a consistent effort to support technique with the perspective of what has gone before. Mere juggling through a therapeutic bag of tricks is put aside in favor of a more subtle view of the informed therapist reacting spontaneously but with a spontaneity which takes its sustenance from a deeper affirmation of basic principle and method.

This book is divided into six sections. The first part, Historical Background, presents some of the influences which inclined Perls in the directions so familiar to many of us. It is a carefully presented panorama which attends to the mentors Perls had from whom he drew the threads he wove into his own formulations. In addition, there are the events, the coincidences of time and geography that he lived through. Edward Smith gives us a balanced picture of the exciting thinking to which Perls was exposed and the skillful synthesis of his distillations from those teachings which is the hallmark of his peculiar genius.

Irma Lee Shepherd expresses well the importance of relating to what exists outside oneself. She distinguishes between the complete independence from environmental support that some felt Perls implied and a sensitive and differentiated way of relating—"separate, not independent, but separate and different." Another essential observation she makes cannot be remembered too often: Edicts—those distortions that have sprung up around the slavish use of Gestalt technique—are not therapy.

Part II also provides the viewpoint of several contemporary practitioners and their innovations and lively speculations about how Gestalt therapy fits in with some of the current developments in psychotherapeutic thought. Joen Fagan muses articulately about right and left brain lobe functioning and the role Gestalt therapy may play in plumbing some of the inchoate wisdom of the sub-dominant (surely an arbitrarily pejorative term in the light of new discoveries) lobe.

Sheldon Kopp's fine sense of the paradox it is to be a therapist enriches our picture of the magic-healer, charlatan, savior, that must somewhere underlie most of our efforts to relate to another human being in a healing way. His is a touchingly revealing first person account of what it is to be a therapist and how he goes about keeping himself honest in his engagements with others.

Robert Hall adumbrates a model of organismic movement through the awareness cycle. And Denis O'Donovan gives us a ruefully humorous anecdote about a young psych intern and an old guru.

Part III fleshes out the Gestalt view with insights from the Jungian tradition. There is first of all, as Whitmont and Kaufmann remind us, the debt that all existential schools owe to Jung for his affirmation of the creative and constructive side of the unconscious. They also make some illuminating comments on the place of ritual in our lives. Lathrop suggests how Gestalt therapy profits also from Jung's recognition of the importance of the intuitive, perhaps less verbal, elements in human nature.

Part IV explores new possibilities and fresh applications of Gestalt therapy combined with other approaches. Levitsky gives us a carefully detailed account of how he uses hypnosis in conjunction with Gestalt therapy. Dublin presents soundly reasoned, critical observations on the evolution of Perls' position and points out, with gothic clarity, the distinctions which can be made between Gestalt therapy, existential-Gestalt therapy and Perlsian therapy. He expresses the dilemma of the existential therapist who, in the very act of using his craft to assist someone he is working with, may be vulnerable to the accusation of reducing the patient to "it" status instead of the existential "thou." He suggests that this is done, however, in the service of restoring to the patient those parts of himself that he in turn has reduced to "it" status, a provocative argument. Derman describes how a group can be used to amplify a particular theme, resonating to it until it reaches full expression and, hopefully, a movement into closure. Stanley and Cooker unite Rogerian research into the core elements of communication, with Gestalt method as a way of clarifying what goes on in good contact. They also suggest a stimulating application of Gestalt principles as used in the supervision of trainees.

Part V articulates some of the links between Gestalt therapy and the Eastern philosophical tradition. This section is distinguished, however, by its insistence on pointing out the present relevance of certain trends which are first stated in these ancient traditions and which continue to parallel important trends in Gestalt thinking. Greaves makes some comparisons between the Gestalt acceptance of paradox and the Zen koan. Stallone and Gagarin augment this relationship by drawing points of likeness between other forms of Eastern discipline such as transcendental meditation and Taoism.

Finally, in Part VI, Laura Perls elucidates what are for her the essential elements in Gestalt therapy. She reapplies a basic concept, that of support, by observing that the therapist, too, can support what she has to offer in relationship with the patient by calling on everything that she has in the rich background of her experience: music, poetry, story-telling, parables, movement, literature, all to be integrated into enhancing the movement of the patient, with support, into otherwise disowned parts of himself.

This is a rich and varied book, to be read a section at a time. It serves as both a reminder of and a challenge to the diversity and richness that good, pungent Gestalt therapy can have. It reminds us that rather than striving to be Perls we must do what we encourage those who work with us to do—to be all of *ourselves* we can and to live and work at our own growing edge.

MIRIAM POLSTER, PH.D.
Co-Director, Gestalt Training Center
(San Diego, Cal.)

Part I
HISTORICAL BACKGROUND

This section is devoted to an in-depth look at the roots of Gestalt therapy, the several major sources which influenced Perls in the creation of his approach. In addition to showing what elements Perls drew from each of these sources, this historical review places Gestalt therapy in a historical-theoretical perspective, indicating its relationship to other positions and developments in psychiatry and academic psychology. Since these sources have not previously been studied in a detailed manner, many students of Gestalt therapy have been unaware of the traditions in psychiatry and academic psychology to which Gestalt therapy belongs. This section is designed to reduce that imbalance.

1

The Roots of Gestalt Therapy

EDWARD W. L. SMITH, Ph.D.

"Gestalt" is a German word for which there is no adequate English translation. It sort of means whole, configuration, integration, a unique patterning. The technical use of the word in psychology dates back to 1890, to an issue of debate over the nature of perceptual functioning which resulted in a major schism within academic psychology. Today, this same untranslated word is identified with one of the most powerful psychotherapy systems yet to evolve.

No one can make valid claim to extensive knowledge of psychotherapy without being familiar with Gestalt therapy and the contributions of Fritz Perls. Gestalt therapy has grown in its influence to the extent that the *Directory* of the American Academy of Psychotherapists lists it as the sixth most common affiliation. Beyond that, Gestalt therapy has influenced countless therapists who do not claim it as their primary affiliation, but who nonetheless incorporate Gestalt techniques or philosophy into their work. In developing Gestalt therapy, Perls drew upon several diverse traditions, and gleaned from them those elements which he could empirically validate in his living. To understand the position as it is today and the direction it seems to be taking requires a careful training in its past, in those several streams which flowed together through the person of Perls.

Perls' genius was demonstrated not in his combining of elements from several traditions into a unique eclecticism but, rather, in his creation of a new system which in its essence goes far beyond the constituent elements. Gestalt therapy is, in a very real sense, a Gestalt.

It appears that Perls was primarily influenced by five traditions: Psychoanalysis, Reichian Character Analysis, Existential Philosophy, Gestalt

Psychology, and Eastern Religion. In addition to these positions, Perls mentions a number of writers who, at least for a time, held his attention. Among the philosophers that Perls acknowledged are Friedlander, whom Perls saw as one of his gurus, Hegel, Husserl, Kant, Marx, and Vaihinger. Perls spoke of three literary figures with fondness—Huxley, Hesse, and Mark Twain. Taking elements from these several positions and writers, Pearls created his "way."

PSYCHOANALYSIS

Orthodox psychoanalysis served as the seedbed for the early growth of Gestalt therapy. Perls was trained as a Freudian analyst, being analyzed by Harnick and Reich, and supervised by such eminent figures as H. Deutsch, Fenichel, Hirschman, Horney, and Landanner. He also knew Federn and Schilder and had "casual encounters" with Adler, Jung, and The Man Himself, Freud (Perls, 1969c). After immigrating to South Africa in 1934, Perls founded the South African Institute for Psychoanalysis and lived the life of a highly successful analyst for several years (Perls, 1969c).

But after a severe disappointment, perhaps even a rebuff, upon meeting Freud in 1936, Perls became skeptical of psychoanalysis and turned to Zen, then to existentialism. Further evidence that Perls may not have been very highly regarded by at least a significant portion of the psychoanalytic establishment is his relating in his autobiography that Jones once called him an exhibitionist (Perls, 1969c).

Perls' early training in psychoanalysis provided him with an orientation and technique which he could question and doubt, and upon which he could improve, based on his years of analytic experience and his exposure to existential philosophy, Gestalt psychology, Reich, and Zen. But his debt to Freud, for the starting position from which Gestalt therapy was to emerge, was never forgotten. Perls (1969c) declared Freud to be the "Edison of Psychiatry" who changed the descriptive to the dynamic and causal, as well as the Prometheus and Lucifer, the bearers of light. For Perls, Freud was the "saint-devil-genius" (Perls, 1969c).

It was Perls' belief that Freud's discoveries were extremely valuable, but that the philosophy and technique of orthodox psychoanalysis were obsolete (Perls, 1969c). In his first book, *Ego, Hunger, and Aggression,* Perls (1969a) delineated his transition from orthodox psychoanalysis to the position that was later to be named Gestalt therapy. Central to his departure from the classical position was Perls' dictum that working with behavior which is not of the "here-and-now" is a waste of time. He saw the historically-oriented thinking of Freud's method as obsolete.

In terms of his revision of the psychoanalytic position, Perls (1969a) set forth three criticisms of Freud: (1) the treatment of psychological facts as if they exist in isolation from the organism as a whole; (2) the use of a linear association psychology as a basis for a four-dimensional system; (3) the neglect of the phenomenon of differentiation.

As a result, Perls offered the following revisions: (1) replacement of the psychological by the holistic organismic concept; (2) replacement of association psychology by the field theory of gestalt psychology; and (3) application of differential thinking based on Friedlander's notion of "creative indifference." Differential thinking resembles the dialectical theories of Hegel and Marx. Basically, it is the view that a given event is related to a zero point from which differentiation into opposites takes place. It follows, then, that opposites within the same context are more closely related to each other than either one is to any other concept. The underlying essence becomes clear through an alertness to the zero point from which the differentiation takes place.

After crediting Freud with performing a great service by analyzing the sex instinct, Perls (1969a) proceeded to analyze the *hunger instinct* in a similar fashion. Whereas the anus is behind and relates to the past (a terminal point), the mouth is in front and relates to the future (a beginning point). In terms of the developmental stages of using the mouth, there are four: (1) pre-natal; (2) pre-dental or suckling; (3) incisor or biting; and (4) molar or biting and chewing. Although aggression can be a part of any instinct, it is most closely related to hunger. It follows that the economic regulation of aggression relates to proper organismic use of the oral apparatus, particularly the teeth. Corresponding to the stages of oral development, then, are *assimilation* (biting and chewing, destroying the structure), *partial introjection* (biting off a piece, but not destroying the sub-structure), and *introjection* (sucking in, swallowing whole with no destruction of structure.

To be assimilated and made an integral part of one's self, the substance, be it physical or "mental" food, must be digested, which requires a destruction of the structure of the substance. Mental food not adequately chewed becomes an introject, and is subject to one of three fates. First, it can be vomited like the repeating of an oath or the student's recitation of a memorized list on an examination. Second, it can be defecated through the dynamic of projection (in the vernacular, "laying your shit" on someone else). Third, it can be the source of mental indigestion, the symptom being a suffering from memories (obsession). The inhibition of the natural oral aggression means a reluctance to chew, perhaps even to bite, and thus the substitution of swallowing whole or introjection for the physical and mental digestion necessary for organismic growth. This smooth flow between the realms of physical and mental metabolism shows Perls' development of a model having clear connections with Freud's thought.

In his writing, Perls said relatively little about the other major figures in psychoanalysis (with the exception of Reich, who is discussed later in the present chapter). He did express the opinion that Adler placed too much emphasis on the future in his focus on the lust for power (Perls, 1969a). Perls (1969c) contrasts two of his supervisors by saying that from Fenichel he got "confusion," whereas from Horney, he says warmly, he got human involvement without a lot of technical jargon. To Jung he gave credit for the notion of the introversion-extroversion dimension and criticism for what he saw as Jung's overemphasis of the idea of libido. Rank was criticized as having developed Freud's already historical perspective to its logical absurdity (Perls, 1969a).

Surprisingly, Perls (1969c) relates that he actually had read very little of Freud's works.

As is evident from the above, Freud was important in providing a position in contrast to which Perls could define his own. As Perls (1969c) stated, "I am deeply grateful for how much I developed through standing up against him." Indeed, Freud established the institution of modern psychotherapy, the foundation on which Perls built his own structure.

There have been several significant steps in psychotherapy since Freud. Perls (1969a) calls attention to Reich's making concrete the psychology of resistances through his demonstrations of tension binding in the musculature, Sullivan's emphasis on the importance of self-esteem, Rogers' development of feedback techniques, Berne's concept of game-playing, and the gradual evolution from symptom emphasis, to character emphasis, to existential therapy, to humanistic psychology. And, of course, came Perls' own contributions such as the explication of the here-and-now reality, the organism-as-a-whole, the dominance of the most urgent need, aggression as a biological force, the phobic attitude of neurosis, the organism-environment unity (Perls, 1969a), the contact boundary as the locus of psychological events, and the "withdrawal into the fertile void" (Perls, 1973).

REICHIAN CHARACTER ANALYSIS

An important step in Perls' move away from classical psychoanalysis came about as the result of a suggestion made by one of his supervisors, Karen Horney, that Perls become an analysand of Wilhelm Reich. During 1931 and 1932 Perls was in analysis with Reich, and the following year he participated in a seminar which Reich led (Perls, L., 1972).

The contributions which Reich offered to the world can be arranged conveniently into two somewhat distinct theoretical systems, corresponding to two periods in Reich's adult life. It was from the first period and system that Perls borrowed and for which he expressed appreciation. As for Reich's later period, Perls' opinion was that Reich's fantasy had run wild and the man had eclipsed himself as a mad scientist (Perls, 1969c).

Although Perls did not become a Reichian, he did find what I see as perhaps eight elements in Reich's earlier position which are strongly represented in Gestalt therapy.

First, Perls found in Reich the rule of therapy that remembrances must be accompanied by the appropriate affect (Reich, 1949). This discovery of the necessity of the appropriate feelings concomitant with the thoughts in order for a therapeutic effect to occur was not original with Reich, for Freud himself had spoken of this finding. Freud said, with an apt metaphor, that a neurosis cannot be hanged in effigy. But Reich took an extreme position on this point, putting far more emphasis on the elicitation of powerful feelings and dealing with them in the therapy session than had the classical psychoanalysts. Perls showed his strong belief in this approach by distinguishing the awareness-enhancing experience of psychodramatically returning to the past incident (Perls, 1973) from the emotionally avoidant, purely cognitive "mind-fucking." He went so far as to declare that dealing with anything which is not experienced (felt) in the here-and-now is a waste of time (Perls, 1969a)! One point where Perls differed from Reich was in connection with Reich's view that emotions are disturbers of the peace and are to be gotten rid of. Rather than something undesirable, Perls saw emotions as a natural element in the organism's homeostatic cycles.

Perhaps the most significant contribution of Reich was his bringing the body into psychotherapy. Again, Freud and other early psychoanalysts spoke of the body and body symbolism, but did not develop the idea into a central concept of therapy. Freud stated that the ego is first and foremost a body ego, but then developed his whole theory of resistances in the realm of mental defenses. It remained for Reich to discover the "muscular armor" and thus introduce the notion of resistances as total organismic functions (Perls, 1969c). Reich suggested that the neurotic solution of the infantile instinctual conflict (chronic conflict between instinctual demands and counterdemands of the outer world) is brought about through a generalized alteration in functioning which ultimately crystalizes into a neurotic "character" (Shapiro, 1965). Character is, then, essentially a narcissistic protective mechanism, formed for protection against actual external dangers and retained for protection against instinctual internal dangers. One aspect of the holistic character is the "armor," the muscular rigidities which serve to bind free-floating anxiety.

In addition to calling attention to the resistances in the body realm, Reich broke with the classical psychoanalytic position by introducing intensive body contact into psychotherapy. Through feeling the patient's body, Reich could assess the muscular armoring, locating the focal points of bound anxiety. Perls included much of Reich's body orientation in his system, even stating that the deepest split, long ingrained in our culture, is the mind-body dichotomy. Thus, in therapy, one needs to attend to the patient's nonverbal communications—voice, posture, gestures, and "psychosomatic language" (Perls, 1969b). Perls also encouraged enhanced body awareness and bodily involvement to facilitate organismic completion of emotions, even suggesting exercises to those ends (Perls, Hefferline, and Goodman, 1951).

Consistent with Reich's character armoring, Gestalt therapy includes the concept of "retroflection" as one of the major means of limiting one's awareness of self-functioning. Retroflection refers to the process of negating or blocking an impulse to action through opposing sensorimotor tension. Reich's notion of character armor amounts to a chronic state of retroflection (Enright, 1970). Body contact is sometimes also found in gestalt therapy, although it is not emphasized or formalized into a treatment mode as it is in the neo-Reichian therapies.

The third way in which I see a Reichian influence in Perls' work is in the latter's active, and at times frustrating, confrontive style (Perls, 1973). He himself stated that psychological growth comes only through frustration (Perls, 1969b). The therapist must therefore learn to use a balance of sympathy and frustration. Perls' (1973) way was to frustrate those expressions of the patient which reflect manipulatory techniques, neurotic patterns, and the patient's self-concept, while satisfying the patient's expression of his true self. The therapist's tools are support and frustration. In turn, the therapist's basic responsibility is to challenge all statements and behaviors which, rather than representing the patient's self, are evidence of the patient's lack of self-responsibility. There are times when it seems that the therapist must be cruel in order to be kind (Perls, 1973).

The earlier position of Reich shows an extremely close similarity to this view. Reich's view was that during resistance phases of therapy it is up to the analyst to direct the course, first interpreting that the patient is resisting, then interpreting how the resistance is taking place, and finally interpreting what is being resisted. (Reich used the term "interpretation" in a generic sense, encompassing what other writers would distinguish as reflections, interpretations, and confrontations, i.e., any therapeutic intervention.) Reich suggested that the patient be constantly confronted with his character resistance until he experiences it as something to get rid of. Or, put another way, it is important to undermine the neurosis from the cardinal resistance rather than from the detail resistances (Reich, 1949). Perhaps consistent with his therapeutic style was a personal style for which Perls was well-known—troublemaking, roguish, disruptive, impolite, demanding, a "dirty old man"—such terms were usually used to describe him, with warmth (Fagan, 1971). Interestingly, he credited Reich with teaching him brazenness (Perls, 1969c).

A fourth influence comes from Reich's suggestion that the character resistance is revealed in the "how" of the patient's communications, rather than in the "what" of those communications. The idea expressed herein is that the form or style of communication reflects the character and therefore is more important than the content (Reich, 1949). Several persons can do or say the same thing, and thus individuality and uniqueness are not revealed in the content of the behavior, but each person behaves in his own consistent "style" reflecting his uniqueness. Following this line of thinking, Perls made "why" questions taboo. The patient who asks "why" is usually trying to "hook the environment for support"; he is asking someone else to think for him. The therapist who asks "why" is inviting the patient to rationalize, justify, comply, make excuses, or talk in tautology. As Perls said, there are no ultimate answers to "why." The relevant questions can be answered by "how, where, and when" (Perls, 1969a). Gestalt therapy walks on two legs, according to Perls (1969b)—"now and how." In order to hear the "how," the therapist must listen to the sound, the music of the patient's communications. The appropriate focus is on the voice quality, the postures, the gestures, the psychosomatic language, with the content taking a secondary place, for Perls suggested that in therapy the patient's verbal communication (content) is usually a lie.

Another of Reich's concepts which seems likely to have influenced the development of Perls' view is the notion of the "phase of the breakdown of secondary narcissism." In terms of Reich's (1949) theory, the lasting frustration of primary natural needs leads to a chronic contraction of the armor. This conflict between inhibited primary impulses and the inhibiting character armor leads to the formation of a secondary narcissism (as contrasted to the primary narcissism of the infant which results from his cathecting his own body parts as part-objects of love). That is, as investment of libido in the outside is made more difficult or is withdrawn, the energy builds up within, intensifying a secondary narcissism. Reich spoke of the loosening and dissolution of the characterological protective mechanisms as bringing about a temporary condition of complete helplessness, an aspect of successful treatment which he termed the "phase of the breakdown of secondary narcissism." During this phase the patient moves into a position of strong, freed energy with a concomitant lack of "safe" neurotic controls. It is because of these two factors that this phase of treatment is stormy, often including strong feelings of negative transference.

Perls seems to have included the essence of Reich's dynamic formulation of the phase of breakdown of secondary narcissism in his five-layer model of the neurosis. Perls (1969b; Levitsky and Perls, 1970) was consistent in his conceptual presentation of the layers of neurosis, but was not consistent in his numbering of the layers. Disregarding, then, the arbitrary numbering, the layers emerge as follows. Neurosis is characterized by a cliché layer, or layer of tokens of meaning. Below that is the layer Perls named the Eric Berne or Sigmund Freud layer of playing games, playing roles, behaving "as if." Beneath this phony layer is the impasse, characterized by the phobic attitude. The phobic attitude results in avoidance, and in turn, the feeling of being stuck, lost, empty, confused. Beneath the impasse or phobic layer is the death layer or implosive layer. At this layer, the person is paralyzed by opposing forces; he is trying to pull himself in, hold himself safely together. The implosive layer may unfold into the final layer of explosion. The explosive layer is characterized by the person's authentic experiencing and *ex*-pressing of his emotions. The explosion may be into grief, if a loss had not been assimilated, orgasm, if a sexual block had been present, anger, or joy.

There are striking parallels between Reich's "phase of breakdown of secondary narcissism" and Perls' progression through "impasse, implosion, and explosion." In both cases the essence is the dissolution of organismic (holistic) core defenses in order to emerge, after a "walk through hell," with an authentic (organismically appropriate) behavior. The impasse was defined by Perls (1969b) in terms which sound very much like Reich's concept, saying that the impasse is the position where environmental support or obsolete inner support is no longer adequate and authentic self-support has not yet been achieved.

The important difference between the two men's concepts is that Reich limited his concern to the sexual impulse and establishment of a sex-economic regulation of energy following the "breakdown." Perls clearly developed the concept beyond the point where Reich stopped. Cohn (1970) regards Perls' explication and therapeutic use of the impasse phenomenon as his most important contribution to therapeutic practice. This contribution she describes as Perls' discovery that the skillful separation of conflicts into their duality, and their subsequent reenactment through the "gestalt dialogue," leads to the feelings of helplessness—just as the impasse, enduring the hell of confusion and helplessness, leads to organismic growth. In his later work Perls (1973) referred to such staying with one's confusion as a "withdrawal into the fertile void." If one stays with his techniques of interruption, and his confusion to the utmost, he may experience something like a hypnogogic hallucination or miniature schizophrenic experience leading to a "blinding flash of insight." This phase of therapy is not for the novice or the squeamish, as Reich warned therapists, and is usually applicable in Perls' system.

Perls (1969b) expressed misgivings about anyone calling himself a Gestalt therapist, because that often means that one is a technician, one who has learned to use techniques, but may have little sense and appreciation for the natural individualistic growth process. Perls saw his work as the promotion of the growth process, a process which requires time and a powerful personal commitment. To promote that process of growth Perls ingeniously invented techniques. But the techniques were invented for particular uses and employed only when they fit, even then undergoing modifications into nonce techniques. Perhaps this is another influence Reich had on the young Perls, for Reich (1949) declared emphatically that for any given patient at any given time there is only one technique, and that technique has to be derived from the individual's circumstances. Reich denied that the therapist should ever impose any "ready-made schema" of therapy.

What is perhaps the seventh element of Reichian influence in Gestalt therapy is a pervasive political undercurrent. Reich's political controversies in his later period, with the book burnings, prosecutions, and eventual incarceration, are a matter of historical record. But even in his earlier period, when Perls studied with him, Reich took a political stance with his character analysis. Reich (1949) declared that the therapist's work is in conflict with most of the heavily defended positions of conservative society and, therefore, the therapist will be exposed to enmity, contempt, and slander as long as he maintains his integrity. One can escape the negative sanctions of the conservative society only by making concessions, at the expense of his theoretical and practical convictions, to a social order which is in opposition to the demands of therapy. There is no doubt but that Reich went political because he believed that depth psychology requires the complement of radical politics (Rieff, 1966).

Perls' life seems consistent with this view of Reich's. Perls left Germany in 1933 because of Hitler, left South Africa in 1948, and left the United States in 1969 because of a dominant political ethos with which he could not be comfortable. As Perls (1969b) saw it, there was a race on in the United States between fascism and humanism, and fascism held the lead. He supported the rebellion which was going on (he said that it had not yet reached the proportions of a revolution). The meaning of life is that it is to be lived, not to be traded, conceptualized, and force-fit into categories. The ultimate joys are not born of manipulation and control, but of authenticity. As Shepherd (1970) has suggested, Gestalt therapy may offer a promise of authenticity that is very difficult to achieve or maintain in this culture. The upshot of this is that, as one successfully experiences Gestalt therapy and thus becomes more fully aware and centered, he will be less tolerant of the destructive forces and conventions in our society. Those who successfully experience Gestalt therapy will likely become less fit for and less adjusted to contemporary society. Gestalt therapy is not a therapy of adjustment, but a therapy of self-actualization.

Some systems of psychotherapy focus only on the remedy of the acute situation, problem, or neurosis. Reich (1949), however, clearly distinguished the "cure" and the "immunization" as aspects of a successful treatment. By this he meant that a successful character analysis not only brings an end to the symptoms of the neurosis but, by virtue of the new character structure puts the patient in a better position to resist the return to neurotic solutions when future problems are encountered. This orientation is expressed by Perls, as well. In his posthumous book, Perls (1973) states that the goal of therapy is to give the patient the means to solve his present problems and any problems which may arise later. Whereas Reich saw this goal as coming about through the dissolution of a neurotic character structure, Perls sees the same goal through the development of self-support. The idea of growing from environmental support or inadequate self-support to authentic self-support may be a step beyond Reich's concept of the establishment of a non-neurotic character structure, but the two notions share a common core. It seems quite clear that Reich's thinking had a very basic influence on Perls in his development of the Gestalt position.

It was rare for Perls to acknowledge another as a good therapist. One of the few who received such recognition, as well as being called a lovely person by Perls (1969c), was Hellmuth Kaiser. The intersection of Perls and Kaiser was in Reich's seminar, and for these reasons I think it is important to look into Kaiser's position (Fierman, 1965).

Under the sponsorship of Freud, Kaiser was trained in orthodox psychoanalysis at the Berlin Institute. But, in time, he grew disconcerted with what he saw as an inefficiency of the classical treatment. Much of psychoanalytic technique seemed to Kaiser to be irrelevant and retained merely because it was dogma. The starting point for Kaiser's departure from Freud was a concept that he learned in Reich's seminar: The "how" of the patient's communication is more important than the "what." Seeing the stylistic component of communication as the elucidator of the patient's resistances, à la Reich, Kaiser shifted his emphasis from "psycho-analysis" to "resistance analysis," later changing the name to "defense analysis." Otto Fenichel seems to have been misled by a paper in which Kaiser described the dramatic "true affective breakthrough" which ensues from successful defense analysis, and he attacked Kaiser as being interested only in promoting abreaction. The attack from the psychoanalytic establishment and the rise of Hitler served as adequate incentive for Kaiser to emigrate. His wandering led him to Italy, Majorca, Switzerland, England, France, Israel, and eventually, through the invitation of Karl Menninger, to the United States.

Having found a home in the United States, Kaiser turned his energies to the further development of his way of psychotherapy. Up to this point in his development, his therapy was basically psychoanalytic, but without the basic rule (free association) and without content interpretation. Now, he took a significant step by coming to see that the patient's behavior could be understood as an attempt to get very close to the therapist, creating an "illusion of fusion." This led to Kaiser's ceasing to view what he did as a technique, and seeing what he did as an approach to therapy. This approach followed from his central thesis that the neurotic communicates in a way such as to give himself the feeling that he is not responsible for his words and actions.

Kaiser's final position can be summarized by the "Universal Triad."

The *universal psychopathology* is the attempt to create in real life the universal "illusion of fusion" (the illusion that one is not alone but is fused with others). The *universal symptom* is "duplicitous communication" (failure to be "behind one's words"). The *universal treatment* is straightforward (nonduplicitous) communication.

This succinct skeleton of a theory can be fleshed out as follows. Whenever one values something not universally valued, wants something others don't want, or makes a decision not supported by authority, the basic fact of his individuality or aloneness is poignantly emphasized. All men share to some degree the illusion of fusion to soften the existential fact of aloneness. The illusion of fusion is given life through religions, teams, clubs, parades, and various organizations. To the extent that one cannot tolerate his aloneness and tries to make real the illusion of fusion, he is neurotic. The neurotic, as one who tries to deny the existential fact of his aloneness, tries to avoid taking personal responsibility for his life. His technique is duplicitous or inauthentic communication. The goal of psychotherapy is the establishment of straightforward communication *per se*. It is through the nonduplicitous communications of the therapist that the patient may find the model and support to gradually move behind his words himself and experience his taking responsibility for his life.

The good therapist is, then, characterized as one who is sensitive to duplicity in others, who is himself relatively free from duplicity, and who has the desire to engage in straightforward communication with relatively noncommunicative persons. Kaiser's therapy is extreme in orientation, being relationship oriented as opposed to technique oriented. The basic rule of therapy is never to withdraw in the patient-therapist encounter, either physical or psychologically.

The similarities between Kaiser and Perls, from their personal lives to their views of therapy, are rather clear. Perhaps the central similarity, and in fact a central theme in both of their views of therapy, is the emphasis on personal responsibility. Perls (1973) saw the importance of coming to self-knowledge, satisfaction, and *self-support*, speaking of the neurotic as one who manipulates others to give him support rather than developing self-support. Kaiser emphasized that the neurotic fails to be behind his words, thus perpetuating the illusion that he is not *self-responsible*. Tobin (1969-70) has alluded to the feeling of worthlessness as being behind Perls' concept of hooking the environment for support and Kaiser's concept of creating in real life the illusion of fusion. In terms of working with the neurotic, Perls and Kaiser again present consistent rules. Kaiser's rule was not to withdraw in the encounter, but to stay nonduplicitously with the patient. Perls (1973) stated the primary responsibility of the therapist as not to let any statement or behavior which is evidence of the patient's lack of self-responsibility go unchallenged. Also of importance is the contempt for dogma and mechanical techniques in therapy which Perls and Kaiser shared.

EXISTENTIALISM

Perls (1969c), in his autobiography, relates that while he lived in Frankfurt he was preoccupied with psychoanalysis and therefore did not get involved with the existentialists there—Buber, Scheler, and Tillich. Even though Perls was not personally involved with the existential thinkers, he found in their thought a basic message which helped him out of the doldrums of his disillusionment with classical psychoanalysis. That basic message, which was also to become basic to gestalt therapy, is that one must take personal responsibility for one's own existence. Perls sometimes rewrote "responsibility" as "response-ability." By this he meant that the basic given in life is ability to personally respond. *Only I can move me, think me, feel me, live me.* The corollary of this is: *I cannot move you, think you, feel you, or live you. I am I and you are you.* When we lose awareness of that existentialum, we find ourselves in the confusing situation of trying to credit or discredit ourselves for what others do, or credit or discredit others for what we do. This confusion is maintained by four mechanisms which Perls (1973) refers to as *introjection, projection, confluence,* and *retroflection.*

In *introjection* the person does what he thinks others would like him to do and thus takes responsibility for what actually belongs elsewhere. *Projection,* on the other hand, is the mechanism whereby one does to someone else what he accuses the other of doing to him, thereby making the other responsible for what originates in himself. When one completely loses contact with the I-you boundary and doesn't know where he stops and another begins, he is in pathological *confluence.* In the case of *retroflection,* one does to himself what he would like to do to another. In each of these cases, but particularly evident in introjection, projection, and confluence, there is a failure to live out personal responsibility.

An especially tenacious occurrence of such denial of personal responsibility is the blaming of outside sources for one's feelings. This special case of projection is reflected in our habitual language by such phrases as "It makes me mad when . . ." or "He makes me mad when . . ." In the first case, some indefinite "it" is made responsible for me; in the latter case, at least there is a definite concrete target, but still someone other than I am responsible for me. These statements do violence to the existential fact that I and only I can think me, move me, feel me, live me. Whenever I deny this and attribute my living to someone or something else, I am living an "as if" existence of considerably lowered vitality. Of course, I can decide that if anyone speaks to me with certain words or with a certain tone of voice then I will feel mad (or hurt, or happy, or whatever). But the decision is mine. Only I can decide me. Just as my feelings are my responsibility, so, too, is my disappointment when it is *my* expectations which others have not met. And I grow more full as I own what is in fact mine.

Closely related to the above is the issue of asking questions. Perls (1969b) suggests that much of questioning is done to torture one's self or others. One can enhance his awareness by changing questions into statements. If an honest question remains (a request for information which one cannot get by himself, but to which another has access), it can then be asked.

Discovering for one's self, as opposed to asking others to find out about something and tell one about it, is one of the steps towards self-support. All really important learning is first-hand. Another aspect of self-support is growing to a point where the need for encouragement and praise from others is minimal. When constant praise from others is sought, one is making each of the others his judge. Maturing, according to Perls (1969b), is the transcendence from environmental support to self-support. It follows from this that a therapist who wants to be helpful may defeat himself more, the harder he tries. To paraphrase Perls, beware of the helpers, for they will help you to your help-lessness.

A further point made by Perls (1969b), profound in its simplicity, is that no one at a given moment can be different from what he is at that moment.

An aspect of Gestalt therapy which is sometimes overlooked or misunderstood is the relationship between therapist and patient. The model which Perls chose for the therapeutic relationship is one delineated by Buber as the "I-Thou" relationship. Buber distinguished two types of relationship, the "I-It" and the "I-Thou." The "I-It" relationship is one of person to object. In this objective, one-up arrangement, values are determined and decisions made unilaterally. In contrast, the "I-Thou" relationship is a subjective one in which two persons mutually coexist. Gestalt therapy is based on the coming together of two persons in an atmosphere where the therapist respects the personhood of his patient.

The patient must bring with him at least a modicum of goodwill. With these conditions met, there can be intimate communication. Without such communication, there can be only isolation and boredom (Perls, 1969b).

In discussing philosophy, Perls (1969b) mentions three types. First is "shouldism," or talk of what should be. Second is "aboutism," or talk about things. Third is "existentialism," the only one of the three addressed to "what is." Perls takes a strong stand in favor of focusing on "what is" rather than "talking about" or trying to decide what "should be." Within this three-type schema, Gestalt therapy is based on "what is." In fact, Perls (1969b) claims Gestalt therapy to be one of only three existential therapies, the other two being Binswanger's daseins therapy and Frankl's logotherapy.

Consistent with its concern with "what is," Gestalt therapy focuses on the immediate moment, the "now." It is the living phenomenon which is of interest in Gestalt therapy, the "here-and-now" phenomenon. Perls (1969b, 1973) saw the neurotic as one who is not aware of the "here-and-now," one who does not see the obvious.

In addition, Perls made several passing references to the ideas of Kierkegaard and Nietzsche, giving evidence of some acquaintance with further existential thought.

The strong influence of existential ideology in Gestalt therapy is perhaps made most evident by the summary statements of the Gestalt approach. Levitsky and Perls (1970), for example, set forth these "rules" for the conducting of Gestalt therapy: (1) The principle of the now (experience in the immediate moment); (2) "I" and "Thou" (realness of therapist and patient, together); (3) "I" language and "It" language (changing "it"s to "I"s to own what is one's own); (4) use of the awareness continuum (patient's focusing on his immediate awareness, thus getting away from the "why" orientation and to the "what" and "how" perspective); (5) no gossiping (rather than talking about others to a third person, the patient speaks directly to them, whether they are present or not); (6) changing questions into statements (accepting genuine questions while refusing questions which cajole or manipulate). It is apparent that adherence to these Gestalt rules provides the setting for an existential encounter, "*I and Thou, Here and Now.*"

Naranjo (1970) offers what he sees as the implicit moral injunctions of Gestalt therapy: (1) Live now (concern with the present as opposed to past or future). (2) Live here (concern with what is present as opposed to that which is absent). (3) Stop imagining (experience what is real). (4) Stop unnecessary thinking (hear, see, smell, taste, touch). (5) Express directly rather than explain, judge, manipulate. (6) Be aware of the unpleasant as well as the pleasant. (7) Reject all "shoulds" and "oughts" which are not one's own. (8) Take full responsibility for one's actions, feelings, and thoughts. (9) Surrender to being as one really is. These injunctions are summarized by Naranjo as valuation of actuality, valuation of awareness, and valuation of wholeness. The belief underlying the injunctions is that one is better off accepting the truth, by being aware of that which is. Psychotherapy, then, means assisting the patient to face that which he tries to avoid (Perls, 1969a).

GESTALT PSYCHOLOGY

That Perls came to call his way of therapy "Gestalt therapy" bears testimony to the ties he saw with the tradition of Gestalt psychology. Very early he termed his approach "Concentration-Therapy," but later, even though his wife Laura opposed his calling it Gestalt therapy, he made this change (Perls, 1969c).

In Gestalt psychology Perls found the answer to a question which had plagued him. He had come a long way with the existentialists' dictum that one must take responsibility for one's own existence. Still, the existentialists seemed to need external conceptual support, be it psychoanalysis, Judaism, Christianity, the freedom movement, or whatever. Perls' question was: Is there a way out? After reading Lewin, Wertheimer, and Köhler, he answered, yes, and it came from an approach called Gestalt psychology. Most important for him was the idea of the unfinished situation, the incomplete Gestalt. He suggested that the most interesting and important property of Gestalt is its dynamic, the need of a strong Gestalt to come to a closure (Perls, 1969c). The completing of incomplete Gestalten is, then, the essence of personal responsibility.

Perls found many valuable ideas in the Gestalt position. To adequately understand these contributions requires an historical excursion into academic psychology.

Academic psychology emerged from philosophy and physiology. Philosophy provided the problems while physiology and, later, physics provided the models and techniques for empirical investigation. The line of thought being traced herein conveniently can begin with the first professional philosopher, Immanuel Kant. In his very difficult book, *The Critique of Pure Reason* (1781), Kant attempted to set forth a theory of knowledge which woud incorporate both reason and experience. The central question which served as his starting point was: If the "knower" and the "known" are not distinct, then what are they and how are they related? Or, in his style: How are synthetical judgments *a priori* possible? This is the essential problem of pure reason. (A judgment is a thought in which we assert that a given predicate applies to a given subject. There are two types of relationship possible between the subject and the predicate—experience and entailment. Corresponding to the two types of relationship are two kinds of judgment—synthetical and analytical. The synthetical judgment, such as, "This man is bald," differs from the analytical judgment, such as, "Bald men have no hair," in that in the former, the predicate is not contained in the subject. Universal and necessary connections are asserted in an *a priori* judgment, whereas this is not true of *a posteriori* judgments.)

In coming to an answer to his problem, Kant distinguished "form" and "content." Kant proceeded to argue that if we know the *types* of judgments one can make or, in other words, the basic ways in which the mind organizes experience, we would have *a priori* knowledge. This knowledge concerns a *form*, a knowledge about all experience of a given class, but not knowledge of a particular experience which is a specific *content*. Kant concluded from this argument that all knowledge begins with experience, but that all knowledge does not arise out of experience (Jones, 1952). Kant proceeded into his "Metaphysical Deduction" of the twelve different synthetical operations, but at this point he had already left his mark on that which would become psychology.

Important here for psychology was the notion that the mind is not a passive recorder of external events, but rather that it orders its perceptions through an active process. Highly important aspects of this ordering are the *a priori* synthetic terms of space and time.

During the latter half of the nineteenth century Kant's theory was modified by a number of thinkers known as neo-Kantians. A materialistic, even mechanical turn was taken by Herbart, who came to see the soul as one of the units of cells which constitute the organism. Mach suggested that the world is simply the sum of all of our sensations which are the content of consciousness.

One influential group of neo-Kantians, known as the Marburg school, led by Hermann Cohen, then Paul Natorp and Ernest Cassirer, actually carried Kant's thinking one step further. They boldly suggested that science does not discover truth, but constructs truth. In so doing, the mind is governed by certain formal principles (*a priori* synthetics) which determine the structure of experience.

The other neo-Kantian group, the Baden school, headed by Windelband

and Rickert, introduced the idea of values into the thinking of the times. They suggested that certain abstract *a priori* principles (i.e., values) govern all cognitive, esthetic, and practical experience. Another contribution made by the Baden group was their discussion of the appropriate methods of research of the cultural sciences and the natural sciences. They suggested that, although both cultural and natural sciences are empirical, the natural sciences deal with general laws and the cultural sciences deal with the unique, individual case. The methods of investigation, therefore, need be nomothetic and idiographic, respectively. An important difference here is that the idiophenomena are concerned with values rather than natural causation (Wolman, 1960). These revolutionary ideas are even today a major focus of controversy in academic psychology.

Other ideological developments, in addition to the work of the neo-Kantians, were contributing to the development of psychology. One such major development was Husserl's attempt to unravel the complexity of Kant's heritage through a "phenomenological reduction" (Wolman, 1960). Phenomenology, according to Husserl, is prior to psychology, for it addresses itself to the subjective process by which phenomena are presented. The only thing which cannot be doubted is that humans experience, and the naive, "un-sophist-icated" attention to experience is phenomenology.

The major influence which this philosophical heritage had upon academic psychology was the concept that perception of the world is not a totally objective process, but that the perceiving mind contributes organization to this external data.

By the end of the nineteenth century German psychology was represented by two foci, "act" and "content." The respective primary representatives of these foci were Brentano and Wundt (Boring, 1950).

Turning attention first to the content psychology, we find the clear beginnings of experimental psychology. The content emphasis was vivified by a new philosophy of analytical empiricism (which evolved into today's logical positivism). In outlining the problem of psychology, Wundt emphasized the analysis of conscious processes into elements and the determination of the laws and manner of these connections. The result was the experimentally oriented "Structuralism," which provided the seedbed from which the "individual differences" and eventually the psychometric movement grew. In addition to Wundt, other psychologists who found themselves in the content camp were such remembered figures as Avenarius, Ebbinghaus, Hering, Külpe (early), Mach (early), Messer (early), Müller, Stumpf (early), and Titchener.

In contrast, act psychology sprang directly from the philosophical tradition of neo-Kantianism and phenomenology, and was not as inclined toward laboratory experimentation as was the content psychology. The position of act psychology, or the Austrian school, as it came to be known, was well represented, in addition to Brentano, by men such as Benussi, Cornelius, Ehrenfels, Hering, Külpe (late), Lipps, Mach (late), Meinong, Messer (late), Stumpf (late), and Witasek. (Note that several of the men found their way from the content to the act camp.)

Brentano is responsible for calling attention to a two-part process in perception. First is the "act" of perceiving, and it is followed by the "content" or the what of the perception.

The experimental work of the Austrian school tended to be in the areas of space-perception and esthetics. Through such work, Ehrenfels, in a paper published in 1890, delineated a doctrine of "Gestaltqualitäten" or form qualities. This doctrine was set in opposition to the content school's doctrine of perception as simply a composite of elementary sensations.

In discussing "Gestaltqualität," Ehrenfels used an explanation of the following type. A square can be formed from four lines. The lines are the "Fundamente." The product is a "Grundlage." But, the quality of "squareness" is a "Gestaltqualität" (Boring, 1950). Put very simply into a well-known cliché, the whole is more than the sum of the parts. (Note that the method used here by Ehrenfels was empirical, but was not experimental.)

Ehrenfels deserves to be remembered for his early description of types and properties of "Gestaltqualitäten." He distinguished, for instance, temporal "Gestaltqualitäten," such as a musical melody or warming and cooling, from the non-temporal. His basic criteria for a "Gestaltqualitäten" were: (1) superordination (not just a sum of elements, e.g., notes become a melody); (2) transposibility (the form can be found with different contents, e.g., a melody can be transposed to a new key).

Further development in the Austrian school came with Meinong and Cornelius. Meinong elaborated Ehrenfels' views, but in so doing came to see founding contents, or "inferiora," and founded contents, or the "superius," thus returning somewhat to a content emphasis. Cornelius, in turn, saw the "Gestaltqualität" not as a founded content, but as a founded attribute. Such a founded attribute comes about through an "act" of founding, and is disestablished when given analytical attention (Boring, 1950).

Thus, the Austrian school was a step beyond the content school, but only halfway to the position of "Gestaltpsychologie." It appears that in their reaction against the elementism of content psychology, the Austrian school merely sought an element at another level. The bold step of denying the need for the assumption of the existence of real elements was made by the men of "Gestaltpsychologie."

Much of the experimental work in perception conducted during the end of the last century and the beginning of the present century provided data which supported the emerging gestalt psychology. Jaensch, for instance, is remembered for his attracting attention to the phenomenon of eidetic imagery (Woodworth and Schlosberg, 1954). In one sense, eidetic imagery is the retention of an entire, extensive visual gestalt. The subject who experiences eidetic imagery remembers not just an essence or translation of the visual image, but the actual image in its wholeness.

A clever demonstration of the emergence of Gestalten as elements come together was provided by Katz. By observing and comparing what he distinguished as surface color, volumic color, and film color, Katz showed that color and space are not independent elements (Boring, 1950). The same color, blue for instance, does not look the same when it is painted on a surface, tints a transparent film, or appears to fill an expanse, as in a clear summer sky. Color and space interact to allow for the formation of a particular Gestalt.

Denmark's best known psychologist, Rubin, also contributed to the emerging Gestalt psychology. His very central contribution came from his extensive work with the figure-ground relationship. According to Rubin, figure and ground differ in terms of five major phenomena. *First,* the figure has form, while the ground tends to be formless. *Second,* the ground appears to extend continuously behind the figure without being interrupted by the figure. *Third,* the figure has a quality of "thingness," while the ground has a quality of undifferentiated material. *Fourth,* the figure appears nearer than the ground. And *fifth,* it is the figure rather than the ground which is more impressive, better remembered, and more apt to be given meaning. Two of the important discoveries which Rubin made were the tendency to see the same figure-ground organization in a given visual field on repeated exposure (figural persistence) and the non-recognition of a field after a figure-ground reversal (Woodworth and Schlosberg, 1954). Although Rubin's work was in the realm of visual perception, his elucidation of the figure-ground phenomena has led to considerable understanding in other realms. Vernon, for instance, has demonstrated the figure-ground phenomena in audition, and Woodworth and Schlosberg apply these phenomena to the study of social kinesics by viewing any phasic movement as figure while the supporting posture is ground (Woodworth and Schlosberg, 1954).

The phenomenological investigations of men such as Jaensch, Katz, and Rubin provided an extremely important antecedent to Gestalt psychology. Other important antecedents came, as I have shown, from the Austrian school.

Gestalt psychology began, in a sense, as a protest movement. The protest was against "structuralism" with its analysis of consciousness into elements and the exclusion of values from the data. Alongside the Gestalt protest came another protest movement, "behaviorism." The latter also protested structuralism, focusing a major criticism at structuralism's method of "intro-spectionism." The solution for behaviorism was complete exclusion of "consciousness" from the kingdom of scientific psychology.

In order to place these movements in perspective I will briefly review some of the developments in psychology up to the teen years of the current century: Kant distinguished "form" and "content" in perception. Windelband described two approaches of study, the "idiographic" and the "nomothetic." Husserl introduced the "phenomenological reduction." With Brentano, Kant's "form" became "act," and Wundt focused on the "content" to create the position of structuralism with philosophical underpinning in analytical empiricism. The split in academic psychology was then the "act," or Austrian school, versus "elements," or structuralism. Structuralism was the forerunner of experimental psychology. As structuralism began to wane, a new position of "functionalism" grew from it. Functionalism was represented by several versions—American, English, French, and German. American functionalism, strongly shaped by the "pragmatism" of James and Dewey, eventually became behaviorism under the direction or Watson and the philosophical justification of logical positivism. The French version of functionalism, led by Binet, merged with the early, but sparse work in "individual differences" to form an applied area, the "psychometric tradition." While structuralism underwent these movements, the Austrian school grew, with influence from the phenomenological work in perception, into "Gestalt psychology."

So, in the teen years of the twentieth century, academic psychology was constituted of behaviorism (nomothetic-experimental) and Gestalt psychology (idiographic, phenomenological). Gestalt psychology set itself against both structuralism, with its analysis of consciousness into elements and exclusion of values, and behaviorism, with its exclusion of consciousness itself (Köhler, 1947). But, by this time, circa 1913, behaviorism was in the second phase of its own protest against structuralism, the first phase being the American functionalism from which behaviorism grew. It is very understandable, then, that when gestalt psychology reached America it was not given much attention (Boring, 1950). First, it was attacking an issue (structuralism) pretty much put to rest by functionalism/behaviorism, and second, it was attacking the popular and emerging behaviorism of Watson.

Although, as we have seen, Ehrenfels had introduced the idea of the Gestalt as early as 1890, the birthdate of Gestalt psychology is traditionally placed at 1912. It was in that year that Max Wertheimer, assisted by Kurt Koffka and Wolfgang Köhler, conducted his experiments on perceived motion. Wertheimer found that when two lines are visually presented serially, and one slightly distant from the other, an inter-stimulus interval can be reached such that it appears that one line has been presented in motion. This apparent movement, which is the basis for motion pictures, was named by Wertheimer the "phi phenomenon." Wertheimer concluded that in addition to the content in this experiment, the stationary lines, there was a uniting factor which resulted in the phenomenal experience of motion, an emergent Gestalt. In the case of a series of flashing lights, there can be a sense of motion without content, or movement without anything that moves, the "pure phi phenomenon." Wertheimer was adamant in his rejection of the "bundle hypothesis" (mere accumulation of elements into a congeries to form a perception). Wertheimer, who, incidentally, took his doctorate with Kulpe, did not publish very much, but left that activity to his two close colleagues.

Koffka and Köhler, both of whom took their doctorates with Stumpf, carried the major load of publishing the Gestalt doctrine. Koffka, perhaps the least original of the three in his thinking, was the most productive in his writing.

Köhler took advantage of his prolonged stay on the Spanish island of Tenerife during World War I to conduct an important series of Gestalt experiments. Using apes and chickens as experimental subjects, he studied visual Gestalt formation. An easy step for him was to move from the study of perception to the study of learning, for he came to see learning as essentially a subtopic of perception. One has learned when one has perceived the appropriate relationships, when one has put together the elements of the learning problem into a Gestalt. Based on his careful phenomenological studies of problem solving, Köhler concluded that the problem of learning is secondary to the problem of perception, for the key to learning is the discovery of the right response, which is dependent upon the "structuring of the field" or Gestalt formation. When one has created the Gestalt, one experiences sudden "Einsicht" or insight, one's awareness is elevated to a new level, one understands. That moment of sudden insight may come like a flash, with a sense of "aha!" True insight, the proof positive of learning, is characterized by reproducibility of the behavior and applicability to new situations. That is, if one has learned a new behavior, one can repeat that behavior at a future time and can apply that behavior to other situations which are not identical to the original situation in which the learning occurred.

So it was that even though Gestalt psychology began and had its greatest success in the study of perception, it soon moved into the study of learning (Hilgard, 1956). Köhler's theory of "insight learning" was posed as an alternative to the "trial-and-error" learning of Thorndike, which was based on the "law of effect." In terms of popularity in academe, Thorndike's reinforcement-based trial-and-error learning, or a portion of it, won out. Actually, in his 1911 book, *Animal Intelligence*, Thorndike stated a rather complex law of effect. Whenever the animal is "reinforced" (receives satisfaction) for a behavior (that behavior often just happening through trial-and-error), he tends in similar situations, on future occasions, to repeat that behavior. Thorndike proceeded to distinguish two reactions to the reinforcement: (1) the "confirming" reaction, which is an inevitable and automatic physiological reaction; (2) the informative reaction, or cognitive effect. Although Thorndike believed that the law of effect is applicable both to animal and human learning, the cognitive factors may be of special importance in the latter (Postman, 1962). Unfortunately, I think, behaviorism chose to deal with that automatic, physiological confirming reaction to an almost total exclusion of the cognitive informative reaction. Thus, only a part of Thorndike's law-of-effect, that part which explicitly excludes insight or understanding, was taken as a basis for the academic mainstream learning theories of Hull and Skinner (Hilgard, 1956).

Gestalt psychology viewed learning as a perceptual problem—the discovery of a correct response, this discovery depending upon the appropriate structuring of the perceptual field. Learning situations give rise to disequilibria and thus, tension. The tension is reduced and cognitive equilibrium reestablished with the completion of the Gestalt of the perceptual field. The "law of closure" (see below) is thus an alternative to the "law of effect" (Hilgard, 1956).

The Gestalt psychology position can be summarized as follows. Gestalt psychology deals with "wholes" and the basic data are "phenomena."

Many of the properties of the whole are "emergent," inherent in no single part, but perceived when the parts come together. Thus, Gestalt psychology often is concerned with "fields" (a dynamic system or whole in which a change in any part affects the entire system). Organization of the field is in terms of "figure" and "ground." A "good form" persists and tends to recur. A "strong form" coheres and resists disintegration through analysis or fusion with other forms. A "closed form" is both good and strong, whereas an "open form" tends toward "closure" by completing itself as a good form. Organizations are "stable"; once formed they tend to persist or to recur with the reinstatement of the same situation or the recurrence of a part of that organization. "Adjacent" units (in time or in space) and units which are "similar" in quality tend to combine. Organization tends toward "meaningful objects." Organized object forms tend to be preserved even as stimulus conditions change ("object constancy"). Organization, form, and object character usually depend on "relations of parts, not on the particular characteristics of the parts themselves" (Boring, 1950). The general guiding principle in perception is the "Law of Pragnanz," or the goal-directed tendency to restore cognitive equilibrium after a disequilibrium has occurred in the perceptual field. That is, there is an intention toward a good gestalt. The "Law of Pragnanz" is served by three closely related processes, according to Wulf: "leveling," or changing the field organization in the direction of symmetry and good distribution; "sharpening," or accentuating of the essential figural elements; and "normalizing," or making the figure clear and simple (Wolman, 1960).

Gestalt psychology was most purely represented by Wertheimer, Koffka, Köhler, and Gelb. These men set forth a position in psychology which was an alternative to the other major position, behaviorism. These four, beyond establishing a theoretical position, focused on the topic of perception, and subsumed learning under the topic. Then, Kurt Lewin and Kurt Goldstein extended this theoretical position into the realm of "personality."

Lewin was associated with Wertheimer and Köhler after World War I, and thus brought a direct and personal contact with Gestalt psychology to his study of personality. His basic position can be summarized as follows: (1) Behavior is a function of the existing field (the totality of the co-existing, mutually interdependent factors of the person and environment) at the moment of the behavior. (2) Analysis of behavior begins with the situation as a "whole," and proceeds by differentiation of component parts. (3) The concrete person in the concrete situation can be represented by a mathematical model (Hall and Lindzey, 1970). His mathematical model is based on topology (the mathematics of spatial relations), hodology (the science of paths), and vector geometry (vectors, characterized by direction, magnitude, and point of application, represent dynamic relationships).

Thus, Lewin's approach to the study of personality is an ecological one. He conceives of the person as a part of a dynamic field, wherein any change in a part of that person or a part of that environment is manifested throughout the system, or Gestalt. The facts of this dynamic field may be empirical (objective) or phenomenal (subjective). And, although Lewin specifies a third dimension of reality-unreality and a fourth dimension of psychological past, present, future in his model, his decided emphasis is on the present, the contemporaneous facts. The principle of contemporaneity states that only present facts explain behavior.

Motivation is based on a tension reduction model. A need, arising in the person, increases tension, releases energy, imparts value to objects in the environment, and creates force in the person. Needs, then, alternate among three states—hunger (positive valence), satiation (neutral valence), and oversatiation (negative valence). Lewin further distinguishes between needs (a general class of objects is sufficient for satiation) and quasi-needs (a highly specific object is necessary for satiation).

The details of Lewin's field theory are complex and involve a peculiar and extensive vocabulary. But appreciation of Lewin's influence, fortunately, is not contingent upon a mastery of the language of hodology. It is the fantastic amount and far-reaching impact of the research based on Lewin's position that demands respect and appreciation. The areas of research given greatest attention by Lewin and his followers fall under the general rubrics of child development and social psychology. The topics include group dynamics, social action, level of aspiration, interrupted activities, psychological satiation, regression and conflict (Hall and Lindzey, 1970). In fact, a large part of the current scene in social psychology can be traced through such persons as Atkinson, Barker, Cantril, Dembo, Festinger, Heider, Karsten, Katz, Kounin, Robeach, Sears, and Zeigarnik to Lewin.

Perls related in his autobiography that he had read Lewin. He also referred to Lewin and alluded to the work of one of Lewin's students in *Ego, Hunger, and Aggression* (Perls, 1969a). His allusion is to research concerning a phenomenon of unfinished tasks, the eponym being Zeigarnik.

The Zeigarnik Effect is a phenomenon found when comparing the short-term memory for finished and unfinished tasks. Based on Lewin's tension system hypothesis (when one begins a task there is a high level of tension, that tension being reduced upon task completion), Zeigarnik hypothesized that the unfinished tasks would be remembered better, because of the remaining tension, than would the finished tasks. And, indeed, this is what she found. Further research has revealed the kinds of conditions under which the phenomenon occurs (Woodworth and Schlosberg, 1954). Of particular interest is the discovery that under conditions where the subject is fearful of failure in the task being performed, interruption of that task results in a reversed Zeigarnik Effect (completed tasks are remembered better than those not completed). Whereas Zeigarnik used covert tasks in her research (thinking situations), another of Lewin's students, Ovsiankina, extended the work to overt activities (doing situations). Ovsiankina found, consistent with Zeigarnik's work, that subjects tend to spontaneously resume interrupted activities when left in a free situation (Kounin, 1963).

Although Perls knew Wertheimer, Koffka, Köhler, and Lewin only through their writing, he had direct contact with Goldstein and Gelb. In 1926 Perls worked as an assistant to Goldstein at the Institute for Brain-injured Soldiers.

Goldstein made a smooth and ingenious transition from Gestalt psychology as a study of perception to Gestalt psychology as a study of the whole person. His position came to be known as "organismic theory," best set forth in *The Organism* (1939). A diligent researcher, Goldstein contributed greatly to knowledge of language and language disturbances and to the understanding of the psychological effects of brain injury. His studies of brain damage culminated in a 1942 publication, *After-Effects of Brain Injuries in War*, and a test battery for the assessment of brain damage (The Goldstein-Scheerer Battery) which has greatly influenced the later developments in brain damage assessment.

In Goldstein's view the primary organization of organismic functioning is figure-ground. Natural figures are those which are preferred and flexible, whereas unnatural figures are those which are imposed and rigid. Behavior is of three types: performances (voluntary, consciously experienced activities); attitudes (inner experiences, feelings); and processes (bodily functions). In addition, behavior may be viewed along a concrete-abstract dimension. This concrete-abstract distinction in assessing behavior is one of Goldstein's most important conceptual contributions. Concrete behavior is a direct, automatic reaction to the stimulus configuration as one perceives it. In contrast, abstract behavior involves thinking about the stimulus pattern—what does it mean, how can it be used, what are its conceptual properties, what is its relation to other stimulus patterns— and acting upon the configuration.

Goldstein used three dynamic concepts in his view of the organism: first, the "equalization processes," or the tension reduction systems which keep the organism centered or balanced; second, the processes of getting what one wants in the world, or the ways of "coming to terms with the environment"; and third, another of Goldstein's major conceptual contributions, the notion of "self-actualization." In his theory, self-actualization is the sovereign motive of the organism, all of the many apparent drives being merely expressions of this master motive. Self-actualization is the creative trend of human nature whereby the person unfolds his potential into the realm of the actual. The satisfaction of any specific need becomes figure when it is the temporally immediate prerequisite for the self-realization of the total organism. In turn, Goldstein emphasizes the conscious aspects of motivation.

Of particular interest to the student of Gestalt therapy is Goldstein's view of anxiety. Perls, in his autobiography, quotes Goldstein as saying that anxiety is the result of catastrophic expectations. That is, one experiences anxiety when he looks to the future and expects unbearable things to happen to him. This is, in a sense, a rehearsal for calamity. Goldstein goes on to suggest that anxiety can lead to detachment and isolation of the organismic parts—a splitting of the personality. Another direct influence which Goldstein had on Perls was the emphasis on care in speaking. Goldstein suggested that loss of categorical thinking (inability to abstract and classify) results in a limitation of orientation and of action. Perls, throughout his writing, points out the importance of using words which express the precise meaning of what one wants to convey. Pathology, he states, produces both distortion of word meaning (incorrect vocabulary) and wrong application of grammar (incorrect syntax). In order to improve one's mentality, Perls suggests the study of semantics as the best safeguard against the frigidity of the palate (Perls, 1969a). He encourages one to learn the value of each word, to appreciate the power hidden in the "logos." Avoidance of ego language (use of the "I" rather than "it" or "you" when speaking of one's own experience) and avoidance of personal responsibility are closely related.

In addition to Goldstein, three more men came to be associated with the organismic position: Andras Angyal, Prescott Lecky, and Abraham Maslow (Hall and Lindzey, 1970).

Angyal drew heavily upon the vocabulary and concepts of Gestalt psychology in the formulation of his particular position. In many ways his position resembles that of Lewin. He, like Lewin, emphasized the ecological view that it is impossible to meaningfully separate the organism from the environment. His "systems" analysis is somewhat like Lewin's field theory. And, finally, Angyal, like Lewin, developed a complex, idiosyncratic language in his theory. His views are presented in two books (Angyal, 1941, 1965).

In terms of special contributions to organismic theory, Angyal offers an interesting concept which bears on interpersonal relationships. Tension exists between the person and the environment as an existential fact. This tension may lead to "self-expansion" (an integrative principle which proceeds by successive stages of differentiation and integration), which has two aspects. The first aspect, "autonomy," consists of expansion of the organism by assimilation and mastering the environment—"self-determination." The second aspect, "homonomy," consists of fitting into the environment and participating in something larger than the self—"self-surrender." In homonomy the person may submerge his self through union with a social group, nature, or even an omnipotent being. Specific motives derived from homonomy include desires for love, esthetic experience, religious sentiments, patriotism, and so forth. Of particular interest is Angyal's stress on the rhythm of self-expansion through stages of self-determination and self-surrender. He also, like Jung, suggests the growth potential of the rhythmic cycle of regression and return to the present level of functioning.

Another important concept in Angyal's thinking is his "theory of universal ambiguity." The personality has a dual organization much like an ambiguous figure used in the study of visual perception. The elements of the personality are the same, but there are two organizations or Gestalten possible, one neurotic and one healthy. This theory of universal ambiguity precludes the view that a person is healthy, but has thus and so wrong with him. The implication dictates against a symptomatic treatment and calls for a treatment of the organismic whole.

Lecky's major thrust into organismic theory concerns "self-consistency," and is explicated in his 1945 book by that name. His idea is that the individual resists experiences which do not fit his own structure of values and assimilates those that do fit. Left to his own innate powers for growth, man has the ability to create a unified (self-consistent) personality.

Of the four major organismic theorists, Maslow has had the greatest impact on academic psychology. Just as Goldstein was the bridge from Gestalt psychology to organismic theory, Maslow was the bridge from organismic theory to "humanistic psychology," with which his name has become almost a synonym. Maslow's major emphasis was on the development of a humanistic science dealing with consciousness, ethics, individuality, purpose, and value. He saw this a complement to the extant mechanistic science, which was seriously limited as an approach to the study of man. Maslow's research focus was on the healthy, creative, well-functioning person.

Maslow's conclusions about man are as follows. Man has an essential nature, with needs, capacities, and tendencies which are to some extent characteristic of the species and to some extent unique to the individual. Full, normal development consists of actualizing this essential nature; that is, growth comes from within. Psychopathology results from the denial or the twisting of man's essential nature (Maslow, 1954). This essential nature is delicate and subtle, and easily overcome by habit, cultural pressure, and wrong attitudes. But even if overcome, it doesn't entirely disappear. It persists underground, always pressing for actualization (Maslow, 1968).

A major contribution of Maslow's thinking is his view of human motivation. In his theory he distinguishes between "basic needs," such as hunger, affection, security, self-esteem, and "metaneeds," such as justice, goodness, beatuy, order, and unity. Whereas the basic needs are based on deficiency and are arranged hierarchically, the metaneeds are based on growth and are of equal potency, being easily substituted for one another. In most instances the basic needs are prepotent over the metaneeds.

From the writings of Goldstein, Angyal, Lecky, and Maslow, a coherent position of organismic theory evolved. These are the major facets of that position: (1) The normal personality is characterized by unity, integration, consistency, and coherence. Pathology is defined by the converse. (2) Analysis of the person begins with the whole and proceeds by a differentiation of that whole into its aspects. (3) The individual is unified and motivated by a sovereign drive—self-actualization or self-realization. (4) The influence of the inherent potentialities is emphasized, while the influence of external forces is minimized. (5) The vocabulary and principles of Gestalt psychology are used. (6) The emphasis in research is idiographic (the comprehensive study of the single case).

Although not an organismic psychologist, General Jan Smuts, a South African statesman, soldier, and philosopher, made a contribution to organismic theory which was acknowledged by Perls. In his 1926 book *Holism and Evolution,* he coined the term "holism" from the Greek "holos" (meaning complete, whole, entire) and presented impressive support for the holistic (organismic, gestalt) view.

This, then, is the Gestalt psychology/organismic theory from which Perls drew heavily. He read Wertheimer, Köhler, and Lewin, and had personal contact with Goldstein, Gelb, and Smuts. Perls' writing is replete with the vocabulary and concepts of the gestalt-organismic position, from his "basic law of organismic regulation" (the figure-ground formation which is strongest at a given time will temporarily take over the control of the total organism) and his view of learning as discovery, to his discussion of self-actualization.

Perls actually used the term "Gestalt" to refer to two levels of the completion phenomenon. On the one hand is the Gestalt of the person, or the wholeness which can come about through self-actualization; in terms of Gestalt therapy, the Gestalt of the person is furthered by the re-owning of the split-off parts of the personality. On the other hand is the behavioral Gestalt—the wholeness which comes about when tasks undertaken are completed. Following the discoveries of Zeigarnik and Ovsiankina, Perls extended the notion of completion of unfinished tasks into a long-term model and developed therapy techniques for the finishing of one's "unfinished business" from even the distant past. Gestalt therapy, then, attends to the Gestalt at two levels, the personality Gestalt and the behavioral Gestalt.

But, even so, as Perls himself said, he was never accepted by the academic Gestaltists. In spite of this, Perls showed his gratitude, both in dedicating his first book to the memory of Max Wertheimer and in his poem (Perls, 1969c):

> Reality is nothing but
> The sum of all awareness
> As you experience here and now.
> The ultimate of science thus appears
> As Husserl's unit of phenomenon
> And Ehrenfeld's* discovery:
> The irreducible phenomenon of all
> Awareness, the one he named
> And we still call
> GESTALT.

Eastern Religion

Although psychoanalysis, Reichian character analysis, existential philosophy, and Gestalt psychology are the major sources of the elements of

---

* This spelling of "Ehrenfels" appears in *In and Out the Garbage Pail*.

Gestalt therapy, much of the flavor of Gestalt therapy comes from Perls' borrowing from Eastern religion, or more specifically from Taoism and Zen Buddhism. As early as in the writing of *Ego, Hunger, and Aggression* (1969a) in 1947, Perls spoke of the Chinese symbols Wu Gi (the circle of non-beginning) and Tai Gi (the Yin Yang, or circle of progressive differentiation into opposites). These symbols were his Eastern examples of the concept of differentiation about which Freud (the "antithetical sense of primal words") and Friedlander *(Creative indifference)* had written. The Wu Gi and Tai Gi are apt symbols for this central flavor of Gestalt therapy—a "slowing down" and "getting in touch with." The Gestalt approach is to experience fully, which oftentimes means getting in touch with primary, undifferentiated feeling, and then progressively differentiating the feeling until both of the poles are recognized. Through such a process, which requires a slowing down of one's intentional physical and mental activity to the natural rhythm of one's total organismic experience, one can learn that opposites within the same context are more closely related than either of the opposites is to any other concept. (This is true both in the realm of feeling and the physical realm, e.g., loving-hating, fucking-fighting.) And herein lies a paradox—the likeness of the not alike.

Paradox is, of course, pervasive in Eastern thought. And paradox lends a special flavor to gestalt therapy. A central paradox is the paradox of change, intriguingly stated by Beisser (1970). The paradox is that one grows by becoming more of what he is, not by trying to be different. As Perls (1973) stated, man transcends himself only through his true nature. I cannot be other than what it is my nature to be, so to try to make myself different is destined to failure, as such a pursuit is in violation of my integrity. I am I, and the best for me is to be as fully I as I can. This means I cannot decide what I should be and shape myself in that direction without loss of myself. What I must do is know my nature and allow that nature to flow, unfold, and be. Such a sacred regard for nature is central to Taoism and Zen, and has been incorporated into the thinking of the humanistic psychologists.

Taking this paradox of change a step further, Gestalt therapy can be seen as a system of not undoing rather than of doing (Naranjo, 1970). A simple example is the patient who wants to stop smoking. Some therapists would put into action a technique to make this smoking behavior cease. That is, they would see the need for doing something, either on the part of the patient, the therapist himself, or both. An alternate view is to see the patient as doing something already, and this doing as not consistent with his nature (i.e., to breathe smoke is not natural). The question of how can I stop smoking becomes, in this framework, an absurd question. The problem here is not one of initiating action; rather, the action in progress is the problem. And how does one not do a specific act? The Roshi, or Zen master, would perhaps simply sit quietly in response to such a question. If the act is in violation of my nature, then that act is an undoing of my natural flow or process. My salvation comes through allowing my flow, that is, not interfering with my natural process, not undoing my nature.

In Taoism is found the growth principle of creating a void so that nature can develop there. This is a process of standing out of the way of the flow. Perls, Hefferline, and Goodman (1951) followed this principle by discouraging a compelling of one's self and encouraging instead that one clear the ground of whatever obstacles, including one's self, might be standing in one's way. Or, as he said many times, "Don't push your river!"

A further aspect of the paradoxical view of change is the Gestalt way of dealing with unwanted thoughts or feelings. Perls, Hefferline, and Goodman (1951) suggest that the only way to get rid of an unwanted thought or feeling is first to accept it and then to allow it expression. This means to accept what is, or to bring one's self in harmony with nature, as the Taoist might say. The Gestalt therapist might say, paradoxically, to the patient who is trying to avoid and control his unwanted sadness, "Feel your pain just as much as you do!"

Another paradox of Gestalt therapy is expressed in Perls' (1973) statement that sometimes the therapist must be cruel in order to be kind. What Perls is saying is that the therapist is obligated to behave in ways which facilitate the growth of the patient. At times when the patient is trying to manipulate the therapist into thinking, feeling, or acting for him, the least facilitative thing which the therapist could do would be to be helpful. The therapist's kindness at such times would be reflected in behavior which on the surface would likely appear to be unkind, uncaring, calloused, even cruel. The Gestalt therapist, like the Zen master, knows that growth comes out of frustration, and that secondhand information about reality cannot substitute for life experience. Such "cruelty" is often upsetting to the Westerner when he reads of Zen practices. From the time the young man leaves home to journey to the Dojo (monastery) he meets with frustrations and confusions, perhaps in time even a slap in the face from the Roshi (Suzuki, 1965).

Perls (1973) strongly emphasized the importance of giving up ambition and the pursuit of artificial goals. The only appropriate goal is the realization of one's true nature. As biological beings our lives are connected with nature, ensconced in the process of nature, while as social beings we live "as if" existences in which reality, fantasy, and pretending become confused (Perls, 1969c). This "as if" existence is the Maya of Eastern thought (Perls, 1969b). Maya hangs as a veil between reality and us, making the perception of "what is" difficult and much of our perception illusory. Zen and Gestalt therapy, each in its own way, seek to lift the Maya and bring its followers into the enlightenment of immediate contact with reality. To describe this immediate, and sometimes dramatic, re-contacting of reality, Perls (1973) borrowed a word from the East, calling the experience a mini-satori. Through satori one realizes that concepts such as "good" and "bad" are not facts of nature, but only one's judgmental reactions to nature (Perls, 1969a).

A further Taoist or Zen flavor in Perls' work is his care not to over-emphasize the importance of thinking. It is the constant use of one's mental computer which prevents one from fully seeing, hearing, tasting, smelling, and touching nature. Thought removes one from immediate contact with nature and must therefore be suspended when it is contact which is needed. Perls was fond of saying that you must lose your mind to come to your senses. The Eastern sages said you must make yourself empty so that you can be filled. Gestalt therapy and the Eastern religions each offer their particular paths to the suspension of thought.

Interestingly, Perls did not agree entirely with some of the Eastern techniques. For instance, he disparaged meditation techniques such as Zazen by seeing them as "education towards catatonia" (Perls, 1969c). It seems likely that this opinion was not based on Perls' personal experience, and may even have been an uncredited reference to a 1931 article by Franz Alexander (1961) entitled "Buddhistic training as an artificial catatonia."

At any rate, the Eastern flavor in Gestalt therapy is unmistakable. Perls (1969c) himself relates that after his disappointment with Freud in 1936 he turned strongly to Zen. And, in his foreword to Perls' 1973 book, Robert Spitzer mentions the importance of 20 further years of experience with such things as Eastern religions and meditation in Perls' theoretical update.

REFERENCES

ALEXANDER, F.: *The Scope of Psychoanalysis, 1921-1961: Selected Papers of Franz Alexander*. New York: Basic Books, 1961.

ANGYAL, A.: *Foundations for a Science of Personality*. New York: Commonwealth Fund, 1941.

ANGYAL, A.: *Neurosis and Treatment: A Holistic Theory*. New York: Wiley, 1965.

BEISSER, A.: The paradoxical theory of change. In J. Fagan and I. Shepherd (Eds.), *Gestalt Therapy Now*. Palo Alto, Cal.: Science and Behavior Books, 1970.

BORING, E.: A History of Experimental Psychology. New York: Appleton-Century-Crofts, 1950.

COHN, R.: Therapy in groups: Psychoanalytic, experiential, and gestalt. In J. Fagan and I. Shepherd (Eds.), *Gestalt Therapy Now*. Palo Alto, Cal.: Science and Behavior Books, 1970.

ENRIGHT, J.: An introduction to gestalt techniques. In J. Fagan and I. Shepherd (Eds.), *Gestalt Therapy Now*. Palo Alto, Cal.: Science and Behavior Books, 1970.

FAGAN, J.: The importance of Fritz Perls having been. *Voices*, 7:1, 16-17, 1971 .

FIERMAN, L. (Ed.): *Effective Psychotherapy: The Contribution of Hellmuth Kaiser*. New York: Free Press, 1965.

GOLDSTEIN, K.: *The Organism*. New York: American Book Co., 1939.

GOLDSTEIN, K.: *After-Effects of Brain Injuries in War*. New York: Grune & Stratton, 1942.

HALL, C., and LINDZEY, G.: *Theories of Personality*. New York: Wiley, 1970.

HILGARD, E.: *Theories of Learning*. New York: Appleton-Century-Crofts, 1956.

JONES, W.: *A History of Western Philosophy, Vol. II*. New York: Harcourt, Brace & World, 1952.

KOHLER, W.: *Gestalt Psychology*. New York: Liveright, 1947.

KOUNIN, J.: Field theory in psychology: Kurt Lewin. In J. Wepman and R. Heine (Eds.), *Concepts of Personality*. Chicago: Aldine, 1963.

LECKY, P.: *Self-Consistency*. New York: Island Press, 1945.

LEVITSKY, A., and PERLS, F.: The rules and games of gestalt therapy. In J. Fagan and I. Shepherd (Eds.), *Gestalt Therapy Now*. Palo Alto, Cal.: Science and Behavior Books, 1970.

MASLOW, A.: *Motivation and Personality*. New York: Harper, 1954.

MASLOW, A.: *Toward a Psychology of Being*. Princeton: Van Nostrand, 1968.

NARANJO, C.: Present-centeredness: Technique, prescription, and ideal. In J. Fagan and I. Shepherd (Eds.), *Gestalt Therapy Now*. Palo Alto, Cal.: Science and Behavior Books, 1970.

PERLS, F.: *Ego, Hunger, and Aggression*. New York: Vintage, 1969(a).

PERLS, F.: *Gestalt Therapy Verbatim*. Moab, Utah: Real People Press, 1969(b).

PERLS, F.: *In and Out the Garbage Pail*. Lafayette, Cal.: Real People Press, 1969(c).

PERLS, F.: Four lectures. In J. Fagan and I. Shepherd (Eds.), *Gestalt Therapy Now*. Palo Alto, Cal.: Science and Behavior Books, 1970.

PERLS, F.: *The Gestalt Approach and Eye Witness to Therapy*. Palo Alto, Cal.: Science and Behavior Books, 1973.

PERLS, F., HEFFERLINE, R., and GOODMAN, P.: *Gestalt Therapy: Excitement and Growth in the Human Personality*. New York: Dell, 1951.

PERLS, L.: Personal communication, 1972.

POSTMAN, L.: Rewards and punishments in human learning. In L. Postman (Ed.), *Psychology in the Making*. New York: Knopf, 1962.

REICH, W.: *Character Analysis*. New York: Noonday Press, 1949.

RIEFF, P.: *The Triumph of the Therapeutic*. New York: Harper & Row, 1966.

SHAPIRO, D.: *Neurotic Styles*. New York: Basic Books, 1965.

SHEPHERD, I.: Limitations and cautions in the gestalt approach. In J. Fagan and I. Shepherd (Eds.), *Gestalt Therapy Now*. Palo Alto, Cal.: Science and Behavior Books, 1970.

SMUTS, J.: *Holism and Evolution*. New York: Macmillan, 1926.

SUZUKI, D.: *The Training of the Zen Buddhist Monk*. New York: University Books, 1965.

TOBIN, S.: Self-support, wholeness, and gestalt therapy. *Voices*, 5:4, 5-12, 1969-70.

WOLMAN, B.: *Contemporary Theories and Systems in Psychology*. New York: Harper, 1960.

Woodworth, R., and Schlosberg, H.: *Experimental Psychology*. New York: Holt, Rinehart, & Winston, 1954.

Part II

FURTHER EXPLICATIONS OF GESTALT THERAPY

It is appropriate that this section open with Irma Lee Shepherd's presentation of the Gestalt approach as an open-ended, experimental approach, thereby unbounded by dogma or artificial "party lines." As such, as she shows, the Gestalt approach continues to evolve, pushed to its growing edge by other systems, techniques, methods.

Central to the Gestalt approach, too, is the concept of organismic flow, that natural homeostatic energy cycle whereby needs arise and needs are met. Perhaps all problems in living are simply interruptions of this natural flow. Robert Hall has developed a model which greatly aids in the understanding of this organismic flow. In his chapter he has offered a graphic paradigm and a carefully worked through discussion of the stages in the flow cycle.

Joen Fagan has viewed Gestalt therapy in terms of the currently expanding research into "right and left lobe brain functioning." In doing so, in her careful and thorough manner, she has contributed importantly to the theoretical understanding of the dynamics of the Gestalt therapy process. In addition, her chapter suggests research directions and invites theoretical speculation.

In his chapter on the "trickster-healer," Sheldon Kopp has presented a provocative view of the role of the therapist. He deals with the "technique-person" dimension in terms of the long tradition of the healer. He has offered a thought-stimulating handling of an important psychotherapy issue.

Denis O'Donovan has provided chapter six . . . and a view of Fritz.

2

Gestalt Therapy as an Open-Ended System

IRMA LEE SHEPHERD, Ph.D.

I see open-endedness as being one of the basic assumptions in the Gestalt approach: the view that personality is the constant interaction and integration of a number of functions—perceptual, physiological, cognitive—in relationship to the environment. Any effort to concretize or dogmatize this ongoing system in a rigid way is a violation of the nature of reality. This definition or way of looking at reality as process, as ongoing, has its corroborative expressions in physics and astronomy and other efforts at looking at the whole of life. Thus, I think that's the major point out of which, as a theory, the system itself is integrative.

Fritz said very specifically that he saw creativity as the ability to see all of the possibilities in the "now" and to take advantage of what is available; to respond in such a way to a need or wish that one fully uses the awareness process, sees the many possibilities, selects the one most satisfying at the time, taking into account the potential consequences, then moves on to the next situation in a constant contacting, responding, integrating, and assimilating way. Any system that doesn't do this, such as therapy, or scientific methodology, becomes rigid and codified, and immediately begins to cut out some of the potential aspects of reality, narrowing the possibilities of eliciting or discovering truth on other levels. This limits both theory and practitioners.

Another aspect of the Gestalt approach that is very important to me is that therapy requires the full participation of the practitioner—that there is no way to be involved in another's process without the ongoing

---

This chapter is based on a recorded conversation between Irma Lee Shepherd and Edward W. L. Smith.

of my own process. If I, too, am constantly changing and open to change, then what happens in the experience of the person with whom I am working cannot fail to touch me.

I think one of the tragedies of the psychoanalytic movement was that Freud became afraid that his central ideas might get lost in innovations. This fear was valid, to a degree, for there is danger in taking partial knowledge of a system and contaminating it with too easy eclecticism. Freud was concerned that the impact he was having would be lost through perversions and variations and elaborations of his theory which would violate some of the assumptions he thought basic. He became dogmatic, and closed to ideas such as the larger dimensions of consciousness in which Jung was interested. He also placed strong limits on his followers who wanted to look at the larger environmental impact, the social context. He was disturbed by what he saw as efforts on the part of the individuals involved to take away his place of leadership and power that was so hard-earned, or to soften his theory. I do not believe this was a problem for Fritz or others who understand clearly the assumptions in the Gestalt approach both experientially and cognitively-theoretically.

One of the basic premises in Gestalt theory describes excitement as being generated when the organism contacts something new, leading to the creation of a new Gestalt or new experience. That is, the immediate internal reinforcer is that something new, valuable, exciting, enhancing is occurring, and I am involved in that new experience as I am aware and responding. This can be an idea or a sensory experience or an observation of what's happening with the patient. My being able then to watch and marvel at what this person is able to do in mobilizing his own self-support and excitment systems, to move from a bad place to a good place, is so intrinsically rewarding that it's difficult to wish to rigidify, or to hang onto the past, or to make a tradition or ritual of the therapeutic processes or the living processes. One becomes so enamored of the emergingness that this may even lead to a reluctance on the part of the Gestalt therapist to talk about or to write about or to attempt, even for purposes of intellectual verbal sharing, to make concrete that which is best apprehended directly from experience.

So those are some of the first assumptions that I think about in supporting an open-ended, ongoing position. I also think of the importance of the relationship of the person of the theorist to the development of a theory. Fritz was an integrating individual. He was widely interested in many aspects of experience and many disciplines. He dabbled here and there, and while he was dilettantish in some areas of his dabbling, he was thorough in others. He had wide cultural interests and a broad educational background, which ranged from the scientific through the artistic. As he focused his energy, his stance toward living and thinking was to follow that which interested him most and then to find ways of integrating that into the foundations that he had already built out of previous interests and experiences.

Given his isolation in South Africa and the professional vacuum that he wandered into, he had an opportunity to pull together his interest in Reich, Gestalt psychology, existentialism, certain psychoanalytic ideas, his work in theatre, his interest in creativity, and his interest in aesthetics coming out of the Bauhaus and the circle of bohemian artists that he had become a quiet and observing part of in Berlin. All these resources were available when he had the time and isolation for integrating them.

And he didn't stop there. As is evident in reading *Hunger and Aggression* and then on through *Garbage Pail*, his ideas were open to changing, to evolving, and he made elegant elaborations of awareness theory. He was very willing to incorporate from Zen and from Charlotte Selver. He learned much from her and gave her credit for deepening his understanding of awareness. He appreciated the writings of Alan Watts and saw many parallels to Gestalt awareness theory in descriptions of Zen. He had little use for the discipline required in Zen training.

Fritz made thorough use of most of the contextual settings in which he placed himself. He valued his Esalen years for adding to his own understanding of himself in relationship to the people there. He was open to the environment, to cultural and aesthetic resources, and to all kinds of human beings. He was open both in the immediate sense and in the larger, theoretical sense. In his later films and lectures, one hears him talking about "writing your life script," referring to "games" and ego states, incorporating some of Eric Berne's language and ideas about personality. Fritz's formulation of "top-dog and under-dog" was more dynamic than Freud's superego and id, and he appreciated Eric's more refined definition in "Parent-Adult-Child." He was contemptuous, however, of keeping these ego states on an intellectual-cognitive level, and felt that nothing would really change if someone simply thought about themselves in this way. Active contact of those processes as they came into awareness was necessary for working through and integration of splits. Many practitioners of transactional analysis now make frequent use of the "empty chair" to resolve conflicts among ego states.

Fritz moved with his own times. He started out as an individual therapist, then he said, "Individual therapy is passé and group therapy is the thing." Later he wrote a paper in which he said, "Group therapy is passé and the workshop is the thing." His next position was that "Workshops are passé, the Kibbutz or the community wherein one can have a larger, longer, more whole, rounded experience that can lead to discovery and powerful change is the way." And he moved. He moved geographically in support of his movement into new ideas. I'm not saying that all of this was Fritz's openness. Some of his moves may have been in response to places within himself that he closed off, but by and large he was a very open, fresh person through his 76 years, open to what was happening around him, and open then to theoretical input and integration in his own way. I'm thinking of the extensive work he did with the people in his workshops on the West Coast in further developing recognition of the importance of the nonverbal. He worked with postural, gestural, motoric avenues to get into important unfinished business. He brought in people who were trained as movement therapists and art therapists, and he incorporated his own experiences with the work of Ida Rolf in structural integration. So, from both the theory and the person of Fritz I took a great deal of support for being open to whatever develops within the profession that I can integrate into my own experience and into my work in a logical, evolving process.

There are several cautions to be noted in working with other approaches. One, obviously, is getting sufficient training and knowledge to be competent in application. Another is the risk of getting carried away by one aspect or approach and then closing one's awareness to other important cues from the individual; arbitrarily deciding on a bioenergetics exercise without some very important listening to cues from the person in advance may well be an example. The therapist who goes with his own cognitive process and does not interact with messages coming from the patient may foster an addictive path of just heavy emotional expression in which there is no facilitation of integration. This is one of my criticisms of some of the primal work. It seems to me that sometimes a person has a powerful experience but there's not enough of a cognitive framework available for him to integrate that in a way that makes a cognitive-affective difference. I believe that growth experiences have to partake of all of the systems within the process for real movement to continue. I believe that part of the role of the therapist is helping the individual focus his awareness, not just have experiences, in the same way that the education of a child is in helping him to focus his awareness and maintain some flexibility of focus. The danger there lies in so narrowing the points of focus and in socializing in such a limited way that the child loses the possibilities of other ways of seeing.

When I say, "Gestalt approach to therapy," that seems to leave me with more doors than to say "Gestalt therapy," and maybe I'm begging the point here. Fritz's last book is called *The Gestalt Approach*. This volume represents the finest distillation, as I see it, of Gestalt theory. Fritz referred to his work as an integrative approach. He really was not enamored of the word "Gestalt." I think he preferred "experiential," but it already had connotations of the Atlanta Psychiatric Clinic approach. The word "experience" encompasses more than the word "Gestalt" because the latter has a limited scientific meaning and it really cannot be translated into English. It's one of those shades of meaning that's very difficult to translate. Those of us who are not German simply have to intuit the shades of meaning.

The Gestalt view of man is "man-in-the-environment," "man-as-a-part-of-nature." It's very clearly a system that's based on a theory of energy —that ultimate matter, the ultimate "stuff," is energy, and one of the characteristics of this energy apparently is awareness, possibly on all levels. This basis makes it fairly easy for me to have a cosmology that is process; as such, then, I can talk about a Gestalt philosophy of life, or Gestalt as a way of living. It's a way of living, a way of knowing, or it embodies a way of knowing; it embodies a responsibility-ethical system.

Within the experience of awareness and contact with myself, with another person, with the environment, I can have that heightened awareness that is often described in religious writings, in poetry, in literature of devotion. With some kinds of awareness there is evoked in me, a sense of awe and wonder and gratitude that feels completing for a period of time, fulfilling, realizing, making real, actualizing, making actual, a powerful sense of contact with what is, and that becomes part of the basic support that allows me to open myself to other ways. When this is shared with another human being, there is added a dimension of unity, a kind of confluence that is in itself enhancing and supporting.

In the Gestalt system there are many peak experiences, resolutions of dichotomies and integration of polarities in what may be described as "a small Zen satori." Thus, much of the elegant and rich wisdom of the East and the West becomes available to me in its distilled essence when I am open. One of the excitements in therapy is finding the blocks to this in myself and other people, and helping remove these.

When I think of the issue of support, I think of the importance of differentiation—of moving from almost total confluence at birth and in infancy towards separateness. One of the tasks of the child is to get enough support from the environment to survive and begin to take over more and more of his own self-direction. One of the important factors is that he begins to see himself as separate, not independent, but separate and different from his mother and other adults around him, and that he moves more and more into the development of his own center and experiencing himself as the center of his existence. The process includes identification and being confluent with the parent, taking over the parent's values for a while, then having enough support from the parent to be different, to be separate, to begin to think for himself, to make choices and to see and accept the consequences of those choices.

This process, the separating and centering of oneself behind one's own eyes, is the most powerful self-support. One of the skills here is to recognize the needs that I can't meet for myself, that I can only have met in relationship to another person. I can't really look into my own eyes, except in a mirror, and a mirror doesn't give me the kind of communication and contact that is an important need. I can't hug myself very well, not nearly as well as another person can. The need for loving is an international, interpersonal one that's important in my regard for myself. The most self-supporting person is one who is quite clear about his real boundaries and reasonably clear about the difference between his needs and wants, so that he doesn't get pitched into panic about survival when he doesn't get what he wants from others. Now I *need* air, and my organism will respond with panic at being deprived of air. I need ongoing contacts with people, and something in me would be diminished if I were utterly isolated at this point in my life. At the same time, the kind of contact that I may be having with people adds to my sense of my own difference and separation. Being able to be in solid, caring touch with other persons may lead me to withdrawing from interpersonal contact more and more and opening myself up to internal experiences.

Sometimes I think of myself as a two-way gate, where there is a vast realm of contact and communication with energy, and with forms I don't precisely know. My internal being is my gate to that—this is what meditation does. Perhaps going inside with awareness gets me in touch with archetypes, with other aspects of awareness that seem to be limitless and circling. I tried to diagram this once by drawing two lines crossing in an elongated χ. The fore part is the global confluences of my past and my contact with the world which narrows as I differentiate myself to a point of being one pointed, centered, yet it stays open at the same time, intensely focused and opening again, now to what feels like immediate contact with the universe—a new and limitless confluence, oneness with all that is. As I drew this symbol one time and looked at it, I realized all I had to do was round it out and I had the symbol for infinity, which implies continuous and ongoing process.

Sometimes, as a therapist, I am also a gate to that dimension for others. I see myself as focusing my attention, my responsiveness, and my action in such a way that I help individuals move from the confluences of their growing-up, the introjections and the projections, so that they begin to take their own power back inside themselves. They become more focused and one-pointed, separated, differentiated and self-supporting. At the same time, sometimes I think I am the gate to the other dimension, that if I can hold the door open long enough they see things through me that ricochet back into themselves. It's that kind of thing, that neither I nor they are the limits of. And that requires openness to all kinds of unfamiliar personal and interpersonal experiences which carry with them threat and fright of madness, that are unsettling and uncontrolled and unpredictable, and can be very quickly interpreted as madness and chaos.

One of Fritz's powerful gifts was the extending of insights from the field of linguistics, emphasizing the force of language in shaping experience, especially in diminishing the individual's sense of responsibility (meaning responsiveness to his own experience) by the ways in which he describes experience. The language usages that Fritz and others have highlighted—"it" for "I," the confluent "we," the projected "they," using passive verbs instead of active—provide an exciting and powerful tool for correcting the distancing experience that goes with mechanical, coldly objective language.

Recent widespread usage of these corrections has led, in some instances, to rather thoughtless and rigid application giving rise to Gestalt commandments and a new set of "shoulds" no less restricting than the ones they supplanted. I have been especially conscious of the misuse by some therapists of the suggestion to change "I can't" statements to "I won't." This has seemed to me to be a way for therapists to express their impatience by saying to the patient, in essence, "It's very obvious that you can do what you want to at this moment and that you are just refusing to."

I believe that while an individual may choose to see himself as impotent rather than risk changing some habitual ways, there are also some genuine existential "I can'ts," and "I will" is based on awareness. Given the kinds of education and the kinds of life experiences most of us grow up with, we eliminate, for survival's sake, some awareness of various aspects of our own power and resources. Often this is conditioned on a preverbal or nonverbal level and there is almost no way to consciously make anyone aware of what so terrifies him when the stimulus itself sets off an immediate defensive response. To tell a patient that he is resisting may be quite true, but to expect him at that moment to respond in a different way is, I believe, a kind of therapeutic put-down or put-off. The person who doesn't change when the technique is applied becomes a threat to the therapist's sense of himself as an effective therapist who "should" get this person through his block, through his defense. The therapist may be venting his frustration on the patient.

I believe such situations are most appropriately dealt with by going beyond the usual "hot seat—empty chair" procedures for dealing with introjected parents, etc., and supplementing them with experiences that permit sensory input at deeper levels, almost the hypnotic states, states of altered consciousness that parallel the early states that the child was in when negative, destructive messages were put in. This is similar to Pesso's psychomotor approach, which provides a very powerful reparenting experience when the person needs to have sensory experience. Fritz dealt with this very nicely by having a person be his own ideal parent. "What did you want your parents to say? Now, be the parent that says that."

I think it's true we can hear on this level sometimes and it's quite possible for the message to filter down into a deep resolving place. At other times, however, I believe there are other kinds of requirements that may be sensory, in which the sound has to come from a male voice or a female voice and the words must go to that place of primitive pain in order to be corrective. At these times, there has to be a restructuring of the setting, of the emotional, physiological sensory state, in such a way that the input comes from some outside source. Pesso says it well in terms of our needing inside us parent archetypes: fathers who protect us and support us, and mothers who love and nurture us. Once established, these integral presences become a powerful source of self-support. I do indeed believe that each person must ultimately take this over, but may well need to hear and experience it from outside first.

Much of this is done in fantasy. The integrative power of fantasy and its real feeling power is very, very healing, but I think sometimes there has to be the literal physical stimulus, and fantasy alone cannot close the gap. I think that with the healing of those developmental deficits in self-support, the person is far, far more able to take from other fantasy experiences, from meditation, from reflection, a sense of being able to receive loving energy from the sky, the trees and sunlight and a direct experiencing of energy in the air (prahna) in breathing.

There is also an experience of being loved by life, which doesn't have to be mediated through another person for me to feel loved and valued in the universe by the universe. But I think that's way up the line on a developmental scale. It's an error if people try to get there before they are there by avoiding dealing with their chronic pain. Fritz said in one of his last films, "What is Gestalt?", that we have become phobic about pain, the pain that's just there in growing up. I don't think yoga and meditation, whether Christian or Hasidic or Eastern, can fill in some of those experiences if there is a gap there. That is exactly the task of psychotherapy. . . .

With the psychotic person, one of the gaps is insufficient sensory input, or input so noxious and so terrifying that much sensory awareness was cut off or had to be distorted in order to be even remotely tolerated. An example is from a colleague who has been working with a severely schizophrenic woman, now doing well and functioning as a professional. Her statement was, "I am just now beginning to feel real. I am just now beginning to really be in my body, to feel connected to and responsive to processes in my body. Now I know what is meant by being real, rather than just thinking of myself as a person all these years." That's both exciting and frightening. To get there, to realness, she had to work through terror and to let herself receive much early mothering.

Another danger, I think, is that with all the vast array of techniques and procedures for keeping a person focused in his own experience the therapist can avoid interaction. This was not true for the really good Gestalt therapists, Fritz, Jim Simkin, and a number of others. One of Fritz's many definitions in Gestalt therapy was, "I and thou, here and now." In the hands of a frightened therapist, however, these procedures become a marvelous way of working exclusively as a director. While I think that may be very appropriate at times, it may also allow a more threatened therapist to be objective and yet appear and act involved. The Gestalt approach allows the therapist to focus on the block within the patient which prevents communication and which has to be dealt with there before genuine exchange can take place. But for the therapist to minimize the importance of process between himself and the patient as an ever-constant ground of support is an error. The other error would be in being so confluent with the patient that objective observation of the obvious blocks in the patient is limited and the self-limiting processes are never dealt with.

I think there is a general misunderstanding that Gestalt work is all "sturm und drang." If people limit their experience to episodic workshops where the focus is on intense and powerful working through of unfinished business, then the impression is given that Gestalt work involves only the release of powerful feelings. Recently, a girl came to a workshop, and towards the end she wanted to do something and get something for herself. She had the idea that it was going to have to be something huge and awful that would, of course, feel *bad*, that she would go into all her bad feelings. What she was really in touch with at that moment was her sense of appreciation for having participated in vicarious ways, in an empathic way, with so many people. I focused with her on just the fact that she had been willing to speak at this point and was letting herself be the center of attention, and that may be sufficient for her for that time. Just by my supporting and directing her to her own responses to her somewhat limited actions, she became aware of her sense of pleasure and pride in herself for having come to a workshop that was initially frightening, having witnessed a lot of powerful work, and having let herself weep with some people. She was feeling good about all that, but didn't know how to support her good feelings. Her realization of that was a lovely experience for her, for me, and for the group. In fact, I think of such experiences as probably as important work for her as the working through the death of a spouse or the other terribly dramatic experiences with which others were dealing. The gentle, delightful, playful, limited kinds of unowned or unintegrated experiences are just as important as the more powerful and dramatic ones.

Another confusion among practitioners is between well-supported compassion touching the integrity of the other person who is in need of support and the so-called Red Cross nurse rushing in to take over to do for the person that which he can do for himself. Some Gestalt therapists work so hard to make sure they are not Red Cross nurses (often accurately perceiving manipulations of the other person), that they may make the opposite error and withhold some of their own loving responsiveness, the powerful human force available to them, when a patient needs it. So, when to support and when not to is another decision point, and a difficult one to reach. There can be errors in either direction. The way I check out for myself is by asking, "What am I getting out of this?"—whether this is related to my need to feel important or be compassionate or loving. If this is a genuine expression, I don't have anything invested in whether the person accepts it or not. If I offer who I am at the moment and the person makes use of my presence and support in whatever way I express in a way that's mutually instantaneously negotiated, then that feels like part of the process, versus smothering, infantilizing, putting in too much information, and serving up too much projection. It's a fine balance. Self-knowledge is the corrective for this, constant self-knowing and constant self-contact.

I've been talking in detail about the effects of the open-endedness of the Gestalt approach in the person and work of the therapist. Now, I would like to look at possible integrations of insights about personality and procedures developed in other therapeutic systems. Certainly one of the most powerful antecedents of the Gestalt approach was Reich's influence and impact on Fritz both as a person-psychotherapist and as a theoretician. Many of the developments of the Reichian approach, if not incorporated too rigidly in the person of the practitioner, offer ways of extending procedures in the Gestalt approach. For example, exaggerating physical movement: a tiny tapping movement may lead to pounding with the fist on a knee, then to pounding on a pillow, beating on a mattress. The whole person may become involved in movement, and assisting the development of this into a full-fledged temper tantrum may give him experience with the rage which he has been afraid to have.

There are problems that accrue, however, if too much focus is placed just on the physical expression without a chance for the person to deal with the symbolic processes that are also there. Staying with the body for extensive periods of time, as in the work of Feldenkrais or Charlotte Selver, is useful to anyone interested in expanding his awareness or sensory embodiment. When body armor becomes rigid, Charlotte Selver's approach often leads to the release of muscle tension in really amazing ways, changing chronic postures and chronic restrictions in the musculature.

Rolfing is another intervention that carries powerful, evocative reactions to early trauma or early decisions to hold a powerful affect in physically. Rolfing loosens muscles so that more flexibility and more options are possible. The person is no longer restricted by past attitudes that he may have pretty well worked through in feeling, but that still are represented by stiff muscles and postures. Rolfing may give that additional latitude so that the individual may gain more mobility of movement and expression. That makes sense to me, as do practices that involve joyous physical expression, such as dancing movement, which can be a way of both pleasuring the body and energizing it so as to keep the system more open and responsive.

Any of the movement therapies which help the person reacquire freedom to move, to express and to experience himself bodily in the world, can be used as elaboration or an extension of the Gestalt approach, as art and music offer other kinds of nonverbal exploring and development of awareness and expression. One of the dimensions that bioenergetics makes an effort to work through is freeing sounds, freeing those verbal expressions that children have such immediate access to in screaming and shouting. Fear of singing, speaking, or making sounds can be dealt with by the Gestalt approach and can be enhanced by the use of the expertise and skill of therapists trained in body work, speech and voice, recreation and play.

Also important in relationship to Gestalt is the dimension of expanded awareness—the processes of meditation that facilitate centering, listening, stillness, staying in the now. The slow opening of awareness in our interior may also lead to discovery of demons and introjects, or of powers and presences. All can be faced and dealt with within the Gestalt approach. I support and encourage and delight in people I work with moving in the direction of gaining more skill in contacting the deeper dimensions of self.

To me, there is considerable value in some of the formulations in transactional analysis and rational emotive therapy—specifically, becoming aware of the ways in which my thinking both sets up and limits and stirs up and contaminates my feeling experience, so that any way that I have of getting onto those self-torture games, as Fritz called them (Self-Improvement Game, Great Expectations, Self Ideal, etc.), is worthwhile.

So, the therapies that offer ways of thinking about thinking seem useful to me. I learn what I can and take from them to integrate those ideas that are congruent with me and my own experience to this point in time. I avoid those approaches that seem to me to be anti-organismic or coercive or forcing or restricting or narrowing. Among the more useful approaches, certainly the work of Ira Progoff and Jung, focusing on the power of symbolic processes, is important. In one sense the work in Gestalt touches archetypes. Recently I've been doing a fantasy trip which I'm calling *The Search for the Lost Child*. Individuals often discover in this fantasy that the child who is lost is of the opposite sex, which can be thought of as how the animus or anima got lost or diminished or tucked away. The Gestalt work is thus focused on the effort to recontact and then to assimilate and integrate that energy into a balanced person. The work of the Jungians is a point of focusing and contacting in terms of theory that offers excitement to me. As such, I can take that in as a resource, as an alternative way of thinking about the people I work with which frees my creativity for improvising experiments that may facilitate their contacting themselves in richer, deeper ways.

A useful concept from TA is the idea of critical decisions that a child makes at a point in time to survive, but which becomes a defensive approach to reality as conditions change, no longer appropriate. The Gestalt process teases out that decision and makes it real. The patient can enter the present and have a change to say, "This is not appropriate now; it is not true of my world, and I don't have to continue operating under the power of a frightened three-year-old." I find concepts from TA and from symbolic processes very useful to effect some kinds of integration.

I am always appreciative of those colleagues of mine who operate within a psychoanalytic framework but who are open and integrative in their work. I think that they have a respect for process and they also have a respect for the unconscious, a powerful respect for those processes that sometimes effect change without really emerging into awareness. My preferred style is to know, but I surely recognize that change occurs on other levels and sometimes outside awareness. This gives me appreciation for the experiential school that focuses so heavily on letting process alone and supporting it only by the person of the therapist. I believe that the Gestalt approach allows for some refinement in that and may increase the facilitation of process by more specific focusing on aspects of it that the experiential therapist might let go by or may only get to much later. I continue to take support from that respect for process—person process —that is evident in the work of some of those who call themselves experiential, and also that of some of the existentialists. I can imagine that many of the existential therapists are finding more excitement in the Gestalt approach, and some who ten years ago called themselves existential may now be describing themselves as "Experiential-Gestalt."

Fritz called the behaviorists "existentialists" in that they worked in the present. I am very clear about the important role of learning in the Gestalt approach and the use of many procedures familiar to any therapist working in a behavioral style, such as the use of relaxation, breathing, repetition and practice, and, certainly, reinforcement. The internal experience of the patient as he tries new ways of speaking and acting brought to his awareness becomes a powerful incentive for sustaining behavior changes. More collaboration and study of the potentialities of behavioral principles for the Gestalt therapist is certainly indicated.

In summary, I've tried to look at a number of dimensions of the Gestalt approach as an open system based on its basic assumptions of reality as process. The open-endedness of the theory makes it possible for the thoughtful therapist to be in constant development of his skills, with input from many therapeutic systems available for examination. Such a system may evolve into future forms not recognizable as we see it today, but likely maintaining a dynamic core. The ancient descriptions of reality in East and West seem to have stayed intact, even if dynamic and changing and strangely circular. That which was new becomes old, jaded, and lost, rediscovered, redefined, new, becomes old, *ad infinitum?*

3

A Schema of the Gestalt Concept of the
Organismic Flow and Its Disturbance

ROBERT A. HALL, M.D.

This schema is a graphic presentation of the stages of the phasic homeostatic flow of the organism, according to the Gestalt conception. It also schematizes the disturbed characteristics of these stages in psychopathology, as seen by the clinical psychotherapist.

The graph uses the horizontal axis to represent the flow of time. The energy level of the organism is represented by the vertical axis. A sinusoidal curve is the function used since it is a cyclical "wave" function which is more accurately representative than the circle, for example, of the flow from one resting point, through a perturbation-behavior unit, to a subsequent and different point of rest. Stages in the flow of the healthy, undisturbed cycle are shown above the sinusoidal curve and are labeled "0" through "8" and "0'." Corresponding stages in the pathological cycle are shown below this curve and are labeled similarly in parentheses.

Stage "0." The healthy cycle begins at the nodal point of the *resting* state (lower left). This has qualities of integration and centeredness. There are feelings of fullness and self-acceptance. The feeling of "just being" is comfortable. This is the "fertile void," the organismic ground from which all figure must arise. There is peaceful "no-thingness" in the Zen sense, and in its ultimate development by those who have mastered the oriental arts of meditation there is a sense of cosmic identification with the universal. This state is pregnant with the limitless range of potential developments for the fully alive person. "What interesting thing might happen next?" is the quiet, confident, open, poised question.

Stage "1." Then something does happen. A fresh organismic *deficit* or *surplus* arises. For example a physiological deficit of tissue hydration occurs.

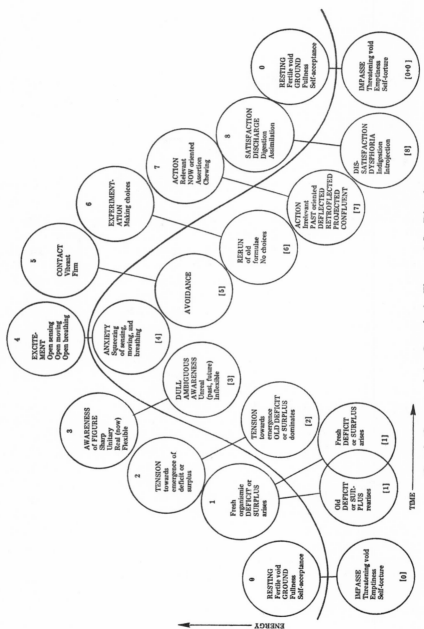

Gestalt Concept of the Organismic Flow and Its Disturbance

Stage "2." The water deficit leads to the development of a *tension* towards the emergence into awareness of the feeling of thirst.

Stage "3." The feeling of thirst emerges into clear, sharp *awareness*. This awareness is unitary in that it is not diffused by competing needs. The awareness is existent and real in that it relates to the dominant need of the person *now*. It is not dissipated by attention to the non-existent past or future. Also, good awareness function has the property of "hierarchical flexibility" by being able to freely switch should a more urgent need arise. For example, awareness switches from thirst to the smell of the smoke that heralds a fire in the kitchen. A most important quality of full awareness is one which strongly suggests the adaptive basis for its existence as a biological phenomenon. Awareness has the remarkable quality of promptly and powerfully raising the energy level of the organism to one which is appropriate to support the action necessary to meet a particular emerging need.

Stage "4." The alert, energized organism is now in the phase of *excitement*. Physiologically, the organism has entered into a state of activation of the sympathetic portion of the autonomic nervous system. This activates functions which support action. The eyes are fully open, the pupils dilated. The other senses are more open to stimuli. The motor system is activated, more open to movement. Cardiovascular and other support systems for sensing and moving are activated. There is a heightened metabolism. Especially notable is the opened, deepened, free breathing which provides the additional aeration necessary to support the heightened metabolic rate.

Stage "5." Excitement moves the organism towards *contact*. Contact is made with aspects of the non-self (environment) which offer potential resources for dealing with the deficit or surplus. Good contact has the lively quality of vibrance. It is firm, yet not "deadlocked," as in the stare. Contact is made, broken, remade, moves on. It is energetic, pulsating in relation to clearly defined contact boundaries with clear recognition of what is "I" and what is "not I" (in contrast to confluence).

Stage "6." Freely ranging contact allows *experimentation*. Possibilities are opened up for innovation, for finding alternate ways of meeting needs. Choices can be made of easier or more fulfilling behaviors.

Stage "7." Experiment and choice set the stage for definitive *action*, which then has the quality of relevance. This means orientation to the optimal aspects for fulfillment in the existential reality of now. The action engages the full, healthy, self-assertive, aggressive resources of the organism. Following Perls' recognition of the preeminent significance of the processes involved in nutrition for psychological as well as physical metabolism, Gestalt theory emphasizes the importance of thorough "chewing" of all "food" from the environment.

Stage "8." Now it is possible for *satisfaction* to occur. The intakes from the environment are chewed up, tasted, and destructured. They can be digested and assimilated, made part of one's own being. And that which does not taste good can be spit out. Here, the physiological state is predominance of the parasympathetic nervous system. This augments activities associated with the destructuring, absorption, and restructuring of what has been taken in. The organism is ready to return to the new resting nodal point, "0'."

The pathological cycle is seen, in the theory of Gestalt psychotherapy, as the consequence of self-interference with the normal flow. This is generally characterized by preoccupation with the unrealities of past, future, fantasy, and the substitutive dummy thinking ("mind fucking"). There is consequent loss of engagement with the real existential now. Much frightening of the self occurs, typical under the pressure from "top-dog" introjects. The top-dog always "knows" what terrible catastrophes will befall the person, especially if he risks innovative and assertive behavior. He thus keeps himself in a state of chronic frustration, anxiety, and depression.

This concept of the psychopathological cycle is most easily applied to the neuroses and psychosomatic disorders, but can also be seen in the psychoses and character disorders. The schema traces this cycle from a low energy nodal point called the *impasse* (stage [0]). This is characterized by the person feeling stuck and empty. The void is experienced as threatening rather than fertile. Nothingness is poorly tolerated. Instead of peacefulness, the experience is that of feeling haunted by the vague ghosts of uncompleted prior Gestalts arising from the graveyard of accumulated unfinished business from the past. These may be the focus of self-torturing. Like all proper ghosts, they seek resurrection. And so they re-arise, and compete with a fresh deficit or surplus in stage [1]. In stage [2] they often dominate at the expense of here-and-now organismic needs. This does violence to the homeostatic process. It is comparable to a railroad sidetracking a carload of fresh strawberries in order to try to deliver last week's wilted lettuce; neither one arrives at market in usable shape. "Market" in the case of the organism is an awareness which is dull and ambiguous due to the splitting of attention between competing figures (stage [3]). The awareness also has an unreal quality associated with the dilution of attention towards what IS now by attention towards what was or what may be. Furthermore, there is diminished flexibility of the awareness process. In the extreme (as in psychosis), life-threatening signals do not receive the preeminent access to awareness needed for survival. The disturbed awareness is then succeeded by anxiety in place of excitement (stage [4]). One of Perls' important discoveries is that anxiety is excitement unsupported by adequate oxygenation. Along with squeezing off of the senses and body motility, the anxious person squeezes off breathing. Just when it is most needed, respiration becomes blocked and shallow. (Many people can readily demonstrate the validity of this proposition by merely enhancing their breathing when anxiety is experienced. They will discover that anxiety is transmuted into excitement.) The anxious, poorly energized person then avoids good contact with the environment (stage [5]). Then, instead of experimentation, the person refers back to and reruns old "canned" formulae from his "tape library" of stale, anachronistic behavioral responses (stage [6]). No real (now-relevant) choices are made. For example, one tries to manipulate someone to meet a need for affection in the same way they (perhaps successfully) manipulated mother in childhood. There is a wide repertoire of deflected, retroflected, projection-based, and confluent behaviors which are irrelevant and past oriented (stage [7]). They lead to dissatisfaction and dysphoria (stage [8]). Having failed to assert himself or herself and chew, the person then suffers psychological if not physical indigestion as intakes from the environment are "swallowed whole" (introjected) without assimilation. Then there is return to another point of impasse. This has been labelled $[0 + 0']$ in recognition of the fact that the person has not only failed to deal with his old unfinished needs, but has accumulated an additional burden of unfinished business.

Like all abstractions, this schema suffers from inherent limitations and inaccuracies. These stem from such factors as arbitrariness, logical imperfections, the exaggeration of polarities, and especially from incompleteness. The other side of the coin is that this diagram is at least a beginning attempt to be graphically specific and concise about an important theoretical orientation to the understanding of human behavior and its aberration. As such it may have value for the teaching of Gestalt therapy. It may also be found to have application as framework for making more precise experimental hypotheses for research in normal behavior, psychopathology, and psychotherapy.

4

The Gestalt Approach as "Right Lobe" Therapy

JOEN FAGAN, Ph.D.

If we divide schools of psychotherapy along a continuum between the poles of cognitive and emotional-expressive, there is no doubt where the Gestalt approach lies—not quite so far down the line as primal therapy or bioenergetics, but still well to the left of center. In the late 1960's, when Gestalt therapy was first becoming widely known, the model presented by Perls was the workshop "hotseat," where a participant, only a few minutes after telling Fritz his name, might be engaged in an explosive reenactment of a childhood scene. Other variations of Gestalt practice and theory, such as Kempler's (1974) insistence on an immediate powerful encounter with the families he works with and Naranjo's (1970) proposal of a radical present-centeredness as a way of life are similar in their opposition to any forms of analysis, conceptualization, and distancing. Even the more conservative Gestalt therapists expect routinely that patients will experience intense emotional states, relive early conflicts with vividness, and show strong bodily expressions of anger, despair, etc.

A recent paper by Sanders (1974) examines abreactive therapies, including primal, bioenergetics, and Gestalt, from the standpoint of split-brain research, and suggests that the techniques developed by these approaches constitute a "royal road" to the right lobe or non-dominant hemisphere. A similar viewpoint is expressed by Ornstein (1972) who lists Gestalt therapy as an alternate route to the present-centeredness sought by meditation, not only to evoke right lobe functioning but also as containing "the seeds of a new synthesis." Finally, Galin (1974), in a sophisticated and tightly reasoned paper, suggests that present knowledge of hemispheric specialization provides a framework for thinking about

58

repression and psychological defense mechanisms. He parallel's Freud's descriptions of primary process with right lobe functions, and suggests hypotheses that might account for functional disconnections between hemispheres in persons with intact brains that would clarify a variety of psychopathological symptoms. His paper suggests that perhaps genuine cross-fertilization between neuropsychology and psychiatry is now possible.

These three viewpoints are all presented by persons whose background is experimental psychology or neuropsychology rather than psychotherapy. The purpose of the present paper is to connect Sanders', Ornstein's and Galin's thinking to therapeutic techniques, especially those of Gestalt therapy. First, findings of recent research on hemispheric localization of function will be presented, followed by related theories, then schools of therapy examined and Gestalt procedures detailed. The base of excitement underlying this paper is that recent research in a number of areas relating brain functioning to behavior and/or experience is offering strong possibilities of a theoretical underpinning that will facilitate the study and understanding of psychotherapy, as well as a rapprochement of the "left" side of psychology (verbal, behavioral, logical, scientific) with the "right" (intuitive, experiencing, imaging, therapeutic).

HEMISPHERIC SPECIALIZATION

Recognition of speech and language as localized in the left or dominant lobe dates back to Broca over a hundred years ago. Shortly afterwards, Jackson suggested that the two lobes had different functions; however, only the left hemisphere was of interest to neurologists for many years. Only several decades into this century did a few studies, primarily based on patients with right hemisphere injuries, begin to appear, suggesting deficits in visual perception, spatial relations, and musical skills. A series of steps, including Penfield's electrical stimulation of intact brains during brain surgery and Myers and Sperry's study of animal perception and learning following section of the corpus callosum, led to the successful efforts of Bogen and Vogel to control epileptic seizures by commissurotomy (see Gazzaniga, 1970 and Pines, 1974). The significance of this procedure was that it made available a number of subjects, many without massive hemisphere damage, whose right and left lobe functioning could be studied by simple variations on type of stimulus presentation and type of response mode. Input to half of the brain could be achieved by stimulating the contralateral visual field or hand, and output could be controlled by specifying the type of response (verbal or motor) or by using the contralateral hand.

The theoretical importance of the early findings for the understanding of brain functioning has encouraged a rapid flowering of studies of lateralization in *S*s with intact brains by means of such procedures as tachistoscopic presentation to half of the visual field (Swanson, 1974), eye movement direction during response to questions (Kinsbourne, 1974, Schwartz, 1974), patterns of interference between tasks performed simultaneously, such as speaking or singing while engaged in motor tasks (Hicks, 1974), and EEG studies of alpha asymmetry with verbal and spacial tasks. In addition, studies of altered states of consciousness, including meditation and biofeedback procedures, appear to have direct implications for hemispheric localization.

Since research and findings in the area of hemispheric specialization are undergoing such rapid change, summarizing the current state of knowledge is risky business. However, a list of apparently safe generalizations will be given, drawn largely from the following sources: Gazzaniga (1970), Nebes (1974), Ornstein (1972), and Galin (1974).

1. LEFT LOBE

  General: Cognitive style is to process data by sequential analysis of abstract symbolic "bits." This involves logical, temporal cause-effect emphases. Types of data used are words and other symbols such as mathematical. Attention and perceptual input are focused on written or oral speech and motor output is concentrated on speech and writing.

  Specific: The left lobe contains centers for language and symbolic comprehension, language memory, speech, reading, and association of names with objects. It also has main motor control over the right side of the body and the speech musculature.

2. RIGHT LOBE

  General: Cognitive style is to process data in a holistic, integrative way, for purposes of pattern recognition and orientation. This involves simultaneous processing of a number of sensory and kinesthetic cues. Output is by expressive movement and gestures, manipulation of objects, and drawing.

  Specific: The right lobe is concerned with sensory perception, including visual perception of shape and pattern, especially if complex, and 3-dimensional; spatial relationships, visual memory; musical perception and expression. It has primary motor control over the left side of the body. More hypothetically, the right lobe may be primarily involved in imaging, dreaming, emotional experiencing and expression, and body image.

3. COOPERATION/COMPETITION:

The halves of the brain alternate being "on" and competing for motor channels. The side most competent for the function involved—competence involving probably both speed of response and ability to achieve positive reinforcement—"wins," inhibiting all or part of the other hemisphere. The suppressed lobe may interfere with or cue the dominant side. Forms of meditation may result in synchronization (Orme-Johnson, 1974) and integration may be possible and even neccessary for creativity (Bogen and Bogen, 1969). Hypothetically, training and past experiences may result in perceptual and output selection which could result in one side of the brain being "on" a disproportionate amount of time.

RELATED THEORIES

A number of theories, drawn largely or partially from brain research, have amplified aspects of consciousness or cognitive states. Deikman (1971) hypothesizes and describes bimodal consciousness consisting of an action mode and a receptive mode. The action mode, characterized by beta waves, focal attention, logic, and dominance of form over sensory characteristics, has as its aim manipulating and changing the environment. The goal of the receptive mode is the intake of information, and the sensory-perceptual system is dominant with diffuse attending, paralogical thought, and blurred boundaries. Deikman believes that the receptive mode originates and dominates in infancy, but is gradually submerged by the action mode. He notes that it is possible to shift modes by shifting components, e.g., relaxing muscles. The essence of the action mode is language; love, mystical states, and psychotic states belong in the receptive.

Weil (1972), following experiences with and research on altered states of consciousness, especially as related to marijuana usage, proposed two ways of using the mind or of thinking, which he calls "straight" and "stoned." Straight thinking is ordinary thinking, with five characteristics or tendencies: (1) knowing through the intellect, which is confused with "mind," (2) being attached to the senses and through them to external reality, (3) paying attention to outward forms rather than to inner concepts, (4) perceiving differences rather than similarities between phenomena, and (5) negative thinking, pessimism, and despair. Stoned thinking, which includes altered states of consciousness, is the mirror image of straight thinking, including as components: (a) reliance on intuition as well as intellection, (b) acceptance of the ambivalent nature of things, (c) experience of infinity in its positive aspect (as in peak experiences).

Ornstein (1972), basing his position directly on research findings coming from split brain and hemispheric specialization studies, proposes two major modes of consciousness, the analytic and holistic, which he views as being complementary, both being necessary for genuine achievement. He is more interested in examining holistic consciousness since it is more neglected by Western psychology. He views Eastern approaches, including meditation and meditative techniques, as ways of "opening up" the right lobe, with Zen, Yoga, and Sufi exercises involving the dehabituation and deautomation of ordinary left lobe consciousness. These all involve ways of focusing attention in either very limited or very broad ways (see also Naranjo and Ornstein, 1971). Techniques include use of geometric and visual forms, crafts, dreams, music and chanting, and special language forms, including parables. Finally, he includes a few Western contributions to tapping right lobe functioning and assisting in integration; two therapeutic approaches are psychosynthesis and Gestalt therapy. "The process of Gestalt therapy is an alternate route to the present-centeredness sought in meditation" (p. 218).

Watzlawick and his coworkers (1967) detail two patterns of communication, which they describe as digital and analogic. Digital communication is dependent on arbitrary symbolic coding, i.e., language. It is logical, precise, complex, and versatile, and is capable of abstraction, negation, and truth functions. Analogic communication, which includes virtually all nonverbal communication, is more ambiguous and atemporal, and since it can be understood across cultures (i.e., sign language or intentional gestures) or even across animal species, it is more generally valid. The main function of digital communication is to deal with and transmit content or information; analogic communication deals with relationships, and serves as metacommunication indicating how a given message is to be received. When attempts are made to translate from digital to analogic communication, information is lost; going from analogic to digital involves uncertainty due to the variety of "meanings" possible.

Watzlawick describes a number of psychiatric symptoms which can be seen as coming from confused translations from one system to the other.

"Psychotherapy is undoubtedly concerned with the correct and the corrective digitalization of the analogic; in fact, the success or failure of any interpretation will depend both on the therapist's ability to translate from the one mode to the other, and on the patient's readiness to exchange his own digitalization for the more appropriate and less distressing ones" (p. 100).

These four positions, one concerned with perception, two with consciousness, and one with communication, or, viewed another way, input, throughput and output, describe almost identical patterns. One of the men most directly involved with split brain research, (Bogen, 1974), has broadened these two modes even further, paralleling the descriptions of hemispheric functions derived from neurological studies with theories from anthropologists, linguists, philosophers, psychologists, therapists, and developmentalists. In conclusion and anticipation, he states:

> The hypothesis which is the main burden of this paper may be summarized as follows:
> One of the most obvious and fundamental features of the cerebrum is that it is double. Various kinds of evidence, especially from hemispherectomy, have made it clear that one hemisphere is sufficient to sustain a personality or mind. We may then conclude that the individual with two intact hemispheres has the capacity for two distinct minds. This conclusion finds its experimental proof in the split-brain animal whose two hemispheres can be trained to perceive, consider, and act independently. In the human, where *propositional* thought is typically lateralized to one hemisphere, the other hemisphere evidently specializes in a different mode of thought, which may be called *appositional.*
> The rules or methods by which propositional thought is elaborated on "this" side of the brain (the side which speaks, reads, and writes) have been subjected to analyses of syntax, semantics, mathematical logic, etc. for many years. The rules by which appositional thought is elaborated on the other side of the brain will need study for many years to come (Bogen, 1974, p. 119).

Psychotherapy

Freud's early work with patients, including his use of hypnosis, often involved powerful emotional expressions, both with respect to transference feelings and also abreaction and catharsis of early memories. Uncomfortable with the amount of feeling aroused and increasingly doubtful about its usefulness in producing long-term personality change, he opted for the more controlled method of free association. Given Freud's mastery of verbal skills and his logical scientific bent, it is hardly surprising that he produced a "left lobe" therapy, expressed as *"Where there is id, let there be ego."* However, his assigning of meaning to dreams, images, slips of the tongue, and body expressions of conflict make his writings a compendium of right lobe expressions and hypotheses. This is seen most especially in his description of primary process. Therapeutically, however, Freud viewed alogical productions, intensity of emotions, and altered states of consciousness as deflections of energy or waste products to be cleared up, if possible, or at least controlled by appropriate socially regulated release. Even sexuality was to serve genital discharge and instinctual release and relief, not intimacy, excitement, or relationship. Freud admitted that he could not understand women, or creativity, or emotion (e.g., why libido could not be easily attached to a new object (!) if the old relationship were severed by death or desertion).

Many of the therapists who rebelled against Freud emphasized various aspects of right lobe functioning: Ferenzi's use of physical deprivation to evoke emotion in sessions; Rank's emphasis of artistic expression and counter-will; Jung's exploration of symbols and symbolic expressions as sources of wisdom, not pathology; and, most thoroughly, Reich's emphasis on body, sexuality, nonverbal therapeutic approaches, and rebelliousness against cultural mores.

Perls, in addition to his therapeutic experience with Reich, was exposed to many other "right lobe" influences: Goldstein's holism, Buber's contrast of I-Thou with I-It relationships; Gestalt psychology; and the influence of his wife, Laura, and her training in body work. Feeling rejected by Freud and the psychoanalytic leaders and isolated in South Africa, Fritz began to experiment with and synthesize other approaches. In a personal communication, he gave the following account of the beginning of Gestalt therapy. The patient was an accomplished violinist whose presenting problem was inability to perform as a soloist, although his playing as an orchestra member was extremely skilled. Fritz began working with him in classical analysis and quickly located the expected oedipal interpretation: Orchestral playing for the patient was following father's lead; solo work was asserting himself as an equal. However, the symptom remained. Finally, having exhausted all analytic approaches and interpretations, Fritz asked the patient to bring his violin to a session and play. He began standing, and very quickly his playing worsened, becoming shaky and erratic. Fritz noted that this was accompanied by much body sway and that his feet were close together so that he was awkwardly off-balance. By calling this to his attention and getting him to stand with more support and balance, Fritz cured his problem in one minute!

Following this dramatic demonstration of the value of direct observation of body cues, Fritz began increasingly to attend to body cues and suggest behavioral experiments. The end result in Gestalt therapy was Fritz taking the extreme position that "talking about" and interpretation were to be avoided as completely as possible in favor of awareness and experiencing.

> Gestalt therapy is an experiential therapy, rather than a verbal or an interpretive therapy. We ask our patients not to talk about their traumas and their problems in the removed area of the past tense and memory, but to *re-experience* their problems and their traumas . . . in the here and now. . . . We ask the patient to become aware of his gestures, of his breathing, of his emotions, of his voice, and of his facial expressions as much as of his pressing thoughts (Perls, 1973, p. 63-64).
> Just as talking about oneself is a resistance against experiencing oneself, so the memory of an experience—simply talking about it—leaves it isolated as a deposit of the past. . . . The neurotic's memory is more than simply a hunting ground for the archeologists. . . . It is the uncompleted event, which is still alive and interrupted, waiting to be assimilated and integrated. It is here and now, in the present, that this assimilation must take place (Perls, 1973, p. 65-66).

The Gestalt approach can be described as viewing pathology as incomplete Gestalten or experiences, involving strong emotion or interrupted action or expression where either insufficient support was available or active suppression occurred. Similar patterns of interruption and avoidance continue in the present and interfere with current activities. The conflict between that which seeks expression and that which prevents it is usually presented in a right lobe—left lobe framework. One side is viewed as nonverbal: expressive, body-involving, emotional, impulsive, childish, "wrong." The other side is verbal, logical, warning, parental, "right." The patient may be consciously aware of the "under-dog" position or have access only to vague blockages; almost always, however, he is conscious of the "top-dog" verbal arguments. The main thrust of therapy is to bring the split into awareness, to allow full experiencing of the conflict by evoking the behavioral and experiential Gestalt, and by supporting a different pattern of experiencing and symbolization that will lead to completion or "centering."

For example, a woman comes into a therapy session reporting that she has felt upset following a visit with her mother. Her mother's sadness has left her feeling helpless and bothered, and her telling herself that she should not feel that way has not made any difference. The therapist notes that her hand keeps slapping her thigh and asks what her hand is saying. *"You've got to listen."* The therapist suggests that she say this to mother. Her words to mother, visualized as sitting on a chair across from her, quickly turn to *"I want to hurt you,"* but the accompanying angry tears are choked back. The therapist gives her a pillow and tells her to choke the pillow instead of herself. Squeezing the pillow leads to her shaking it, hitting it repeatedly on the floor, and finally stomping up and down on it. Full bodily expression of anger has now been loosed, accompanied by a flood of accusations: *"I'm furious at your acting so helpless; at your blaming father and making him into a villain; of warning us about him so we'd stay away from him and keep close to you."* She pauses and looks at her pillow-mother coldly and knowingly. *"That's what you've been doing all these years—using that phony act to keep us tied to you. The amount of time I've wasted feeling sorry for you when I should have been sorry for myself or Dad!"* Her fury is renewed as she forcefully enacts her determination not to be caught again in such a way. More calmly, now, she finishes the dialogue by telling her mother how she will respond differently at their next meeting. She stops, feeling clear, powerful, and much relieved. Her perception of the situation has changed, and with it the words she uses to symbolize and describe, as well as her experiential and behavioral responses. The therapist behaviors involved suppressing her usual verbal descriptions, evoking body cues by calling attention to them and giving them verbal and physical avenues of expression, and supporting the process by physical presence and occasional suggestions.

This process will be examined by listing various cues used by Gestalt therapists to locate areas of conflict and techniques to define the split as sharply as possible. This is usually done by interfering with or "turning off" left lobe verbal functioning and evoking body response and affect.

> In order to avoid living a life of discovering the world and ourselves, we often take the short-cut of getting information. This is what you did right now—you asked me for information. But you could have set out and discovered what you are phobic about or what somebody else is phobic about—what you or they avoid. But instead you ask me to feed your computer, your thinking system (Perls, 1970, p. 25).

Perls, in working with someone, might start out with the problem the person presents, or with the awareness continuum which involves asking the patient to stay in contact with and report his moment-to-moment awareness. As the patient begins speaking, the therapist then watches for any of the cues given below, not in a diagnostic sense of then knowing or planning with clarity where the process will lead, but with a continuing interweaving of awareness and response.

PATIENT CUES	THERAPIST RESPONSES
pauses, hesitations, interruptions	"What's happening?"
conflicts represented in words ("I'd like to . . . but I can't . . .")	"Which of these are you in most contact with . . . put the other side in the empty chair . . . begin a dialogue . . ."
incongruities between verbal statements and bodily expressions ("I'm angry at . . ." accompanied by a smile or said in a placating tone)	"Are you aware you're smiling?" "What is your tone of voice saying?" "Keep saying, 'I'm angry.'" "Exaggerate your smile, your tone of voice."
repetitive gesture	"What is your hand saying?"
retroflection (fists clenched, throat, jaw muscles tight)	"Hit the pillow." "Choke someone else." "Tighten your muscles as much as you can."
"It was good . . ." "They don't want . . ."	"Change *It* (*They*) to *I*."

Other ways of interrupting usual verbal patterns include responding to language literally and/or metaphorically *("I'm feeling low. . . ." "Would you lie down on the floor?" "I'm depressed. . . ." "Push down on my shoulders and depress me.")*, asking the person to repeat phrases, to say the opposite of what he just said, and to shift style by using short sentences or making questions into statements. Ways of increasing emotional emphases include making the patient assume a body posture appropriate for his words; use emotionally loaded words; and especially, enact or visualize past scenes in which the person alternately plays both roles, speaking as if to the actual person involved (the "empty chair"), with heavy use of imaging and fantasy.

In summary, most of the techniques and procedures used by Gestalt therapists appear to disrupt left lobe functions and to evoke right lobe perception and memories in order to allow past and present experiences to be more adequately symbolized and integrated. These procedures have been found valuable in solving problems and emotional discomforts which have resisted left lobe analyses. In the process, Gestalt therapists have devised an armarmentarium of approaches to the right lobe that may be of value to neuropsychologists attempting to evoke and study hemispheric specialization, as well as serving as hypotheses to additional functions.

REFERENCES

BOGEN, J. E.: The other side of the brain: An appositional mind. In R. E. Ornstein (Ed.), *The Nature of Human Consciousness: A Book of Readings*. New York: Viking, 1974.

BOGEN, J. E., and BOGEN, G. M.: The other side of the brain: III: The corpus callosum and creativity. *Bull. Los Angeles Neurol. Soc.*, 34:191-220, 1969.

DEIKMAN, A. J.: Bimodal consciousness. *Arch. Gen. Psychiat.*, 25:481-489, 1971.

GALIN, D.: Implications for psychiatry of left and right cerebral specialization. *Arch. Gen. Psychiat.*, 31:572-583, 1974.

GAZZANIGA, M. S.: *The Bisected Brain*. New York: Appleton-Century-Crofts, 1970.

HICKS, R. E.: Hemispheric sharing of vocal and unimanual performance. Paper delivered at the American Psychological Association, New Orleans, Aug. 1974.

KEMPLER, W.: *Principles of Gestalt Family Therapy*. Oslo, Norway: Nordahls Trykkeri, 1974.

KINSBOURNE, M.: Cerebral representation of cognitive style: Evidence from gaze and gesture. Paper delivered at American Psychological Association, New Orleans, Aug. 1974.

NARANJO, C.: Present-centeredness: Technique, prescription and ideal. In J. Fagan and I. L. Shepherd (Eds.), *Gestalt Therapy Now*. Palo Alto: Science and Behavior Books, 1970.

NARANJO, C., and ORNSTEIN, R. E.: *On the Psychology of Meditation*. New York: Viking, 1971.

NEBES, R. D.: Hemispheric specialization in commissurotomized man. *Psychol. Bull.*, 81:1-14, 1974.

ORME-JOHNSON, D.: An experimental analysis of the effects of transcendental meditation on reaction time. Paper delivered at American Psychological Association, New Orleans, Aug. 1974.

ORNSTEIN, R. E.: *The Psychology of Consciousness*. New York: Viking, 1972.

PERLS, F. S.: Four lectures. In J. Fagan and I. L. Shepherd (Eds.), *Gestalt Therapy Now*. Palo Alto: Science and Behavior Books, 1970.

PERLS, F. S.: *The Gestalt Approach*. Palo Alto: Science and Behavior Books, 1973.

PINES, M.: *The Brain Changers; Scientists and the New Mind Control*. New York: Harcourt Brace Jovanovich, 1974.

SANDERS, J. R.: What can split-brain research tell us about abreactive therapies? Paper delivered at SEPA, Fort Lauderdale, Fla., April 1974.

SCHWARTZ, G. E.: *Hemispheric Asymmetry and Emotion: Bilateral EEG and Lateral Eye Movements*. Paper delivered at American Psychological Association, New Orleans, Aug., 1974.

SWANSON, J. M.: *Unilateral Input, Attention, and Performance in RT Experiments*. Paper delivered at American Psychological Association, New Orleans, Aug., 1974.

WATZLAWICK, P., BEAVIN, J., and JACKSON, D.: *Pragmatics of Human Communication*. New York: W. W. Norton, 1967.

WEIL, A.: *The Natural Mind*. Boston: Houghton Mifflin, 1972.

5

The Trickster-Healer

SHELDON B. KOPP, Ph.D.

So brilliant was his intuition and so powerful were his techniques that sometimes it took Perls only minutes to reach the person on the hotseat. You might be some stuck, rigid, long-dead character, seeking help and yet fearing that it would come and change things. He would put you on the hotseat and then do his magic. If you were willing to work, it was almost as though he could reach over, take hold of the zipper on your facade, and pull it down so quickly that your tortured soul would fall out onto the floor between the two of you.

Despite the power and the brilliance, such techniques are only good for openers, and much more work must be done if feelings are to be worked through and life to be lived more fully (Kopp, 1971, p. 146).

In every time, in every place, some men have sought the help, the guidance, the leadership, the healing hands of others. Sometimes it is the curing of the soul.

In either case, he who is appointed savior is expected to have powers which transcend the patient's more human foibles. The role of healer, of course, is not just an appointed office but, like town-drunk or village-idiot, it is in part a voluntary position. And so the temptation to play out the corrupting power trip originates not only with the patient's dependent hope to be cured, but with the healer's arrogant presumption of placing himself above other men as well.

By way of example, the start of the relationship between the psycho-therapist and his patient has been described as resembling that of a *sorcerer*

Another version of this chapter appears in Dr. Kopp's book, *The Hanged Man*, Palo Alto, Cal.: Science and Behavior Books, 1975.

and his *apprentice* (Guggenbuhl-Craig, 1971). The patient, of course, hopes to find a good and all-powerful parent, that magician-savior who will use supernatural powers to work the wonders that can cure all ills, solve all problems, and bring everlasting happiness.

The sorcerer-and-apprentice fantasies of the patient match exactly the power fascination of the guru who would heal others. It is quite likely that for a while they will both go mad, consensually validating the illusion that the therapist knows more than the patient about the most profound parameters of life, and that this wisdom and power will some day belong to the apprentice if only the young supplicant submits, surrenders, and hangs around long enough.

The forerunners of today's intrapsychic healers are many. The contemporary psychotherapist is foreshadowed in those individual visionaries who were the gurus of other times and other places. The heritage of the contemporary guru includes healing metaphors of the Zen master, the Hasidic rabbi, the fourth century Christian hermit monk, of wizards, medicine men and magi (Kopp, 1971). In his earliest and most primordial form, the healer appeared as the paleolithic *shaman*, the helper, healer and guide of the earliest hunting and gathering societies. Before man planted crops, domesticated animals or settled for one god and his priests, before all of that progress, he looked to the shaman for spiritual leadership.

As primitive harbinger of later archetypal savior figures, the shaman was a suffering hero, a wounded healer who had to die and be reborn if he was to be able to mediate the redemption of his community, the other members of his tough-minded hunting band. He begins his own tortured pilgrimage as a fuck-up, a misfit youth. In overcoming his own personal agonies he comes to be in a position to guide others on their spiritual pilgrimages. His source of power is his personal vision, acquired in the solitude of wilderness ordeals, during which he must make his way without instruction or preplanned pattern.

His self-tortured growth-experiences breed sensitivity to the pain of others, and a deep need to turn-on others to the power of their own visions, to be available as a spiritual companion as they undertake their own adventures. But the shaman is no gentle saint, no milksop Christ. Like Jesus in the temple when He wildly swung chains to drive out the money-changers, the shaman is like a titan to a god, a devil to an angel. There is a powerful contrast between "the wild, quarrelsome, dangerous shamans and the people who were so polite to each other that they were like brothers-in-law" (Campbell, 1972, p. 162).

This lustily surging irritability can be frightening, at times even dangerous, but, too, it is that very primordial force which is the healer's power source. The principle of personal abandon which powers the primitive shaman may be found in the mystics, the poets and the artists of more developed cultures. The shamanistic trance is a regressive spiritual flight during which this guru leaves the everyday world behind, discourses with the spirits and wings to those heavens and hells of the soul which are the wellsprings of archetypal potency. Christ himself demands abandon when he advises one who hesitates as though trapped by earthly duties, telling him, "Let the dead bury their dead"; so too when he tells the materialistically reluctant rich man, "Sell all that you have . . . and follow me."

Never mind the rules! Forget conventional wisdom and morality if you would be healed, saved, made free! Augustine says, "Love God, and do what thou wilt!" while Luther admonishes the men of his age to "Sin bravely!"

The classical pre-figure for the healer who must stand against the gods if he is to save the world is that hero of humanistic enlightenment, Prometheus. This fire-bringer was the supreme trickster, the super-shaman. When Zeus hid the fire from man, Prometheus stole it returning it to earth where man could once again have its power, its warmth, and its light. Indeed Zeus' punitive withholding of the fire was itself an act of vengeance brought on by Prometheus' having dared to fool the very gods. Prometheus had served up burnt offerings in which he wrapped in fat the poorest parts of the slaughtered beast, putting the best parts in another bundle and so tricking Zeus into choosing foolishly, leaving the best parts of the meat for man.

In symbolic retribution, Zeus chained Prometheus to a rock and sent an eagle to eat his liver. Poor bastard, his immortal liver grew anew each night only to be devoured by the eagle again by day. And so his torture continued until he was at last rescued by Hercules.

It Isn't Nice to Fool Mother Nature!

So it is that the savior-healer has his archetypal forerunner in the trickster-hero. At its worst, the *shadow* of the healer is the charlatan. The evil underlay of the guru is that dark brother who sometimes surfaces as the quack or the false prophet. It is a form of corruption, or chronic temptation to a power trip, the daily personal menace of every honest therapist to which he must constantly be alert. The trickster-figure (Jung, 1959) in his less sinister forms is merely an imp, a fool or a buffoon, a practical joker of the Punch and Judy Show genre.

The trickster appears in the picaresque mythology of settings as diverse as Ancient Greece, Medieval Europe, the Orient, Africa, and the Semitic world. He is the primitive tricky spider of the animal world, the alchemical figure Mercurius, Satan the ape of God, Tom Thumb and Stupid Hans of fairy tales. He is the peasants' poltergeist, Loki the Norse helper and trouble maker, or a carnival clown. When not a shaman or witch doctor, he may appear as Hermes, the divine trickster of Greek mythology. That particular guide of souls was both a god of wisdom and a patron of magic. Later to become the messenger of greater gods, Hermes was cunning from birth. On the very first day of his life, he is said to have both invented the lyre and stolen Apollo's cattle.

As always, he is both benefactor and buffoon, combining the dual image of both creator and destroyer. In his more serious moments, he is a cuture-hero who appears in an account of the earth's creation or of the world's transformation. But always, he is a spirit of disorder, one who operates with laughter and with irony outside of the fixed bounds of custom, law, and conventional wisdom. He is a hungry, highly-sexed wanderer who both plays tricks and is as easily duped by others. But "if we laugh at him, he grins at us. What happens to him, happens to us" (Radin, 1972, p. 25).

He is a shameless arch-deceiver. Among some American Indians, for instance, the coyote, who is the personification of this trickster-hero, is often seen as a mischievious intermix of Eros and Pan. And so a Shagit Indian poem (Rothenberg, 1972, p. 271) tells that:

> One day when Coyote
> was walking through Snoqualmic Pass,
> he met a young woman.
>
> What do you have in your pack?
>
> she said.
>
> Fish eggs.
>
> Can I have some?
>
> If you close your eyes
> and hold up your dress.
>
> The woman did as she was told.
>
> Higher.
>
> Hold your dress over your head.

Then Coyote stepped out of his trousers
and walked up to the woman.

> Stand still
> so I can reach the lace.
>
> I can't.
> There's something crawling between my legs.
>
> Keep your dress up.
> It's a bumble bee. I'll get it.

The woman dropped her dress.

> You weren't fast enough.
> It stung me.

Sometimes the shaman plays more malicious jokes on people, and is in danger of retaliatory sorcery of black magic. Even the *appearance of evil* is not easily tolerated in one who is expected to be a savior. But trickery has always been a part of the healing process. By no means need it be sinister. In the healing techniques of the shaman of the Nuba mountains, whose patients are tough-minded hunters, it consists "principally in the ability to hide about his person and to produce at will small quartz pebbles and bits of stick; and, of hardly less importance than this sleight of hand, the power of looking preternaturally solemn, as if he were the possessor of knowledge quite hidden from ordinary men" (Spencer and Gillen, 1968, p. 255).

In the contemporary ministry of the healing of neuroses, trickery is certainly not the *only* mode of approach used by the therapist, but it's not a bad beginning. Lao Tzu (Waley, 1958, p. 187) advises us to "Be where they ain't" when he counsels that:

> What is in the end to be shrunk
> Must first be stretched.
> Whatever is to be weakened
> Must begin by being made strong.
> What is to be overthrown
> Must begin by being set up.
> He who would be a taker
> Must begin as a giver.

"*Be where they ain't!*" is a tactical rule-of-thumb for meeting patients during the opening phase of psychotherapy. Of course, we all understand that any categorizing of the therapy process into Phase I, Phase II, Phase III et seq. is merely a playful way of setting up make-believe classifications, a fictional hedge to be raised at those times when we feel that we can no longer stand working in the boundlessly flowing stream of the ever-changing process of live interactions with another separate human being. It offers the therapist the momentarily soothing illusion of order in the overwhelming chaos of ongoing life. Theorizing is only our way of telling ourselves wonderous fairy tales, just as psychological interpretation is our way of telling comforting stories to our patients. Enjoy my tale if you can. It is not at all necessary that you believe it.

At those times when the entropic ambiguity of my work makes me feel as though I might lose my Self as well as my way, I am tempted to try to understand what it is that I am doing. Those are not at all the best of times. At the best of times, I can enjoy the creative freedom of not even trying to understand. ·Yet, since there *are* those times when I analyze, theorize, pretend to myself that there is no truth to the Truth that "This is as clear as it ever gets" I might as well share the experience as not share it.

Most recently the story has gone something like this: Once upon a time all therapy was divided into three parts, called Phase I, Phase II, and Phase III. Phase I, the Opening or Judo Phase, begins with the patient presenting the symptoms which are his ticket of admission to the cosmic light-show which in our day is called psychotherapy. He does his opening number and the therapist fucks up his trip by being where he ain't (more about this below). This phase lasts from a few sessions to several months, during which the patient usually gives up his presenting complaints. He may either terminate at this point, having settled for relief, or go on to Phase II as a function of having become curious about his life and wanting a more intimate relationship with the therapist.

Should he enter Phase II, the Middle or Intimacy Phase, he and the therapist will be rewarded by a period of several months to several years of continuing closeness, having come beyond the struggle over contract, and well into a period of love and soulful adventure. For some such couples the healing of wounds gives way to the excitement of a pilgrimage of spiritual growth. One of my many impossible wishes is to become successful enough as a therapist to treat only healthy patients, to leave Phase I to lesser gurus and to restrict my practice to working exclusively with patients who have already been successfully cured.

As Phase II draws toward its completion (in those cases when it does), one member of the couple (almost always the therapist) begins to make noises like "This sure has been wonderful, but there is something spooky or unreal about going on and on this way indefinitely." A brief struggle follows, often ending with the patient terminating precipitously, offering the exit line: "You know I love you Doc, and you've been a great help up till now, but you seem to have gone crazy. I'm leaving."

Should the patient stay, it will be to make his way through Phase III, the Final or Separation Phase. This bittersweet ordeal is so poignantly painful that many therapists make sure to terminate with all of their patients during Phase I or II rather than risk ever going through it at all. Phase III lasts from a few weeks to several months, often with an alternation of false stops and starts along the way. If it is completed successfully, the therapist and the patient give each other up forever. If not, the therapist is forever haunted, and the patient (though they may never meet again) remains in therapy for the rest of his life.

Back to the issue of Phase I tactics. They have been sensitively explored in the character-analytic work of Wilhelm Reich (1949) in which he begins by ignoring the *content* of the patient's complaints in favor of focusing entirely on the style in which they are being presented. Or alternately:

> In individual therapy we may get the patient to focus on his past history. In group therapy, we may encourage the patient's curiosity about the group process. Some of what occurs as the patient reluctantly takes on these tasks is that he can begin to lose himself in the sense of giving himself over to the assigned work. As this unhooks him from his willful, self-sorry demand for someone to give him relief right now, a new possibility arises: The patient can now begin to experience the therapist and the other patients as real people with selves of their own; as people who have meaning outside of himself, who can therefore be meaningful to him, and who can ultimately put him in touch with the meaning of his own life (Kopp, 1971, p. 96).

At this point, the therapist is instructing by indirection, helping the patient to unhook from his old stuck ways, opening him to the possibility of new ways of living (whatever they might turn out to be). The perverse guideline for this instruction is *"Be where they ain't!"*

For the patient who begins with immersion in his own history, the therapist must draw him back again and again to what is going on in the here-and-now. The hysterically emotional, overly impulsive patient must be slowed down to stopping and thinking over what he is doing, while the obsessionally paralyzed thinker can be met with non-rational responses which finally get him too upset to hold back any longer. Patients who are initially too hard on themselves are to be treated gently and indulgently while self-sorry whiners must be confronted with harsh demands which leave no quarter for excuse-making.

This phase can be really hard work, calling for a great deal of self-discipline on the part of the therapist. Ironically, once a young therapist gets the hang of it, it can be a great deal of demonic fun as well. There will, of course, be present the corrupting temptation to simply be clever and manipulative, to succumb to the healer's power trip. I find that the best protection for my avoiding the charlatan in myself is to keep aware of the patient in myself, to renew again and again the image of myself as "the wounded healer" (Guggenbuhl-Craig, 1971, p. 91).

When I do, I am in the best position to trust myself, to follow Carl Whitaker's advice about responding to patients. Don't feed the baby just because the baby cries that he is hungry unless it is a time when the milk is overflowing from your own nipples.

To those who demand clarity, speak metaphorically. Only those who would keep things muddled demand direct confrontation at this stage.

Zen literature provides a handy source-book of such Phase I tactics (Barrett, 1956). Here are a few examples of the Zen master's response to the young monks who sought his instructions by asking for help in their unenlightened ways:

1. *Monk:* "What is the idea of the Patriarch's coming here from the West?"
   Master: "Ask the post over there."
   Monk: "I do not understand."
   Master: "Neither do I" (p. 207).

2. *Monk:* "This ground where we sit is a fine site for a hut."
   Master: "Let your hut alone; how about ultimate things?" (p. 210)

3. *Monk:* "I have come from a distant place with the special intention of seeing you. Will you kindly give me one word of instruction?"
   Master: "Growing old, my back aches today" (p. 225).

4. *Monk:* "What way would you use in the demonstration of Zen thought?"
   Master: Holds up his staff without speaking
   Monk: "Is that all?"
   Master: Silently throws down his staff (p. 208).

Lao Tzu makes it all so very clear when he tells us:

Straightforward words seem paradoxical (Waley, 1958, p. 238).

Of course, the beginning of instruction (whether Zen or psychotherapy) is not the only point at which the healer offers the patient/pilgrim the treat of trick or trick. I'm reminded of an example of such trickery which I offered in a group setting to a patient who had come further along the way. The therapy group began in an ordinary mode that afternoon with a brief initial silence followed by each of us doing his number. Melvin was really into himself, luxuriating in the low-keyed anguish of obsessing about how he was doing. "It's all just no use at all," he whined. "All these months of therapy, and still I'm never really myself." I pointed out that that was the one problem no one could have, as it was never possible for a person not to be himself.

He seemed pleased at the opportunity to go on and explain, to go on and on and on. He described at length how he could not be spontaneous, could not respond in the here-and-now. I offered to help him then and there. If he was open to trusting me for a minute, I would teach him to trust himself by letting him experience the here and now, spontaneously and competently. Offered the opportunity to solve his problems, Melvin was of course understandably reluctant. He eyed me suspiciously but responded to group pressure to at least try.

I was holding a lit cigar in my hand during this exchange. The moment Melvin agreed to trust me, I flipped the smoking butt across the room straight into his lap. Suddenly his whiningly lethargic, gelatinous manner gave way to alert and angry action as he fielded the hot cigar expertly, shouted "God damn you anyway, Kopp," and tossed it back at me with verve and accuracy.

His eyes were wide with wonder and vitality. Uncharacteristically he announced, "I've got some other unfinished business to take care of in this group right now." He blurted out some long-withheld anger toward one of the other men in the group, and then told one of the women how much he cared about her. Crossing the room with clear purpose he hugged her with unrestrained tenderness.

In the midst of the embrace, he began to mutter something about how he might mess this up. But when the group told him to shut up and enjoy himself, he seemed pleased to surrender to the moment once more.

Even when the trickster is not being helpful, he is not necessarily an evil figure. More mischievious than malevolent, his clumsiness, impetuousness, stubbornness, and poor judgment result more often in his getting into ridiculous scrapes than in his creating catastrophes for others. "The trickster is a collective shadow figure, a summation of all of the inferior traits of character in individuals" (Jung, 1959, p. 270). He is the epitome of the fallible human being, a collection of foibles and defects which are the mark of human nature. So it is that he may appear in stories as a jester, a clown, a buffoon, or a fool. It is the cleverness which my mother always zeroed in on when I maneuvered myself into impossible binds. "Smart, smart, smart, and you're dumb!" she would say, with more sympathy than malice.

Coyote, spider, hare, raven or any of the other trickster figures found in American Indian myths are "no merely horny version of a Disney character" (Rothenberg, 1972, p. 422). The profound comic imagination which they represent is that of man not yet free from his animal nature. Look what happens when he defies his nature even in a minor fashion:

As he went wandering around aimlessly he suddenly heard someone speaking. He listened very carefully and it seemed to say, "He who chews me will defecate; he will defecate!" That was what it was saying. "Well, why is this person talking in this manner?" said Trickster. So he walked in the direction from which he had heard the speaking and again he heard, quite near him, someone saying: "He who chews me, he will defecate; he will defecate!" This is what was said. "Well, why does this person talk in such fashion?" said Trickster. Then he walked to the other side. So he continued walking along. Then right at his very side, a voice seemed to say, "He who chews me, he will defecate, he will defecate!" "Well, I wonder who it is who is speaking. I know very well that if I chew it, I will not defecate." But he kept looking around for the speaker and finally discovered, much to his astonishment, that it was a bulb on a bush. The bulb it was that was speaking. So he seized it, put it in his mouth, chewed it, and then swallowed it. He did just this and then went on. "Well, where is the bulb gone that talked so much? Why, indeed, should I defecate? When I feel like defecating, then I shall defecate, no sooner. How could such an object make me defecate!" Thus spoke Trickster. Even as he spoke, however, he began to break wind. "Well this, I suppose, is what it meant. Yet the bulb said I would defecate, and I am merely expelling gas. In any case I am a great man even if I do expel a little gas!" Thus he spoke. As he was talking he again broke wind. This time it was really quite strong. "Well, what a foolish one I am. This is why I am called Foolish One, Trickster." Now he began to break wind again and again. "So this is why the bulb spoke as it did, I suppose." Once more he broke wind. This time it was very loud and his rectum began to smart. "Well, it surely is a great thing!" Then he broke wind again, this time with so much force, that he was propelled forward. "Well, well, it may even make me give another push, but it won't make me defecate," so he exclaimed defiantly. The next time he broke wind, the hind part of his body was raised up by the force of the explosion and he landed on his knees and hands. "Well, go ahead and do it again! Go ahead and do it again!" Then, again, he broke wind. This time the force of the expulsion sent him far up in the air and he landed on the ground, on his stomach. The next time he broke wind, he had to hang on to a log, so high was he thrown. However, he raised himself up and, after a while, landed on the ground, the log on top of him. He was almost killed by the fall. The next time he broke wind, he had to hold on to a tree that stood nearby. It was a poplar and he held on with all his might yet, nevertheless, even then, his feet flopped up in the air. Again, and for the second time, he held on to it when he broke wind and yet he pulled the tree up by the roots. To protect himself, the next time, he went on until he came to a large tree, a large oak tree. Around this he put both his arms. Yet, when he broke wind, he was swung up and his toes struck against the tree. However, he held on.

After that he ran to a place where people were living. When he got there, he shouted, "Say, hurry up and take your lodge down, for a big war party is upon you and you will surely be killed! Come let us get away!" He scared them all so much that they quickly took down their lodge, piled it on Trickster, and then got on him themselves. They likewise placed all the little dogs they had on top of Trickster. Just then he began to break wind again and the force of the expulsion scattered the things on top of him in all directions. They fell far apart from one another. Separated, the people were standing about and shouting to one another; and the dogs scattered here and there, howled at one another. There stood Trickster laughing at them till he ached.

Now he proceeded onward, he seemed to have gotten over his troubles. "Well, this bulb did a lot of talking." he said to himself, "yet it could not make me defecate." But even as he spoke he began to have the desire to defecate, just a very little. "Well, I suppose this is what it meant. It certainly bragged a good deal, however." As he spoke he defecated again. "Well, what a braggart it was! I suppose this is why it said this." As he spoke these last words, he began to defecate a good deal. After a while, as he was sitting down, his body would touch the excrement. Thereupon he got on top of a log and sat down there but, even then, he touched the excrement. Finally, he climbed up a log that was leaning against a tree. However, his body still touched the excrement, so he went up higher. Even then, however, he touched it so he climbed still higher up. Higher and higher he had to go. Nor was he able to stop defecating. Now he was on top of the tree. It was small and quite uncomfortable. Moreover, the excrement began to come up to him.

Even on the limb on which he was sitting he began to defecate. So he tried a different position. Since the limb, however, was very slippery he fell right down into the excrement. Down he fell, down into the dung. In fact he disappeared in it, and it was only with very great difficulty that he was able to get out of it (Radin, 1972, p. 25-27).

At his most powerful, trickster-healer-savior is "the archetype of the hero, the giver of all great boons—the fire-bringer and the teacher of mankind" (Campbell, 1972, p. 274). He is Prometheus unbound, defiant challenger who takes that he might give, suffers that he might heal, tricks the oppressive gods that he might free men to become what they are. But foolishness and fallibility are his other face. And so when in my arrogance as guru I trick myself, at such times wisdom consists in listening to those voices which would warn me against myself. Sometimes my patients help by not taking me seriously. Sometimes "enemies can be very useful" (Guggenbuhl-Craig, 1971, p. 29). In some instances only another trickster can see through my games.

One recent expression of my personal struggle with the treasure-burden of the healer-trickster role is symbolically written in the growing, wearing, and finally in the shaving off of my Old Testament-Mephistophelian-Psychoanalyst-Magican Beard. Many years ago I grew a full beard, for the fun of it and as a matter of simple vanity. Partly it was my sense of theater at work, taking on a hirsute prop, part of the costume of my trade, much like the leopard's teeth that witch doctors wear around their necks.

I loved the attention it drew at the time, before Madison Avenue turned my stigmata into high fashion. Back then it gave me a small measure of protection, because men who wore beards were not expected to be polite. My fantasy image of my newly-bearded self was that of an amalgam of a ferocious wildman, an untamed shaman, and simultaneously that of an older, wise prophet and archetypal father. I loved it when a patient said that I looked like a "Santa Claus for the bad children."

Later on when illness turned my life upside down and I returned to therapy as a patient once more, the shifting configurations within me took me to new places, and I knew I had to give up this badge of power. I had found my way once more past my despair and was ready to live again. I wanted to reclaim my innocence, to see what my original face had looked like before I was born. I was ready to be more available, more openly vulnerable. It was scary but one of my sons assured me that if I got into a struggle with someone I could not intimidate, I could show him a photo of how tough I had looked with my beard.

When things occur to me in my head, I most often say them, at times too impulsively. My wife is a far more private person than I. When I talked with her about my decision to shave, as always she supported my wish to do what I chose. She also had let me know that she thought it would be a good thing to let my mouth show so people could see it as well as hear it speak. She pointed out that the sound was more misleading than the sight, since the appearance of my mouth was more tremblingly vulnerable than the strong words which it emitted. And then she floored me (as she so often does) by pointing out that I must have finally come to terms with my grief over my mother's death. I had not realized that it was that summer, seven years earlier, that I had first chosen to grow a stoic mask.

I was tempted to wait and shave while I was away on vacation, but I felt the separation and return to my patients would be complex enough without adding that dramatic and unexpected transfiguration. My patients, both individually and in group, perceived my changed appearance in a generally consistent way, but the meaning they attributed to it polarized them right down the middle. Almost all of my patients saw me as more human, more ordinary, less powerful, but half were delighted, while the rest were scared that they would have to give up their projections and take full responsibility for their own lives and for the ways in which they treated me.

As for myself, I was trying to abdicate as guru, to be closer to others, to let my weaknesses show so that I could ask for and get more sympathy and help. I am weary of making that life-long Moses-trip, tired of leading others to the Promised Land, seeing it only from the mountain-top, and having to remain outside while others enter. And yet I know that I will never be safe from the burdens and temptations of the healer-trickster trek which is my life. At times, I believe that all I am up to, for now, is learning the most magically powerful and most gently healing trick of them all, *the trick of no tricks*.

REFERENCES

BARRETT, W. (Ed.): *Zen Buddhism: Selected Writings of D. T. Suzuki.* A Doubleday Anchor Book. Garden City, N. Y.: Doubleday, 1956.

CAMPBELL, J.: *The Flight of the Wild Gander, Explorations in the Mythological Dimension.* A Gateway Edition. Chicago: Henry Regnery, 1972.

GUGGENBUHL-CRAIG, A.: *Power in the Helping Professions.* New York: Spring Publications, 1971.

JUNG, C.: On the Psychology of the Trickster-Figure. In *Collected Works of C. G. Jung,* Trans. by R. F. C. Hull. 2nd ed., Vol. 9, *The Archetypes and the Collective Unconscious.* Bollinger Series XX. Princeton, N. J.: Princeton U. Press, 1959.

KOPP, S.: *Guru: Metaphors from a Psychotherapist.* Palo Alto: Science and Behavior Books, 1971.

RADIN, P.: *The Trickster: A Study in American Indian Mythology*, with Commentaries by K. Kerenyi and C. G. Jung, Introductory Essay by Stanley Diamond. New York: Schocken Books, 1972.

REICH, W.: *Character Analysis*. New York: Orgone Institute Press, 1949.

ROTHENBERG, J. (Ed.): *Shaking the Pumpkin: Traditional Poetry of the Indians of North America*. A Doubleday Anchor Book. English version of this poem by Carl Cary. Garden City, N. Y.: Doubleday, 1972.

SPENCER, B., and GILLEN, F.: *The Native Tribes of Central Australia*. London: Macmillan, 1899. Quoted in J. Campbell, *The Masks of God: Primitive Mythology*. New York: Viking, 1968.

WALEY, A.: *The Way and Its Power: A Study of the Tao Te Ching and Its Place in Chinese Thought*. Evergreen Edition. New York: Grove, 1958.

6

Great Diagnosticians
Call for Great Patients

DENIS O'DONOVAN, Ph.D.

"May I help you, sir?"

"Yes, I want to piss."

"I'm sorry. You were headed for the staff men's room. Are you on the staff here?"

"I am not on the staff anywhere."

"Please come with me, sir."

I've worked hard for this day, and I don't want to make a mistake. Today is my first time to be a part of Grand Rounds. A most important guest will interview today's patient, and I (young Dr. Norman) have been chosen to pick the patient.

I'm no fool. I realize that if the task were really important, the faculty would not have assigned it to the residents, and if there were any prestige attached to it, the residents wouldn't have assigned it to the interns. You probably know the old joke I heard in heart surgery, that if sex were more work than fun it would all be assigned to the interns.

I had picked Mrs. Cabazzi to be today's patient, with half an eye on old Dr. Virilacello. Dr. Virilacello might be just the man to get me a residency in psychiatry. He is always talking about religious training leading to sexual hangups, and I have a hunch he knows an awful lot about that. Mrs. Cabazzi is a good-looking dish. I'm not so sure her story that her last three shrinks bedded down with her is the delusion her medical chart calls it. Anyway, if she starts fingering her beads and herself at the same time, this should be a Grand Rounds not easily forgotten.

However . . . a new idea has been growing in my head since I met this bearded stranger. I accompanied him to the patients' men's room, partly out of courtesy and partly to keep an eye on him. The guy has absolutely no small talk. He acts as if I were some flunky assigned to escort him around.

Now the old man's arrogance is beginning to fit into my new idea.

Let us review the symptoms, as Dr. Virilacello would say. Every time I try to get a straight answer out of the old man, he frustrates me. Instead of answering my question, he mutters something about devils or holes in the head.

And that story about Einstein. Out of nowhere, when I had just been telling him something about psychiatry, the old man said, "I spent one afternoon with Einstein. He told me two things are infinite, the universe and human stupidity, and he wasn't completely sure about the universe." Just when I was trying to figure out what that meant, he told me that Einstein was almost as wise as his white cat.

Yes, he is a chapter of *Virilacello on Grandiosity* come to life. We have six guys, upstairs in the ward right now, with beards, who are trying to save the world. But they're young and on drugs. If they would just stop flushing their tranquilizers down the toilet, they would get over it. This one is an old atheist. He's not parading around as the son of God. He's impersonating God. Too cool to put words to his delusion; probably been in a lot of hospitals before. But with those extravagant dramatics, who else could he think he is? And that bizarre clothing!

I have to make my decision fast. In five minutes I have to deliver an interesting patient to the visiting doctor.

Okay . . . Goodbye, Mrs. Cabazzi, hello whatshisname.

"Please come with me, sir."

Dr. Virilacello seemed pleased when I brought in the patient. He fairly beamed at the gorgeously embroidered jump suit the old man wore.

"This is a great honor, Dr. Perls. I'm afraid our patient hasn't arrived yet. Perhaps you would deliver a lecture while we're waiting."

"I'd rather begin immediately and deliver minilectures as I go. Your young Dr. Norman obviously has been delegated to select the patient, and if we are to work in the here and now, we should honor his choice."

So he turned to himself and said, "I notice you smoke constantly. . . ."

Part III
GESTALT THERAPY AND
JUNGIAN PSYCHOLOGY

Gestalt therapy focuses on the process, the "how" rather than the "what" of behavior. The content is seen as less important than the style or pattern of living. Because of Perls' emphasis on process and de-emphasis of content, some Gestalt therapists have looked beyond the Gestalt literature to other areas in search of meaningful discussions of the content of living. And some have found this in the works of Carl Jung and those influenced by him.

I believe that the growing edges of Gestalt therapy are sharpened by the influence of Jungian thought in at least three ways. First, Jung's methods were in the service of the facilitation of growth, or, to use his term, "self-realization." But he, like Perls, saw that the technique, in order to be effective in facilitating growth, had to be tailored to the patient and the situation. So Jung creatively evolved ways of intervention to suit the need. His discussions of these techniques can be a real inspiration. Second, Jung identified and labeled aspects of the personality which are involved in the development of wholeness. He did this both in terms of processes (the attitudes of extraversion and introversion and the ectopsychic processes of thinking, feeling, sensing and intuiting) and of universal contents (the manifestation of the various archetypes through personification, e.g., Child, Earth Mother, Old Wise Man, God or Good, Devil or Evil, Hero, Persona or social facade, Shadow or instinctual animal nature, and so on). The awareness of such processes and content of living can be a useful orientation for the Gestalt therapist. Third, and implicit in the above, is Jung's illumination of the transpersonal realm in psychotherapy. The sensitivity to archetypal manifestations allows the Gestalt therapist to enter the realm of the transpersonal or collective.

85

For an in-depth view of Jung's therapy, I recommend *The Practice of Psychotherapy* (C. G. Jung. Bollingen Foundation: New York, 1954).

This section of the book contains two chapters by people expert in both the Gestalt and Jungian approaches. The first, by Edward Whitmont and Yoram Kaufmann, is a highly thoughtful discussion of theoretical issues where the Jungian ideas significantly broaden the Gestalt view. The second chapter, by Donald Lathrop, provides some comparisons between the men, Jung and Perls. In addition, Lathrop has focused on those Jungian concepts which he believes are most useful to the work of the Gestalt therapist.

7

Analytical Psychology and Gestalt Therapy

EDWARD C. WHITMONT, M.D.
and
YORAM KAUFMANN, Ph.D.

Gestalt approaches have been developed in response and opposition to Freudian psychoanalysis and in unawareness of the theoretical concepts of Jung which have frequently anticipated, and indeed would broaden many of its applications. The following is a short summary of how analytical psychology might affect the use of Gestalt techniques.

WHOLENESS

Analytical psychology bases itself upon a view of the psyche that, while not using that particular term, is quite close to the Gestalt approach. Gestalt is defined as a "functional configuration or synthesis of separate elements of emotion, experience, etc., that constitutes more than the mechanical sum of the parts." Hence, a Gestalt view is basically a holistic view. The striving for wholeness might be said to be the one basic concern that characterizes the entirety of Jung's work. The personality is to find its inherent and potential wholeness by means of a dialectical encounter between the conscious and unconscious aspects of the psyche. Both of these are conceived as autonomous structures operating separately but in need of mutual cooperation, if a dissociation of the personality is to be avoided. Jung's postulate of an unconscious "objective" or transpersonal psyche which is unconscious and capable of operating without and, indeed, even against our conscious intentionality, implies nothing less than that we are not masters in our own houses; that an important part of our motivation arises from sources unknown to us. Psychic functioning includes more than repressed infantile wishes and urges, striving for power, or the results of past conditioning and learned habits, although it does include all of these. The unconscious nonpersonal psyche is a self-regulating organism that functions in terms of a striving for growth and a finding of significance rather than homeostasis. Its intent is to complement, correct and enrich the conscious position. Only if unheeded will it tend to "sabotage."

By virtue of maintaining a constant dialogue with the unconscious side, the human being can progress from a relatively habit-bound, robotlike manner of functioning to a more mature decision-making and problem-solving mode. Thus, analysis in the original dissective meaning of the term is only a first step in psychotherapy. It may involve delving into the past, breaking old patterns of conditioning, reliving past experiences in order to understand how and why certain trends have become established; yet the second, more crucial step is synthesis.

Mistakes and difficulties of the past and malfunctions of the present are to be regarded as the raw material of creative potentialities of the future. The psyche is viewed as a self-correcting system, forever embarked on a search for a perhaps elusive goal of wholeness, namely of becoming and realizing what one is or is "meant to be." This goal, although necessarily modified by cultural and societal standards, is nevertheless highly unique and individual. Jung placed enormous importance upon the necessity of discovering one's individual norm. All too commonly, human beings are viewed in terms of collectively agreed standards or belief systems. While for the sake of avoiding needless external conflicts these will need to be given serious consideration, they cannot be standards for "inner" or intrinsic reality. We need a way of looking at human beings that allows them to share in the common experiences of mankind, but gives them leave to do this in their own individual way.

A holistic approach, therefore, is basically a nonjudgmental one. Psychology cannot simply borrow the medical model of normalcy, since it operates in a different frame of reference. It may be a physiological miracle that most people, given all their different variables and parameters, still have, under most circumstances, a body temperature of 98.6. Given this fact, it is conceptually logical to call this temperature "normal" and consequently any other temperature a deviation. Given a like behavioral circumstance, however, we find that people react in many and varied ways, making a theory of normalcy very tenuous. We can calculate statistical average and discover important general trends, but this "norm" cannot be fixed in a physiological sense; and the trend to equate the "norm" with what is right and, therefore, good has become a kind of judgment in our patriarchal system. We are gradually breaking through to a more personalized sense of the "norm" for the individual, of finding one's own drummer who sets the pace.

Herein lies Jung's approach to pathology. Although some behavior patterns undoubtedly deserve to be considered pathological from the standpoint of the destruction they entail, neurosis was viewed by Jung primarily as an attempt on the part of the psyche to force recognition of a lack in development, especially in the area that needs to be worked on. Neurosis, according to Jung, is not merely a sign of distress, but, if symbolically understood, contains within itself the creative way out of the dilemma. Neurosis can therefore force one toward growth and expansion of awareness. The unconscious is not only potentially destructive but constructive as well. One can say that neurosis is a cry for help, to complete a defective "Gestalt."

The medical model is more symptom than actual culprit. Our Western civilization perceives and conceptualizes in the patriarchal system of "laws" and rules. These rules determine a hierarchial value system which in its vertical organization posits acceptable and nonacceptable modes of behavior. Imbued with a sense of reverence for the law and rule, we cannot but feel guilty, indeed sinful, if we do not fulfill its posits of the "norm." Our habit prefers to interpret any manifestation of psychic trouble as a deviation from the norm rather than approach it in a positive, constructive way. The Jungian approach introduces a more horizontal way of looking at psychic phenomena, attempting not to judge or condemn any difficulty, but to understand it in terms of its own merit and inherent potential. This attitude is soon apparent to an analysand and the atmosphere it engenders leads to a more open relationship between his conscious and unconscious, an atmosphere of "no blame."

The psyche may be viewed as an energy system. Psychic energy Jung called libido. That energy is generated by the tension between polar opposites. Reaching for wholeness requires the establishing of a communication between opposites which leads to an encompassing third. Jung called this a transcendent function; it is a Gestalt that includes and is more than the sum of its opposing parts. One such set of opposites includes consciousness and unconsciousness. In addition to repressed infantile material and introjects of the most significant external figures, the unconscious is also a steering system motivated by archetypal sources of wisdom, basic typical human patterns of behavior, emotion, and perception which anticipate, as well as react to, external stimuli and situations. The unconscious psyche is also a source of instinctual wisdom and, indeed, spiritual guidance.

Conscious and unconscious are complementary. The more one-sided emphasis one finds in a conscious attitude, the greater is its polar unconscious compensation. For example, a fanatic emphasis on peace and tranquility implies the existence of strong unconscious hostile feeling. This does not negate the genuineness of the conscious attitude or, in Freudian terms, posit it as a reaction formation, but rather emphasizes the person's unawareness of the opposing tendency. Far from exposing the conscious attitude as fraudulent, once the compensating opposite has been made conscious it enhances and deepens the conscious position by giving it a wider perspective in relation to conflict and change as the basis for the fullness of life.

Other pairs of opposites may be experienced in terms of active-passive, creative-receptive, and male-female. On the basis of extensive clinical data, Jung came to postulate the existence within the human psyche of a contrasexual element, that is, the existence of a feminine side in men and a masculine side in women. In our terms, then, male and masculine are not synonymous nor are female and feminine. The feminine principle as expressed historically in literature, folklore and mythology embodies qualities of receptivity, passivity, nurture, darkness, allure, changeableness, deception, and earthiness; the masculine, qualities of action, courage, initiative, light, spirit, penetration, rational thought, abstraction, and rigidity. The patriarchal character of our Western culture has placed greater value on the masculine qualities, while depreciating feminine ones. Yet both are necessary and valuable psychologically for inner development: the masculine for the female and the feminine for the male. Being a man implies a predominance of masculine qualities, being a woman a predominance of feminine ones. (Perhaps the neurosis may often consist of not feeling their predominance!) The inability to integrate the contrasexual qualities results in a one-sided caricature—a brute of a man or an ethereal mouse of a woman. Every life situation, optimally dealt with, demands a judicious mixture and interaction of the two principles. Some situations require more of the feminine approach and others more of the masculine. The well developed personality needs access to both sides of himself.

In the therapeutic relationship we meet with the opposites of patient and therapist. In the beginning, the sense of separateness is very marked between the two. The therapist is the healer, the healthy one, the individuated, all-knowing expert. The patient is the injured one, the sufferer, the seeker, the "sick" one. As the therapy process unfolds, the therapist carries for the patient the projection of his shortcomings and unacceptable shadow aspects, but also his potential and unknown ability. Successful analysis entails the assimilation of these projections and reintegration of the two opposites within the person of the patient.

A reliable barometer of the successful progress of the therapy is a transformation from top-dog/under-dog frame of reference to a more egalitarian one. When the analysand recognizes and begins to assimilate the fact that he has an analyst within him, a helper, a wise guide in his life whom he can contact and relate to, the analysis can to all intents and purposes be terminated. The value of this lies not in an abstract knowing but in an actual experiencing. This tests our working hypothesis that the non-personal psyche contains a guiding principle, that is, an innate knowledge of who we are, where we are going, and how we should get there. This guiding principle expresses itself through dreams and other products of the unconscious. It is the unfamiliarity with these elements that necessitates the help of the analyst. He is the expert not by virtue of knowing all the answers, but because he himself has undergone a similar process which has made him familiar with the symbolic means of communication from the unconscious.

The therapy process, however, is not one-sided. The opposites to be integrated into the wholeness pattern are a double pair: the conscious and unconscious positions of *both* analyst and analysand. Confrontation and assimilation of his projections are as important for the analyst as for the analysand. He must also realize at all times that he himself incorporates both of the polarities. A holistic approach, therefore, regards the patient and the therapist not as two separate units, but as two elements of one unity.

It is natural, then, that Jungians consider transference and countertransference as two sides of the same Gestalt. In psychoanalytic tradition, the patient is allowed, even encouraged, to have his transference, but the therapist's countertransference is viewed as a nuisance, to be rigidly controlled, if not ignored. In the Jungian view, the therapeutic relationship creates an energy field of which both transference and countertransference are included as equal polar opposites. In fact, the therapist may use his own emotional reactions as indicators of the nature of the ongoing process. If the therapist discovers himself being overbearing or bullying towards a particular patient, he may ask himself whether his own reaction may not be an indication of the patient's unconscious need to be bullied, whether he has not been caught together with his patient in a master-slave pattern.

A very important and long neglected pair of polar opposites is that of body and mind. Here our western culture has been deeply influenced by the Judeo-Christian traditional value system. The first Commandment categorically separates the idea and spirit of God from its concrete manifestation in nature. The religious experience of God is differentiated and cut off from the experience of that which *is*. The graven images that were forbidden are the ancient forms of visualizing the deity through sacred objects, places, things, etc. This visualization was no longer to be tolerated. The contention that God could be found in nature was branded as heresy throughout the Christian Middle Ages, and was subject to burning at the stake.

Thus we find in Blake the voice of the Devil saying:

"All Bibles or sacred codes have been the causes of the following errors:

1. That Man has two real existing principles: Viz: a Body and a soul.

2. That Energy, called Evil, is alone from the Body; and that Reason call'd Good, is alone from the Soul.

3. That God will torment Man in Eternity for following his Energies.

But the following Contraries to these are True:

1. Man has no Body distinct from his Soul; for that call'd Body is a portion of the Soul discern'd by the five senses, the chief inlets of Soul in this age.

2. Energy is the only life, and is from the Body; and Reason is the bound or outward circumference of Energy.

3. Energy is Eternal Delight." *(The Poetical Works of Wm. Blake,* 1949, p. 248).

The idea of unity of mind and body, therefore, is assigned to the Satanic. Nature is something to be exploited, controlled and manipulated; the masculine attribute of doing becomes the all-important value, whereas the feminine attribute of being is valueless. Being is subordinated to the usefulness of doing. Throughout the Middle Ages, nature, the body, and woman were looked upon as inferior, corrupt, and the source of evil and temptation; they belonged to the Devil.

This Weltanschauung has seeped into our present culture in the form of fear and suspicion of the body and body-contact. We have developed a culture of distance, essentially in the name of the spirit. A certain amount of distance or separateness is essential for ego development, and closeness is not to be confused with merging. In pagan cultures, distance and merging were a divine pair of opposites embodied by Apollo and Dionysis-Eros. Our Christian culture has been predominantly Apollonian. However, in the recent countercultural movements such as the flower children, but also in the encounter movement, an unconscious attempt is being made to restore to Dionysis a rightful place.

Yet we have gone so far as to create different disciplines for these polar opposites. Soul and spirit have been claimed by theology, and science has been left to deal with the material body and the world (nature in a mechanistic sense). The split has continued even into psychology in the form of behavioral psychology on the one hand, and classical psycho-analysis on the other. Even Freud, whose genius it was to introduce the psyche into psychology, believed that ultimately all libido could be traced to somatic sources. For scientific psychology could not at first consider it respectable to grant status to a non-physical soul as an entity *per se*. This felt like a regression into mysticism or theology. Nor has this body-mind separation vanished from our present-day practice of dynamic psychology. Until recently, psychotherapy was limited almost completely to the verbal level. Yet words and concepts have become in-creasingly abstract, cut off from their organic meaning and experience. When we talk about feelings, we do not necessarily experience them or have a body awareness of them. Traditional insight therapy has taught us to understand (Apollo), but not always to realize (Dionysis). Without an awareness of the body corollary, the feeling is not fully experienced.

ENACTMENT

A sense of one's basic attitudes is sometimes brought closer home through nonverbal action than through words. Women especially have said that they integrate a feeling more through a body experience than through verbal insight. Hypnosis, autogenic training, bioenergetics, bio-feedback, and psychedelics have shown us that the deeper layers of affect mobilization are intimately tied to sensory body processes. Alterations and expansion of consciousness go hand in hand with alterations of body activities, body experiences, and inner revelations. To treat the psyche as separate and isolated from the body severely limits therapeutic possibilities. We have acknowledged this fact in principle without making full use of it. But there is an increasing awareness of the value of nonverbal physical expression and enactment methods when used with other insights.

The "techniques" not only expand awareness but allow for the possibility of transcending a given psychic state. Take for example a patient who is compulsively goal-oriented, so intent upon getting to his destination that he cannot live in the present, in the reality of the path he is taking to the goal. He might be asked to simply walk across the room to see it from the other side, and he is asked to get in touch with the way his body feels during the process of walking. He may notice even in his manner of walking how he stumbles over an obstacle put in his path, how his body leans forward awkwardly off balance, sensitive to the slightest push, how insensitive he is to the walking process itself. A possible result of this body experience of ruthless goal orientation may be a new gut-level awareness of his living-for-the-future style of life and may permit a more satisfying here-and-now style to emerge. By allowing an intensive focus on immediate experience it becomes possible to discover ways to transcend it.

In another instance, I wished to bring home to an analysand her tendency to constantly ask for help or relatedness, but to reject it when offered. I asked her to give me something, refusing to specify what. Whatever she offered me, a pen, a paper, a glass of water, I refused, implying, "No, not that," at the same time still asking her to give me something. This went on for some time, but after awhile the message registered that this was the way her constant requests came across to others.

Every emotion or affect can, and perhaps should be, brought to proprioceptive awareness, and thus reality tested in this way. No basic impulse can always be held safely under control. It must be given expression somewhere, sometime, in a constructive or at least relatively harmless fashion. "He who desires but acts not, breeds pestilence," said Blake, and again, "Expect poison from standing waters" (op. cit. p. 250-251). This fact is of significance not only for mental but for physical health as well. Here we may touch the roots of psychosomatic illness.

The extent to which unconscious motivation can be clarified through nonverbal physical expression may be illustrated in the following example from a group session. A man and a woman were involved in a seemingly endless and pointless squabble in which the real issues were becoming more obscured with every word uttered. It was then suggested that they try nonverbally to discover what was at stake. They were instructed to place themselves at opposite corners of the room and, in walking toward each other, to give expression without words of any feeling that might arise. What happened proved a surprise even to the participants! The man moved slowly and ploddingly toward his partner. She however, remained rooted to the spot. As he came nearer, she began to sway in a sinuous dancelike movement, very suggestively; but when he came close enough to reach out to her, she abruptly turned her back. When he tried to turn her back to him, she resisted vigorously, and when he rather clumsily used force, she flew at his throat viciously. They now began wrestling on the floor, at which point I stopped them.

It had become obvious to participants as well as onlookers that the woman was bent on arousing the man's aggression at any cost. She would risk, perhaps even desire, violence in order to be noticed erotically as a woman. Yet when she succeeded, she was unable or unwilling to face the implications of her urges, out of the very sense of inferiority which she projected as rejection on those who would not sufficiently take notice of her. The man, in turn, identified rather naively with the role of "conquering hero," the breaker of hearts, who was unable to resist allurement or guile from a woman and who proved his manhood by a show of plodding strength which disguised his inferiority feeling. The mutual projection of their similar complex became immediately obvious and a matter now of experience once the main dynamics of their behavior were explained to them.

This way of dealing with a conflict constitutes what we call *enactment*. Enactment as described here is not to be confused with acting out. The latter, frowned upon in psychotherapeutic work, is an unconscious, usually quite compulsive, expression of aggressive behavior intended to relieve internal tension. Enactment, on the other hand, is a deliberate and conscious effort to find a nondestructive, often symbolic, expression of otherwise repressed unconscious contents. Temporarily, it may increase rather than relieve internal tension.

In enactment we experience primarily the personal unconscious: those conflicts and difficulties (as well as untapped capabilities) that are specifically our own and arise from our particular life history. Enactment of transpersonal, archetypal contents, on the other hand, constitutes a ritual. In performing a ritual, we participate in a universal human process, a life situation or experience that has always been a part of mankind, and will always be part of the collective human experience: marriage, symbolizing the union of two people; baptism, symbolizing the entrance of a person into a new community; bar mitzvah and initiation rites symbolizing the coming of age (physically and spiritually); the Catholic mass, symbolizing spiritual transformation. It is no coincidence that all these rituals are religious ones since it is the function of religion to connect the individual with the archetypal, transpersonal dimension. A ritual, then, is a deliberate psychodramatic enactment of archetypal Gestalt patterns. Its intent is the evoking of fundamental life currents.

SYMBOLIC EXPERIENCING

In the psychotherapeutic process, rituals suggest themselves when there is a psychological need to concretize a theme of the eternal human condition. For example, a woman in her early thirties came into therapy because of a general malaise and a pervasive, though not severe, depression. This woman, being intelligent, had developed her intellectual capacities, but did not essentially experience herself as feminine. After some years of therapy, she had a profoundly moving dream in which she was initiated into the realm of femininity by a goddess or priestesslike figure. Although the dream was easily understood on an intellectual level, this understanding had little effect. Only when the dream was enacted as a psychodramatic and symbolic initiation ceremony was an actual experience mediated, a phenomenological vividness was created that was dramatically effective in bringing about a psychological change. For what matters most in many instances is the direct experience of the affective energy of the symbol.

Symbols, according to Jung, are not to be confused with signs. Signs are agreed products of societal conventions, substitutes, or shorthand expressions of known facts. Symbols, on the other hand, are spontaneous energy-charged motifs or images that express what is rationally and verbally unexplainable, but nevertheless felt as existing. Symbols always point beyond their possible interpretation. Signs may explain, symbols connect us existentially. Hence, mere verbalization may rob the symbol of most of its transformative capacity. All psychotherapists have had the experience of presenting a laboriously arrived at interpretation only to receive a rather flat, "Yes, so what?" response when the level beyond the rational has not been touched.

For example, a woman dreams that as she approaches what appears to be low mounds of earth, they rear into unscalable mountains. The dream in its starkness is very simple. A straightforward interpretation that the dreamer, in her way of approaching the world, makes mountains out of molehills did not add anything to what both the therapist and the patient knew. It was then suggested by the therapist that she *be* the mountain. She got down on her hands and knees and, after a while, she spontaneously exclaimed, "People are walking all over me!" This provided an additional inflection to the dream. The interpretation became: "Because you let people walk all over you, your small problems become insurmountable ones," and she had experienced it.

A dream is a product of the totality of the psyche, and any element appearing in it, human or inanimate, as well as any action, corresponds to a part of the dreamer. Here, Jung's position parallels that of Perls. Perls, however, operates primarily in terms of outside, relation-induced Gestalt elements, the mother as the actual mother, whereas Jung stresses the need to experience the symbolic significance of basic *a priori* or constitutional factors which can be understood and related to only mythologically, the mother as an archetype, the essence of mother in addition to the actual mother.

An example: a young woman who was subject to seemingly groundless outbursts of rage that punctuated a generally conventional and inhibited personality pattern dreamed that a swineherd killed a morning dove because its twittering bothered him. Dealt with in terms of our conventional association and amplification method, the dream led to a consideration of how her identification with the sensation function, a hardnosed prosaic overconcern with work reality, tended to kill the spiritual, poetic side in her. While this was theoretically quite correct in describing her overall situation, it did not add anything new that had not been discussed and understood before, and it did not touch the affect, the terror of the brutal act. She was now asked to enact the figures of the dream. The swineherd elicited nothing new, but in "being" the dove, she started with a few dancing steps, then stopped suddenly, saying she felt terribly inhibited about going on. Now this was peculiar, since you don't expect dancing from a dove, and the sudden inhibition makes you feel that you have come near to something important. I now suggested that some music might help overcome the inhibition about dancing. As I went to put on a record, I noticed her standing in the middle of the room, panic stricken, with tears pouring down her face. Yet she was unable to offer any explanation. I suggested that she simply hold on to the feeling and express any impression, memory or image that arose. She stretched out her hands and began to cry, "No! No! Keep away, keep away!" Then she described a vision of a gypsy girl, or perhaps a young witch, dancing in a forest glade, being attacked and killed by brutish peasants. This scene we reenacted in a therapy group with various group members playing the part of the peasants threatening her. She now went into one of her typical, hitherto unexplainable, outbursts of rage, showing clearly the landmarks of angry despair and the panic of being cornered helplessly. Her inhibitions, formerly seen merely in personalistic terms of conventional standards, were now experienced in a more profound way as the terror of the young witch connected her with a reality of emotional experiencing heretofore untapped, but also with an affect and energy potential which mere discussion of her dreams had failed to reach.

GROUP THERAPY

It is only relatively recently that therapeutic work in a group setting has been introduced, although spiritual disciplines have, since ancient times, recognized the importance of group cohesion for the enhancement of ritual and worship. Group therapy has been gaining more and more recognition in a increasing number of therapies (Gestalt, Transactional Analysis) and for them it is the treatment of choice. Only recently has this technique been somewhat reluctantly introduced into Jungian therapy.

Jung himself was particularly impressed, as a result of his own experience and his clinical observations, by the immense power of the collective in imposing its will and values on the individual. Thus, in most cases it thwarts and warps the individual development. He was, therefore, primarily concerned with buttressing the individual ego against the prevailing collective consciousness. The paradigmatic myth was that of the Arthurian Knight of the Round Table who was to find his own path through the forest to the Grail; if he chanced upon an already blazed path, he was to veer from it and create another. Jung's own temperament was such that it was more natural for him to deal with the individual and the more introverted individuation process. In the face of growing extroversion, this was indeed timely.

However, despite this bias which has affected most Jungian thought, many therapists have been introducing group work in addition to individual therapy. They have found that for certain patients, at a given stage of their analysis, group work hastens, enhances, and deepens the analytic experience, and introduces new areas that might never have come up or would have taken years to uncover. There is nothing inherently antagonistic to group therapy in Jungian psychology which is essentially a phenomenological approach to the understanding of experience. However, since the Jungian approach is primarily concerned with establishing the personal position relative to individual reality, group therapy will in most instances be considered an adjunct to individual analysis rather than the sole treatment of choice. The propitiousness of group therapy will also need to be examined within the broader psychological state of the individual; it may be countraindicated for some people at certain times.

One of the most important features of group work is that it provides the patient and the analyst with an arena for the experience of behavior at first hand. True, the analyst and the patient work with their own relationship, including the patient's projections within the individual context; but the analyst is only one person, and in his given position can constellate and evoke only a limited number of possible projections. The group provides the individual with a much broader range of reactions. He is first confronted with two very important facets of his personality: his person and his shadow.

The persona is our psychological skin; it is that part of our psyche that we have developed in order to relate to the outside world. Like all Jung's concepts, the persona carries positive and negative potential. The literal translation of the word "persona" is mask, and it refers to the mask worn by actors in Greek and Roman drama, representing their main character or attitude in that drama. A healthy persona functions flexibly and the person adapts easily to the various situations and people with whom he is involved; he relates well and seems to fit in naturally. However, a persona may malfunction in the sense of being too porous or too rigid. In the first case the person loses himself in the encounter; in the latter he sticks out like a sore thumb. It would seem that an elementary knowledge of oneself would include a knowledge of one's persona, but many people, otherwise knowledgeable, have no idea of how they come across to other people. The group, by virtue of number and variability, offers an arena where participants, even the analyst, may discover their impact to be totally other than their own impression of themselves. An ingratiating member may be surprised to find that he is considered extremely hostile, or a modest female member may be considered arrogant and overbearing. On the other hand, a woman who felt her own inferiority very strongly was told that she "came through" with great authority! Thus may a person learn from the projections he evokes how these projections will affect further interaction in the group and in his daily life, or how they have already done so.

The shadow is closely related to the idea of the persona. The shadow is that part of our personality of which we are unaware, but which we are particularly allergic to in others. It is the sum total of those qualities in other people that engage our affectivity. Thus, shadow qualities are those that do not correspond to our conscious ideals; they are what we would *not* like to be, the other side of the coin. The shadow is not merely negative; it is also comprised of our undeveloped qualities. When understood and sympathetically related to these qualities can be creatively channeled into forceful assets. Naturally, the exploration of the shadow is an important part of the individual work, but in the group it becomes more concrete and dramatic through interaction. In the group, attitudes are not only talked about but are "caught" in the moment of action for further clarification. A woman was confronted unanimously by her group peers with what her analyst had been saying for years, but which had until then been only an intellectual problem. When it became an experience of the moment, it became real for her.

The transference-countertransference patterns are likely to be modified in the group setting. On the one hand, it understandably dilutes and potentially eases the transference as each group member's reactions to the therapist are seen in relation to the reaction of the others. On the other hand the therapist's picture of the patient may also be modified in the light of the new reality dimension introduced into many transference illusions. With the support of the group, a transference reaction in a specific situation can peak dramatically and swiftly as, for instance, in cases of enactment and role playing. These transferences are transitory and of short duration.

What the group adds in terms of transference, also, is the constellation of a family-like atmosphere in which jealousies and sibling rivalries are evoked and dealt with. Most groups want their therapist to participate on a more equal level than in individual sessions, and since he is related to more realistically, he tends to share more of himself as himself rather than through the therapist persona.

Dreams, as well as other products of the unconscious, can be dealt with very successfully in the context of the group. When a member shares a dream with the group, other members react to the dream itself as well as to the dreamer in the light of the dream. This often brings about a consensus which goes to the heart of the problem or issue of the dream. Also, by virtue of the dream being shared by the group, it has in a way become much like the "big" dreams of primitive tribes, where a dream of one member is taken as a message to the whole community. Each member is requested to react to the dream as if he or she had dreamt it personally. This leads to further illumination, to possible new meanings of the dream. As an example: a group member dreamt that she saw worms coming out of the woodwork. She felt that it was important for her to share this dream with the group. As she was talking, it became apparent that anger was coming out, anger of which she was unaware. This anger was directed at the therapist for alleged neglect of her. As the group members began reacting to the dream, it became apparent that many others of the group also harbored angry feelings toward the therapist for one reason or another, anger which had not been brought out into the open. The anger, then, was coming out of the woodwork for the whole group. The dream not only facilitated the exploration of these feelings, but resulted in an important discussion as to why the members had not raised their angry feelings. The same procedure can be followed with any unconscious product: a fantasy, a poem, or a painting.

Another aid in understanding a dream is enactment, with various members taking roles, often even of inanimate objects. This has proved to benefit not only the dreamer but the role players as well. It permits elaboration and expansion of the dream; the drama can be carried beyond the actual dream content. We achieve here a process of "directed fantasy" or "active imagination" in the group. These often lead to dramatic realizations and to spontaneous breakthroughs.

As the group progresses, a subtle process sets in which we may call the emergence of the mythology of the group. After interpersonal tensions have more or less been played through, and various strivings for power and domination attempted and put down or achieved, the group members settle into group roles. We may have the seer, the leader, the comforter, the follower, the rebel. There emerges at this point a consensus of what a group, or *this* group, is and how it should function. There develops a strong cohesion toward what is allowed or forbidden, a kind of group morality, and the group tends to punish any infringement. It is encumbent upon the therapist, at this stage, to point out what is going on and to suggest that possible spontaneous overt and covert behavior is inhibited because of the group bond. For instance, a group may decide that members are required to verbally participate in any group discussion, particularly if they are directly addressed. The "black sheep" member, new or old, may decide or be unable to comply, thus bringing upon himself the wrath of the entire group. It is very important that the therapist work against this artificial cohesion, and stand behind the emerging individuality of the balking member. It is equally important that every member learn to find and hold his own individual style against the collective pressure of this "group" spirit. By holding his own against collectivity, he or she moves the group to evolve into a new ethic of being and interacting.

One can say, therefore, that the group constellates the archetype of humanity or the body social. It teaches one what it means to be a human being with a potential that is both negative and positive. The individual experiences himself not as a hapless cog in a wheel of collectivity, but as a responsible, influencing member of the body social against which he may stand in defiance if and when his sense of personal integrity calls him to do so.

REFERENCE

The Poetical Works of William Blake. Oxford University Press, 1949.

8

Jung and Perls: Analytical Psychology and Gestalt

DONALD D. LATHROP, M.D.

Perls and Jung: extraverted sensation and introverted intuition. In the Jungian typology, as it has been elaborated by von Franz (1971), these are opposites. The union of opposites is a primary developmental task of adult life.

All students of life study the same phenomenon, and Perls and Jung are no exceptions. Like all theorists, each made up his own system, his own terminology, his own techniques. And like all theories, they are reflective of the personalities of the men involved.

Both Gestalt and analytical psychology carry us past Freud. Freud permits us to believe the projection in the dream—that it is the father, mother, analyst, or whatever, who bedevils us. The Jungians call this the personal unconscious and take us beyond that to the transpersonal, the collective, the objective, the home of the archetypes. The Gestaltists teach the dreamer (the ego) to acknowledge that he or she comprises all of the elements in the dream. Thus, the Gestalt ego can encompass everything. To a Jungian, the totality of these elements is the Self.

We will consider three of Jung's important contributions to psychology. First, he found the unconscious to be a far more beneficent repository than Freud had. To Freud, the unconscious was a cesspool. To Jung, it was an unending river, as filled with positive elements as with negative ones.

Secondly, Jung described the archetypes. These are basic elements in

My thanks to Ellen Murasaki, M.S.W., Ph.D., member Gestalt Therapy Institute of Los Angeles, for her assistance with Gestalt concepts. I remain responsible for the interpretations.

the unconscious which have subsequently been described by Kopp (in press) and others in terms of patterns.*

The third great contribution of Jung was his typology. This system is immediately useful, clinically applicable, and relatively straightforward. He came upon the typology in his struggle to comprehend why he and Freud were irreconcilably separated. Jung was a phenomenologist, first and foremost; as such, he was obliged to examine what was—without judgment, without preconception.

First, Jung identified two basic attitudes towards experiencing, the extraverted attitude and the introverted attitude. The extravert experiences life outside of himself and gets his answers through other people. "If man thinks, feels, acts, and actually lives in a way that is *directly* correlated with the objective conditions and their demands, he is extraverted" (Jung, 1971). The introvert experiences life inwardly. "The introvert is predominantly subject oriented—toward the inner world of the psychic; to him psychic reality is a relatively concrete experience, sometimes even more concrete than external reality" (Whitmont, 1969). A balance of these two modes is called ambiversion. This term is rarely used, probably because the balance is rarely achieved.

While Freud always saw things in threes, Jung equally diligently saw things in fours. Because Jung also understood life as a balance between irreconcilable opposites, in analytical writings the four elements are often arranged on a crossed axis. On one axis are the two evaluative functions, thinking and feeling. On the opposite axis are the perceptual functions, sensation and intuition. Notice that I have called the types "functions." They are very much ego functions, in addition to being extremely useful definitions of character types.

Both of the evaluative functions are rational. The thinking function utilizes thoughts and inductive and deductive logic, while the feeling function is viscerally based. Feelings are the refined products of emotion, and emotions are like the climate. Feelings are like the living creatures that inhabit the climate. They are defined and limited entities, unlike the emotions.

Feeling is part of the function of ego. Ego has feelings. Ego is possessed and subverted by emotions. For example, most of us learn how to feel anger. When we are driven by rage, we often feel humiliated and frightened afterward.

---

* There patterns become character traits, life-styles, the "script" of one's life. At their roots are these structural elements, the archetypes, immutable, timeless, the imprint of our biological and experiential heritage.

Anger is only one generic feeling. It can be refined into many component feelings.

A mood is the effect upon ego consciousness produced by emotion. With effort and direction, a mood may be transformed into feelings.

Affect is to feeling as harmonics are to pure tone sounds. Affect is an expressive aspect of feeling. Feelings are represented by color, in dreams, for example. Affect is the coloring agent. Without affect, feelings are in black and white.

Sensation is the reality function of perception. "Sensation . . . is a function with which we comprehend the here and now" (von Franz, 1971, p. 28). The Here and Now! The cornerstone of Gestalt. "We pay attention to the obvious, to the utmost surface," is a way Perls describes it. Von Franz warns: "The negative aspect of sensation is that this type gets stuck in concrete reality" (von Franz, 1971, p. 28). Translated, this means that one of the dangers of the Gestalt mode is taking things purely literally.

Intuition is the perceptual function for *inner* reality. Like her teacher Jung, von Franz is highly intuitive. She states: "Intuition is a function by which we conceive possibilities . . . future possibilities or potentialities in the background of a situation (von Franz, 1971, p. 30). Intuitives must look through squinting eyes, see blurred, in order to get their inner perceptions.

Perls says, "a good therapist doesn't listen to the content of the bullshit the patient produces, but to the sound, to the music, to the hesitations" (Perls, 1969a). That is the intuitive function, as practiced in Gestalt.

Every individual needs one of the perceptual functions (sensation-intuition) and one of the evaluative functions (thinking-feeling) to get along. Always, one of these four is better developed than the others. If the best developed is a perceptual function, then an evaluative function is the second best developed. With growth, effort, and maturity a person may develop the function opposite to the secondary one. For a sensation-thinker, that would be feeling. The fourth function, also called the inferior function, remains forever a doorway to the unconscious.

The fourth function is represented in myths and fairy tales as the idiot child, the cripple, the bumbler, the inept. This function is always sent on the hero's journey ill prepared, a laughingstock. It is the classmate voted least likely to succeed.

What happens to it? What becomes of the inferior function in a fully developed personality? It is redeemed. It encounters talking beasts, helpful witchs, and sorcerers. Blindly following its designated path, too lacking in self awareness to realize (what the rest of us know for a certainty) that it is doomed to fail, it comes back bearing the Great Secret. The fourth function never develops in the way the others do. Instead it becomes valued for its special purpose—the messenger from the other side.

The unconscious to Jungians is the wellspring from which all life emerges. Perls wants to avoid the evaluative connotations of the term, ". . . therefore, rather than talking of the unconscious we prefer to talk about the at this moment unaware. This term is much broader and wider than the term 'unconscious' " (Perls, 1973).

The pure intuitive "sees" the limitlessness of the hazy and obscure universe. The pure sensation type sees only what he sees right now. Most of us, using some of each, perceive what lies between these two extremes.

What Perls calls "being in the center," and "the integrated person," (1969a, p. 26), Jung calls individuation. Perls teaches us to deal with the here and now of interpersonal experience. Jung teaches us to deal with the here and now of intrapsychic experience. Perls' discussion between topdog and under-dog in *In and Out the Garbage Pail* (Perls, 1969b) is extraordinarily similar to a technique Jung describes as active imagination.

Gestaltists are technique oriented; Jungians are content oriented. Gestaltists can embrace a short-term process; Jungians deal only in long-term process. Gestaltists deal with the almost universal problem of overvaluation of ego consciousness by teaching the ego to identify with nonego elements. For example, in the Gestalt interpretation of a dream, the dreamer is told to *be* various elements in the dream, none of which are presented as the dreamer (ego). Jungians attempt to deal with this same problem by identifying the nonego elements in the dream as Shadow (the mirror image of the ego), Animus or Anima (the contrasexual, nonego elements), and Self (the ego ideal or wholeness).

Jungians are conservative; Gestaltists are radical. Jungians are obsessive; Gestaltists are impulsive. Jungians savor tradition, enshrining it; Gestaltists are short-term, hedonistic pragmatists. Gestaltists use groups as an essential tool; Jungians shun groups and regard them as dangerous sources of influence from the collective or impersonal unconscious.

Gestaltists relate to the body; Jungians relate to the mind and to the soul. Gestaltists relate to sexuality by embracing it, by acting it out; Jungians relate to sexuality by spiritualizing it. Gestaltists and Jungians both use the transference neurosis but do not resolve it. (Whether this is a reflection of the fact that neither Perls nor Jung had the opportunity to work through their transference neurosis with Freud is a question. For that matter, I question whether anyone ever works through the transference neurosis to complete resolution.) Gestaltists deal with the transference by minimizing it, by focusing on "reality" and on the patient's contemporary problems. Jungians deal with the transference by displacing it onto the nonpersonal figures which represent the archetypes. Both groups also use The Founder (i.e., Fritz and Carl) as a focus for transference.

The issue of transference leads to the final point. Each of these great pioneers struggled with this powerful dynamic force in himself, in his life, in his theory.

Freud believed transference could be analyzed. He believed it could be made the center of the analytic relationship, and then resolved with the scrutiny of the analytic eye. Jung believed there were unanalyzable foundations, archetypes, behind all of the experiences in consciousness, including transference. (Behind the personal mother there stands the great mother.) Archetypes can never be fully analyzed. They can be circumlocuted, amplified, but never reductively analyzed. Perls believed that the real relationship, the one in the present, could be made so compelling that the transference would take care of itself.

All the while, each of these teachers has been and is the object of grand transpersonal transferences. Both Jung and Perls resisted this deification activity, while Freud demanded it. (My favorite statement of Jung that summarizes this subject of his own glorification is that he was glad he was not a Jungian.) Each of these three giants now has shrines to his memory (Zurich, Esalen, Vienna), with apostolates all over America and Europe.

Mankind must have heroes. These three are the heroes for psychological man.

REFERENCES

Jung, C. G.: *The Collected Works of C. G. Jung*, Vol. 6. Princeton, N. J.: Princeton U. Press, 1971. P. 333.

Kopp, S.: *The Hanged Man: Psychotherapy and the Forces of Darkness*. Science and Behavior Books, in press.

Perls, F. S.: *Gestalt Therapy Verbatim*. Lafayette, Cal.: Real People Press, 1969. (a)

Perls, F. S.: *In and Out the Garbage Pail*. Lafayette, Cal.: Real People Press, 1969. (b)

Perls, F. S.: *The Gestalt Approach and Eye Witness Therapy*. Palo Alto: Science and Behavior Books, 1973. P. 53.

von Franz, M. L., and Hillman, J.: *Lectures on Jung's Typology*. New York: Spring Publications, 1971.

Whitmont, E. C.: *The Symbolic Quest*. New York: Putnam's, 1969. P. 139.

Part IV

GESTALT THERAPY INTEGRATED WITH OTHER TECHNIQUES AND SYSTEMS

The present section shows some of the integrations of techniques or systems with Gestalt therapy. Each of these integrations is one which I believe adds something of significance to the Gestalt approach, or provides a point on the growing edge.

In his chapter, Abraham Levitsky shares his mature experience in the use of hypnotic techniques within a Gestalt therapy context. I believe Gestalt therapists may find much in Levitsky's approach to stimulate their delving into the body of knowledge on hypnosis and other altered states of consciousness.

James Dublin has provided a deep theoretical discussion in which he draws a distinction among Perls' style of Gestalt therapy, Gestalt therapy, and a style of Gestalt therapy which freely borrows ideas from existentialism. His examples and theoretically important distinctions of these three positions may well encourage the reader to increase his familiarity with existential thought.

Bruce Derman has written on an integration which he terms the Gestalt Thematic approach. In his chapter he shows how, within a Gestalt group therapy context, he integrates theory and technique from the psychomotor therapy of Albert and Diane Pesso. This chapter may whet the appetite of the reader to read more about psychomotor. My suggestions are Pesso's two books, *Movement in Psychotherapy* (New York: New York University Press, 1969) and *Experience in Action* (New York University Press, 1973).

109

In the final chapter of this section, Charlton Stanley and Philip Cooker have presented an integration which I believe to be of great significance. They have brought together Gestalt therapy and the work on "core" conditions of therapeutic communication as expounded by Rogers, Carkhuff, and Truax. They present their understanding of these two positions, and then discuss a synergistic integration.

9

Combining Hypnosis
with Gestalt Therapy

ABRAHAM LEVITSKY, Ph.D.

I

Since its introduction into modern medicine in the late eighteenth century, hypnosis has had a most colorful and erratic history. At times it has been regarded with wonder and awe. At other times, both the method and its practitioners have been vilified for not living up to the magical expectations which are—understandably—generated by this modality. Cycles of overvaluation and undervaluation are evidently destined to be its fate, not only socially but, as my own experience suggests, in the careers of individual therapists.

Most psychotherapists have experienced the great difficulty of arriving at a sane and balanced view of the broad field of psychotherapy. In the case of both clinical and experimental hypnosis, the difficulties are magnified many times. The dynamics of this situation, at least in part, become more and more discernible. It is necessary to avoid the dangers of two polarities, the fear of exercising power on the one hand, and on the other a tendency to be seduced by unrealistic fantasies of power and influence. Very similar dynamics are evidently at play in the field of psychotherapy itself. Gestalt concepts of growth and centering are likely to throw light even on this problem of social and historical development.

II

It often comes as a surprise that a psychotherapist would be interested in combining Gestalt therapy with hypnosis. Perls, for instance, often downgraded hypnosis, and might very well have been shocked at any

111

efforts to integrate these two modalities. Presumably the basic contradiction is that hypnosis is, par excellence, a method which employs directiveness, suggestion, and persuasion, a kind of "management" of the patient. Gestalt therapy, on the other hand, has as its basic tenets the principles of self-responsibility, of the uniqueness of solutions to life problems, of learning through discovery and experimentation rather than through imitation of others.

Although these contentions have some merit, I do not believe that they see the entire picture. For some years, I have worked on the assumption that any point of view, any school of thought, any principle which enriches our understanding of human behavior has a rightful place in the armamentarium of the therapist. In fact, in one sense it is difficult to see much room for debate on this issue. If we agree that the therapist's most important tool is himself, then obviously he will have the greatest success in imparting those views and attitudes which he has most successfully integrated into his own world-view and life-style. If we agree, furthermore, that the therapist as he works expresses his own unique style, there are going to be a great number of individual styles around, and among these there will be found some "surprising" combinations.

We can go a few steps further. For those of us who place a premium on spontaneity, on psychotherapy as an artistic expression, any practitioner who comes to represent a terribly pure version of any approach is suspect. It is precisely the imitative, the canned, "establishment" kind of procedures on the part of many psychoanalysts that Perls and other Gestaltists have all too justifiably derided. In telling the patient, "Be yourself," we ask him to take on the terrors, the challenges, and the pleasures of individuation, uniqueness, differentness. If we find ourselves merely "talking a good game," paying mere lip service to these ideals but not truly developing our unique therapeutic styles, we are obviously selling ourselves and the patient short.

I was introduced to Gestalt therapy after a number of years of work in clinical and experimental hypnosis. During this time, I had many occasions to observe the remarkable phenomena that can be produced with this modality, such as: relief from physical pain—sometimes momentary, sometimes enduring; temporary relief from severe anxiety states by means of hypnotic sleep; induction of dreams during the interview; age regression with uncovering of hitherto repressed material; temporary relief from cold symptoms through the use of fantasy medication, e.g., fantasied nose drops. At times, results were extraordinarily gratifying. A friend reported that her very successful career in fashion illustration began soon after a hypnotic session in which I asked her to imagine herself working while at her office. Prior to that time, she had had so much tension and self-consciousness that it was practically impossible for her to work in her field. A tennis instructor felt that his level of tournament play was helped appreciably by our technique of imagining himself to be both player and coach, and making appropriate corrections as he visualized his strokes, i.e., as if on a movie screen.

The list could be a very long one. Naturally there were failures. Some people were poor or indifferent subjects (about 15 percent of the general population). Some were good subjects and behaved very convincingly during the hour, but demonstrated no particular benefit afterwards. These facts simply had to be accepted. But the price was right; one could always fall back on other therapeutic approaches. What I did find necessary—and I believe this to be the experience of most hypnotherapists—was to gradually acquire a set of realistic expectations as to what hypnosis could accomplish, and also to arrive at refined views of the problem areas in which it might be applicable. A comprehensive statement on this matter is still fraught with difficulty and beyond the scope of this paper. Authoritative treatments of this question are provided by Meares (1972) and Wolberg (1948).

III

Following are some brief episodes illustrating some of the possibilities of combining hypnosis with Gestalt therapy.

During a group psychotherapy session, a woman starts to express resentment towards her physician. She is tense and blocked, and does not express herself clearly. Acting on a hunch, I take her left arm by the wrist and ask her to let the arm go limp. She quickly relaxes the arm, and I suggest that this relaxation can extend throughout the entire body. Her shoulders sag, her head comes forward, and a flood of tears follows. Soon after, detailed material about her frustrations with the doctor comes out. (Though I had never before used this technique with this patient, I felt I knew her well enough to be confident about the usefulness of this simple application of suggestion and relaxation.)

At a public lecture on hypnosis and Gestalt, I do a demonstration of group hypnosis. In these demonstrations, I am accustomed to having fair to good responses from 75 percent of the audience. I suggest a fantasy trip in which they spend a very active day outdoors. At night they are pleasantly fatigued and sleep deeply. I instruct them to dream and remember the dream. Invariably, several people report dreams afterwards, and with those who are willing, I demonstrate the Gestalt method of working with dreams.

At a weekend workshop on Gestalt and hypnosis, it becomes apparent that one of the women is an amazingly good subject for hypnosis. In fact, the readiness with which she seems to hurl herself into the trance seems to me to have a rather addictive flavor. I offer her an unusual challenge; she is to comply with the mechanical aspects of what I ask, but not go into trance. She agrees, and I begin, "Raise your right arm." It is obvious to us all that she is losing the challenge. Her eyelids flutter, her head droops, her facial muscles sag. I repeat this procedure with her several times before she can "succeed" in staying out of hypnosis. The depth of her compliance needs and her eagerness to give over responsibility to someone else are dramatically highlighted. We do some work on this later in the workshop.

In a Gestalt training group, the atmosphere is relaxed and friendly. An advanced trainee, J., is demonstrating a particular approach of his. It occurs to me that this is an excellent opportunity to try an experiment that I have long wanted to do, namely to have a therapist do therapy while himself under hypnosis. J. agrees, and as I expected, proves to be a good subject. He quickly relaxes and accepts suggestions. I ask him to open his eyes and proceed with his work. As he opens his eyes, he objects that he is much too relaxed to work. I reply that he need not consider this to be "work," that he can do his demonstration and "have fun." He immediately proceeds with verve and confidence. In later feedback from the group, many people comment that in working under post-hypnotic suggestion he displayed crisper timing and was more sure of himself. A surprising sidelight was that, while J. was working with one of our group, another group member experienced a spontaneous age regression to age seven, a time at which he had had a severe leg injury. This situation was complex enough to require that I take over from J. long enough to work through the feelings which had spontaneously surfaced.

A college instructor consults me on an interim basis while his therapist is on vacation. He is somewhat depressed, and reports very annoying tension in the abdominal area. He knows of my interest in hypnosis, and feels this may be of help. It is soon apparent that he is a poor hypnotic subject, and I decide that merely helping him to achieve some degree of trance has something to offer him. I begin the second interview by first lifting his arm and asking him to let it be heavy. Then I ask him to fantasy that this is being done. Again I actually lift the arm, and once again have him fantasy that this is being done. I continue the interview with a variety of approaches—some Gestalt work, some interpretive remarks of his fear of pleasure and relaxation. On about four occasions during the hour, I have him again fantasy that I approach and lift his arm to let it get heavy. Each time I add that the heaviness can be allowed to go down into the legs or up into the head, etc. Towards the end of the sessions, he reports that he seems to have crossed a kind of "border" and achieved far more letting go than he has generally permitted himself. There are tears of relief. He feels the sessions have been fairly successful in providing the interim support he was seeking.

IV

The main point of the foregoing section may be starkly summarized in the statement: *Hypnosis does exist!* Though the mechanisms by which it operates continue to mystify us, though the effects of hypnosis on different individuals under varying circumstances are erratic, we can say that many individuals in hypnotic trance are capable of behaviors which normally elude them. Associations can be more free, inhibitions can be diminished, memories may be more accessible, fantasies can be more vivid and immediate, and emotions can be intensified. It would seem natural, then, to have an interest in incorporating these assets into a total therapeutic program.

In my thinking I have found it useful to assume that the capacity for hypnosis, like the capacity for going to sleep at will, is an ancient, natural, biological function that has atrophied in modern man. We are well aware that many primitive people have the most enviable ability to go to sleep for long or short periods whenever they wish. Many are also capable of sleeping restfully while at the same time remaining alert to possibilities of danger. It is my guess that such a capacity for relaxation and for "self-suggestion" would be correlated with the ability to be an excellent hypnotic subject. I am willing to make the assumption that teaching people to be better and better hypnotic subjects involves restoration of a formerly natural function and provides a very useful skill for which countless applications can be found.

The basic phenomenon in hypnosis is that of suggestibility. We know that in promoting suggestibility the attitude of trust is an enormously important factor. Where there is little trust, suggestibility can be seriously impaired. In this connection, it is both interesting and enlightening to compare the reactions to hypnosis induction in different groups I have worked with. It is no great surprise that in working with groups who have some familiarity with Gestalt therapy and/or the encounter move-ment, I encountered less skepticism, less suspiciousness, and less fearful-ness. More interestingly, one observed a greater willingness to focus on those phenomena which did occur rather than on the suggested pheno-mena which may not have occurred. This kind of group tended to be more psychologically adventurous, and showed greater emotional and imaginative resourcefulness. Minimal or ambiguous instructions were reacted to creatively. Phenomena which did occur "made sense" and were fitted into existing frames of reference. Even when they could not be fitted into a familiar frame of reference, the phenomena could still be accepted and attended to without creating the kind of mystification which might lead to a desire to withdraw or deny. In other words, for people who are more in touch with themselves, more trusting of their own impulses and sensations, the opportunity for new kinds of psychological experiences which hypnosis offers is welcomed. The term *intraceptive* has been used for this sort of openness to ideas and experience.

On the other hand, groups which have had less opportunity for self-exploration react very differently. They are more likely to interrupt themselves with unproductive and head-trippy kinds of questions. They seem to have a motivation for hypnotic effects not to occur. Faced with an ambiguous instruction, they opt for the impossible or ludicrous inter-pretation. In a sense they behave as if they would be happiest if nothing happened so that they need not regard themselves as "weak-minded" (suggestible), nor upset their provincial applecarts. They seize upon the very attitudes which Gestalt therapists try to promote (i.e., an experi-mental openness to experiences, trust in one's own sensations, ability to hear what is actually being said rather than getting tangled in frightening projections of one's own aggressions, etc.) as a rationalization for imput-ing devious motivations to the hypnotist.

The two kinds of reactions to hypnosis may be labeled "the yea-sayer" and "the nay-sayer." Some people see the doughnut and some people see the hole.

V

Having these considerations in mind, it can be readily appreciated that both the spirit and techniques of Gestalt therapy lend themselves readily to trance induction, trance deepening, and trance management. The fol-lowing remarks are designed to point up specific ways in which Gestalt techniques have relevance for work with hypnosis.

A. *Being in the Moment*

The notion of the here and now, the philosophy of being in the moment, is, of course, a keystone of Gestalt therapy. This notion seems simple on the surface, but extensive experience shows over and over again that a true appreciation of this philosophy requires persistent effort. Gestalt therapists have been developing a great range of skills in teaching this attitude.

We need to show the patient how quickly and easily he leaves the now. We help him distinguish between a perception and a fantasy, between a reality and an expectation (particularly a fearful expectation), between a true observation through his sense and a fanciful "thought about." A considerable advantage of this procedure is that it helps so much with the problem of concentration.

All workers with hypnosis have been painfully aware of how easily subjects resist by being unable to concentrate on sensations and perceptions suggested by the hypnotherapist. The focusing and narrowing of the subject's attention provide such a prime advantage in hypnosis, especially during the induction procedure, that this point hardly requires elaboration.

There is another even more intriguing benefit from teaching the patient to stay in the now. As he becomes more skillful at doing this, he is often exhilarated—even astonished—at the richness and novelty of his appreciation of seemingly mundane elements which he formerly took for granted. At times it even partakes of the turned-on feeling associated with the psychedelic drugs. This is a powerful motivator and rapport-getter between patient and therapist. One can say, without even stretching a point, that this total or near-total immersion in immediate experience is itself already the beginning of a hypnotic-like experience which the therapist might choose to broaden, direct, and utilize for specific purposes.

We can go even further. When the patient, when any of us, has succeeded in whole-heartedly being in the now of the real world about him, when he is thoroughly open to the ever-changing richness and knowledge provided by his senses, when he is not confusing his inner patterns of fantasy with what is truly happening around him, then at that very moment he is alive, vital, and spontaneous. At that moment, he has left his neurosis behind and, in the words of Perls, he has "lost his mind and come to his senses." This is always an experience of such impact and so packed with gratification that it is rarely forgotten.

At such a moment the hypnotherapist whose outlook is broadly based and who is grounded not in adherence to any particular "school" but in broad concepts of healthy functioning quickly loses interest in hypnosis or any other technique or gimmick. For such a moment is simply to be savored and enjoyed rather than "used" for some imaginary, non-existent "other" therapeutic goal. We see here the important principle—rather simple in theory but sometimes not so simple in practice—of switching flexibly from one focus to another according to the requirements of the situation. We keep our eye not on any technique per se, but on where the patient is.

It is apparent that the therapist's skill in involving the patient deeply in his sensory observations is easily transferred to the ability to involve him in such a typical Gestalt therapy situation as a fantasy dialogue. It was a commonplace remark on the part of observers of Perls' work with people in the hotseat that the patient's total absorption in his experiences had a "hypnotic" quality. The question naturally arises: Is there any advantage in introducing hypnosis into this procedure? In my experience, there can be a definite advantage, namely that we can then combine the action-laden impact of Gestalt methods with the formidable asset of suggestibility.

For instance, in the case of a fantasy dialogue in which the patient has spoken in a flat voice, typical Gestaltist replies might be:

"Do you hear any anger in your voice?"

"I don't hear any anger in your voice."

"Say it so he hears it!"

We can bring in the suggestive component with: "Go inside yourself. Feel your anger. It can grow stronger and stronger. Express it!"

We can follow up with: "And how do you feel now?"

The two approaches need not be terribly far apart. The goals are precisely the same, namely that the patient experience himself thoroughly and express himself wholeheartedly enough so that he arrives at a finished feeling, i.e., by not having interrupted his internal process.

Does the use of suggestion imply manipulation? This charge is, of course, commonly made against the use of suggestion. Personally, I do not experience this as a serious charge. The therapist may indeed choose to rely on prestige suggestion, and "command" the patient to feel better, or to do this or that. In that case, he is simply regressing to the methods of the late nineteenth century, and not availing himself of all the advances in psychodynamic knowledge that have accrued since then. However, it is in fact far more effective to employ suggestive techniques to assist in uncovering and working through resistances, and to promote the autonomy and inner resources of the patient.

On the question of manipulation, the illustration given of the young woman with a compulsive need to enter the hypnotic trance is deeply relevant. Here the hypnosis itself was seen as the resistance, and was worked with in this light.

B. *Acceptance and Self-Acceptance*

Gestalt therapy has made decisive contributions to a deeper understanding of the nature of acceptance. Even the Rogerian client-centered therapists, for whom the concept of acceptance is so central, might themselves penetrate more deeply into the nature of acceptance by incorporating the insights of Gestalt therapy.

Gestalt groups sometimes play an intriguing form of "acceptance game." Individuals in turn make the statement, "At this moment, I cannot possibly be different than I am." Then one adds some self-descriptive statement, "I feel confused," "I feel scared," "I feel wonderful," etc. The game is then turned around and members take turns with the formulation, "At this moment *you* cannot possibly be different than you are." The speaker chooses some other member of the group and adds his perception: "You look surly," or, "You feel distant."

As with many Gestalt therapy games, a procedure which feels mechanical at first may soon start to feel laden with meaning and emotion. In this game, participants quickly feel the difference between "is" and "should."

Beisser's paper on "The Paradoxical Theory of Change" (1970), was fundamental in helping us articulate with greater awareness a principle with which many Gestaltists were working, but which had not yet been explicitly formulated. He points out, ". . . change occurs when one becomes what he is, not when he tries to become what he is not. Change . . . does take place if one takes the time and effort to be what he is—to be fully invested in his current positions."

In a paper on "Guilt, Self-Criticism and Hypnotic Induction" (1962), I pointed out how the subject's attitude of self-criticism and undue self-expectations provide a common resistance.

Patients in hypnosis will commonly have the attitudes:

"I should be less conscious."

"I shouldn't be able to talk."

"I should be **going** deeper."

"I should have no voluntary control."

In repeatedly exposing the patient to the tyranny of the "should" and helping him be aware of the fact of the "is," the Gestalt therapist is really preparing the patient for the most effective and cooperative orientation to hypnosis. If he can attend sensitively and acceptingly to his impulses of body, thought, and feeling instead of denying or stifling them because they do not conform with some fantasized "should" or concept of what ought to be, then he is truly lending himself to the delicate give and take between patient and therapist which characterizes hypnosis at its best.

Once again I take the opportunity to point out that as patient and therapist approach this sort of communication, the whole question of hypnosis may well become secondary, for it is the unhampered contact and communication between two individuals, hypnotic or otherwise, which are the most powerful curative agents.

There is still another point which bears on the matter of acceptance. The daily work of the hypnotherapist reveals over and over that some individuals respond with quite dramatic manifestations, some with more modest phenomena, and others with few or negligible responses. For the Gestalt therapist, the response itself of the patient to this pattern of successes, "failures," and resistances becomes as much grist for the mill as any other part of the work. Most especially, the reaction of disappointment at the absence of anticipated pyrotechnics can be used not only to help the patient get in touch with his unreal magical fantasies, but even more basically to provide him an opportunity to experience acceptance of where he is and what he is at the moment. This is another example not only of the existential roots of Gestalt therapy, but of the vital existential component of any effective therapeutic approach.

C. *Dealing with Resistances*

As mentioned above, it seems useful to assume that the capacity for hypnosis is a natural function and that little or no ability to enter hypnosis involves "resistance." Gestalt approaches have much to offer in the area of resistance.

As an illustration I return to a favorite technique of mine, the arm-dropping technique. I take the patient's arm by the wrist, asking him to let the arm be limp, to let *me* bear the weight of the arm. Let us assume he has great difficulty with this; he does not let go, I cannot feel the weight of his arm, he maintains his ordinary control. What approaches are possible?

1. Supportive-persuasive: "A lot of people learn as they keep trying; it's just a matter of practice." (This, by the way, is a simple truth; it often works this way, and no more complex approach is necessary.)
2. Interpretive: "Are you afraid to let go? Are you afraid to be held?"
3. Possible Gestalt-oriented approaches:
    a. "See if you can get in touch with where you are holding. Where is the tension and where is there less tension?"
    b. "Make your arm *more* tense; shuttle between tensing and relaxing your arm. Perhaps this can get you in touch with *how* you don't let the arm go. Keep doing it, tense and let go, tense and let go."
    c. Can you say to me, "I won't let it go."

> P: "I won't let it go!"
> T: "What might happen? Are there any fantasies?"
> P: "I might just be a blob and do something foolish!"
> T: "What might that be?"

This kind of exchange obviously starts to move in a familiar direction for the Gestalt therapist. With the release of buried feelings, one can later return to the letting go of the arm-dropping method.
    d. Patient says: "I can't concentrate; my mind wanders."

> T: "Fine, let it wander. Just tell me where it wanders." (Patient recounts the material.)
> T: "Good. Where do you wander now? Now, can you take a deep breath, relax and let your mind wander some more?"

In the last exchange, every experienced hypnotherapist will quickly see the multiplicity of messages involved. The patient has, at one and the same time, been told to do what he wants to do and what the therapist wants him to do, a classic example of paradoxical hypnotic technique at its best.

The Gestalt approach to resistances involves the same principles as the Gestalt approaches to all problems, namely to locate and contact sources of energy, and by freeing and expressing them to make them available for creative use rather than have them bound up, dissociated, pulling against the self. As Perls pointed out on so many occasions, "When in terror, play the terrorist!"

To amplify that a bit, the terrified person is in touch only with his feeling of terror. There is an enormous amount of latent energy there, but it is being squandered in that he is imploding; he is pressing in on himself. We must help him get in touch with his internal terrorist—the powerful, energetic source—and help him see how he is directing this frightening power at himself, the victim. With sufficient ingenuity, we can perhaps translate this energy into some overt physical or verbal action. How often we see that when this negative, bound energy is freed and permitted to flow, it becomes an impressive source of creativity and power, bringing life and vitality to a formerly frozen or constricted person.

One way I have found of using this sort of situation for hypnotic purposes is to have the resistive subject fantasy that he himself is giving suggestions to one or even two other persons. Sometimes I suggest that one of the fantasied subjects be compliant and the other stubborn-resistive. In this way, the resistive patient is persuaded to match his energies against a variety of response patterns, and as a result achieves better perspective on what he himself is doing. In the meantime, of course, his very involvement with this fantasy constitutes his willingness to work with the therapist.

VI

There are a number of techniques which are totally unique to Gestalt therapy, such as use of the awareness continuum, microscopic attention to moment-to-moment experience, dialogues between parts of the body, etc. As unique as any, and quite representative of the spirit of Gestalt therapy, is the so-called "stay with it" approach described by Levitsky and Perls (1970).

On the surface, the thrust of the "stay with it" method seems to represent the very antithesis of the popular concept of hypnosis. Presumably, in hypnosis problems and difficulties are surmounted rather rapidly, with minimal effort and risk on the part of the patient and largely as a result of a somewhat magical injection of confidence and authority on the part of the therapist.

The "stay with it" method, on the other hand, has come to symbolize patient, painstaking, step-by-step confrontation, resolution, and assimilation of painful emotions. In this view, we don't walk around, jump over or try to deny the existence of problems. Rather, we take the risk of experiencing, bearing, and "chewing up" the real pain and discomfort. In this way we learn to distinguish between pain and catastrophe. By not retreating into phobic avoidance, we prevent existential pain from developing into neurotic pain.

Now an interesting feature of hypnosis is that it is possible to employ similar methods of confrontation. In fact, we can do so with remarkable and endless variations. In treating a stutterer, for instance, I have had him imagine that his audience was at the rear of an immensely large auditorium, so large that he could not be heard. Convinced that he could not be heard, he did not stutter. As he approached them, in hypnotic fantasy, anxiety developed and stuttering began. He was given control over his own rate of approaching them, and at various stopping points was questioned as to his feelings and perceptions. With this and similar methods, his speech improved considerably.

As already mentioned, the very nature of hypnosis is that fantasy production is facilitated. Conflictual situations can be endlessly repeated. Time distortion can be used to speed up or slow down the action. A fantasied magnifying glass can be used to focus on particular details. Fantasy drugs, of varying dosage, can be administered. Fantasied "helpers" in the form of friends or associates can be brought in. It is particularly touching for many patients to fantasy the "good parent" in sharp contrast to the actual parent. The particular manner in which we elect to make use of these possibilities will of course be a function of our therapeutic approach, i.e., our view of emotional growth. The transactional analyst will hit on quite different methods of employing hypnosis than the worker with behavior modification. The Gestaltist, with his belief in the careful assimilation of conflictual feelings, will find ways of applying his techniques.

REFERENCES

BEISSER, A.: The paradoxical theory of change. In J. Fagan and I. Shepherd (Eds.) *Gestalt Therapy Now*. Palo Alto: Science and Behavior Books, 1970.

LEVITSKY, A.: Guilt, self-criticism and hypnotic induction. *American Journal of Clinical Hypnosis*, 1962, 5, 2, 127, 130.

LEVITSKY, A. and PERLS, F.: The rules and games of Gestalt therapy. In J. Fagan and I. Shepherd (Eds.) *Gestalt Therapy Now*. Palo Alto: Science and Behavior Books, 1970.

MEARES, A.: *A System of Medical Hypnosis*. New York: Julian Press, 1972.

WOLBERG, L.: *Medical Hypnosis*. New York: Grune and Stratton, 1948.

10

Gestalt Therapy, Existential-Gestalt Therapy and/versus "Perls-ism"

JAMES E. DUBLIN, Ph.D.

Recently I examined Alan Stone's (1972) review of Fagan and Shepherd's (1970) book, *Gestalt Therapy Now*. His disclaimer, that he cannot see what is Gestalt theory applied and that he is struck by the "Perls-ism" he sees (which he calls "adult play therapy"), inspired the three-part title for this essay. A straightforward explication of the theoretical evolution undergone by Perls as he formulated Gestalt therapy theory and operationalized the Gestalt therapy system has not been made. In this four-part essay, I shall attempt one. In the first part, I shall trace Perls' earlier theoretical work, his revision of Freudian and Reichian thought. In the second part, I shall describe Perls' formulation and implementation of a therapy system consistent with and embodying these earlier theoretical notions. Thirdly, I shall attempt to make explicit what in his writings Perls felt theoretically implicit, how the Gestalt therapy system relies on and operationalizes several basic existential tenets. And, finally, I shall give my view of the kind of existentialist Perls was and attempt a start toward sorting out how his personal impact has resulted in an additional but optional form, style, or manner of "doing" Gestalt therapy which is, rightly, perceived as "Perls-ism."

TRANSFORMATION, REVISION, AND EXTENSION OF FREUDIAN AND REICHIAN THEORY

In the first several chapters (especially) of Perls' first book, *Ego, Hunger and Aggression: A Revision of Freud's Theory and Method* (1947), and throughout his second, *Gestalt Therapy: Excitement and Growth in the*

Human Personality (Perls, Hefferline and Goodman, 1951), a theoretical foundation is laid, establishing the basic currents that run throughout his later work, *Gestalt Therapy Verbatim* (1969a), *In and Out the Garbage Pail* (1969b), and "Four Lectures" and "Dream Seminars" (1970, in Fagan and Shepherd, 1970). Perls brings to bear on psychoanalytical and character analytic theory three bodies of theory and data: the Gestalt psychological theory and principles; the holistic, organismic, biological theory of human functioning and growth; and notions of what I would call "affective-behavioral meaning consistency" brought from the study of semantics and certain schools of philosophy, especially the "differential thinking" of Friedlander. His application of these three bodies of knowledge, being done in an integrative, simultaneous way, is somewhat difficult to present systematically, but may best be begun with Perls' holistic, organismic applications.

Perls (1947) gives concrete examples to show that human perception and cognition are, in large measure, motivation-need determined. He presents the human being as a unique system of needs, a system which is self-regulating if not disturbed in this regulatory process. Then he begins to characterize the usual disturbances to this process, as both extra-organismic and intra-organismic in the sense of having been internalized through the adjustment process inherent developmentally. He shows how organismic needs, if not thwarted and if attended to, determine emergent actions which, filling the needs, allow the human organism to return to stasis. And he describes the cyclic aspect of this process.

To be in a relatively tension-free state, says Perls, one needs to listen to the "wisdom of the organism." As had Freud, Perls emphasizes oral, anal, and genital aspects of the organism-environment interchange. However, not satisfied with Freud's ontogenetic hierarchy, he elevates in overall prominence and chronologically extends the oral aspects of development. And to this revised and refined oral-interchange theory, Perls adds a dimension not emphasized by Freud but which forms a core of Gestalt-organismic theory—sensory contact and sensory awareness. At this point (in his thinking), Perls begins (1947) the first of what will be several functional transpositions (or transformations), expansions, and revisions of Freudian and Reichian theory.

First, and perhaps most basically, Perls redefines anxiety, ego, and the relationship between the two. He removes them from the structural context of Freud, functionalizing or dispositionalizing them. Freud's homunculus-like, signal-sending Ego is decapitalized by defining it organismically. Perls presents the human organism not only reactively experiencing excitation, but also appetitionally generating it. And he describes the blocking or thwarting of the expression of both kinds of excitation, generically, as anxiety.

Next, "the Ego" is concretized in its relationship to the experiencing of anxiety, which experiencing is translated in terms of bodily functions, such as heart rate, respiratory changes, etc. Then, Perls (1947; Perls et al., 1951) combines or brings to bear the major principles already worked out by Gestalt neuropsychiatrists and psychologists: Pragnanz, continuation, good figure, closure, etc. Under the general rubric of "figure out of ground" and "the unfinished situation," Perls describes awareness development (equivalent of "ego-building") as a function of attention and concentration which is characterized by contact, sensing, excitement, and Gestalt formation. Thus he in effect redefines Freud's structural ego as confluence, contact point, or boundary *only*. In so doing, Perls develops what could have been operationally defined as something like "Gestalt-Ego-Analysis." But, as a consistent departure from the structuralism and metaphorical nature of "ego," he calls his system, at first, "concentration therapy" (1947), then "Gestalt therapy" (1951).

From the standpoint of theoretical transformation, Perls has only just begun to roll. He has obviously found a powerful new conceptual tool, and generalizes it to conceptions of psychopathology, to psychosexual development theory, and to Freudian and Reichian theory of ego resistances or defenses and character armoring or character defenses. Recognizing that in persons whom we categorize as "neurotic" or "psychotic," another way of talking about "ego functions" is in terms of impairment or disturbance in the usual elasticity of figure-ground formation, Perls generalizes here. He thus functionally establishes what amounts to a Gestalt-formation definition of psychopathology, a unidimensional conception couched in terms of unawareness, described as incompletely formed Gestalten, and called "avoidance." By this conception, Perls subsumes many of the usual ego defensive operations, and lays the foundation for vast methodological implications in terms of de-mystifying "unconsciousness." In effect, Perls "robs" unconsciousness of its libidinal or instinctual reservoir of impulses, describing its explication in terms of contacting, sensing, attending, and concentrating.

Perls simultaneously relates this Gestalt perceptual-cognitive-organismic awareness development process to psychosexual development theory. Unresolved childhood interactions which have left the person deprived of need fulfilment or have thwarted his expressive reaction to his environment are problematic as "unfinished situations," "incompletely formed

Gestalten, "which, in pressing for completion, block other here-and-now behaviors, perceptions, attitudes, etc. Next, Perls sets about functionalizing or dispositionalizing ego resistance and character defenses, again into emotional-organismic terms. Expanding and refining character armoring, he functionally enlivens it, so that it no longer is merely the reactive result of the body not expressing itself outwardly, but is also the continuing efforts of the organism not to express itself outwardly, efforts which take the form of turning back upon self, which Perls calls "retroflection."

Again, Perls simultaneously "carries" psychosexual development theory as another "front." While doing so, he selectively deemphasizes the Freudian anal and Reichian genital aspects of it, emphasizing, expanding, and concretizing oral aspects. He especially revises psychoanalytic notions of introjection and projection by examining them in a concrete, bodily sense and modifying them accordingly. These revisions form a significant enough core of Gestalt therapy theory to warrant detailed description.

Concerning introjection, Perls deemphasizes (1947; Perls et al., 1951), and is later (1969a) to reject, or virtually reject, the concept of the internalized ego-ideal that forms conscience or superego. His manner of deemphasizing this concept amounts to a more literal, as well a dichotomous, definition. Internalization of the ego-ideal in such a way that it becomes part of the conflict-free sphere of functioning, Perls calls something beyond "internalization." He calls it "organismic assimilation," and means about the same as the psychoanalysts meant by "conflict-free ego functioning." But he also conceptualizes functionally what he holds Freud to have missed, the "bad parent" or "toxic" introject, that which (in Perlsian language) the child swallows whole, gulps down without chewing up, or has stuffed down his throat, and which, ingested but undigested, stirs in the organism. Perls points out that, according to Freud, this material needs only to be (again in Perlsian language) emotionally masticated and assimilated. While (in Freudian language) "id" can be "replaced" by "ego," Freud makes no provision, says Perls, for replacing superego, merely for softening it up, or making it more palatable. According to Perls, it may be remasticated and assimilated, or it may be organismically expelled. Here, Perls sees the essence of a concept which he says Freud missed by calling it "id" or "libido"—the infra-ego. This concept will (1969a) become his famous "under-dog" in the top-dog/under-dog ("shoulds" vs "wants") self-split. It is, in fact, the paradigmatic self-split from which Perls expands to the basic principle of reconciling or integrating self-splits, a principle which forms a core part of his finally developed therapy system (1969a, 1969b, 1970).

Concerning projection, Perls (1947; Perls et al., 1951) greatly expands the traditional conception. He describes projections as the result of organismically unassimilated and toxic introjects which the organism would aggress against were they not part of it, and which are therefore "split-off" into the world and perceived as hostile. To this point, his definition does not (functionally) differ significantly from Freud's. But Perls' theory of projection eventually is both essentially different from and more inclusive than the psychoanalytic theory. While in Freudian thinking projection is most often, if not always, the warding off of either sexual or aggressive "impulses" or "wishes," Perls held that its essence, though partly sexual and aggressive, is much more pervasive. He defines projection as disowning and attributing to others any part-self which is experienced as alien to the whole experienced self, and he elevates to theoretical prominence the part played by inhibited oral aggression. Thus, in short, he literalizes and concretizes psychoanalytic theory of introjection and the relationship between that and projection, again by relating these theoretical constructs to observed organismic, bodily functioning. This is to have vast theoretical implications in the therapy system Perls finally comes to, which system is to rely heavily on the concept of bodily, organismically claiming, owning, or assimilating projections by being them bodily, that is, acting them out experientially (1969a).

At this point (the 1940's), calling what he does "concentration therapy," Perls (1947) specifies the skeletal essence of what will become Gestalt therapy, that which, theoretically, must be done: awakening or re-sensitization; undoing retroflections; assimilating projections; regurgitating and/or remasticating introjects; developing a sense of "I-ness" and actuality in the here and now; and reconciling energy-consuming self-splits. Here Perls lays the theoretical foundation stones which will have theoretical-methodological implications for and will become some of the core principles of his later, more formalized therapy system: the "stay with the now on a continuum of awareness"; the "first-person, here-and-now, experiential encounter"; and the "reconciliation" or "centering" principles.

In chapters called "visualization," "body concentration," and "internal silence," Perls formulates essentially what will become the "fantasy trip," the "from here-to-there rhythmic awareness exercises," etc., of his formalized system (1969a, 1970). And here Perls (1947; Perls, et al., 1951) begins to realize further implications of orality and language that only Reich of the psychoanalysts dealt with extensively. That is, he begins to see just the extent to which language can be a form of resistance to awareness of self. As a result, he begins to integrate knowledge and notions from the field of semantics with his theoretical notions about experienced self. In his early (1947) chapters called "sense of actuality," "time," "past and present" and "first person singular," he examines how language as resistance or avoidance relates to "staying with" experience, and, especially, staying in the here and now. He lays the foundation for what will become "owning the 'it' by saying 'I'," "not gossiping," "taking responsibility," and other language "games" of his later therapy system (1969a, 1970, Levitsky and Perls, 1970).

In short, though still functioning at the level of "operational definitions," Perls has by the late 40's and early 50's finished his earlier theoretical work. This work consists of: at least seven transformations and expansions or revisions of existing psychoanalytic theory; integration of these transformed and revised concepts with Gestalt psychological principles and certain principles from semantics and philosophy; further integration of them with, and refinement of, the bodily, characterological armoring principles of Reich; and the simultaneous embodiment of all these integrated principles in a biologically oriented, holistic theory of the developing organism.

Functional Essence of Gestalt Therapy

Having dispositionalized ego as phenomenal self presenting organismically, Perls really has but one general path he can (consistently) follow. His goal is to operationalize a therapy system to help persons awaken or re-awaken, sensitize or re-sensitize, concentrate, stay with the phobic, avoidance-inducing situation to face or encounter the catastrophic expectation—all for the purpose of developing new levels of awareness and finishing unfinished Gestalten. Standing in the way of this awareness development is one generic obstacle, avoidance responses, organismically antagonistic or thwarting responses which preclude or block others. Perls (Perls et al., 1951) sees that while these avoidance responses are unique to the individual in their particular configuration, they do occur in certain regularized ways, which he categories as scomatization, desensitization, introjection, retroflection, and projection (e.g., Enright, 1970).

The basic method of a therapy system purporting to overcome these avoidances must somehow point them out concretely to the patient, as evidenced in bodily reactions, voice and speech patterns, etc. Such a system must be radically phenomenological, dealing always with the actually appearing event. And it has to develop in the patient a sense of

"I-ness" and "now-ness," has to put him into experiential contact with self, dichotomous part-self, and significant others (e.g., parents), for in this experiential contact of the past is where unfinished situations abound and are the source of incompletely formed Gestalten.

There is one last major requirement. Consistent with the organismic and Reichian bodily notions pervading it, such a therapy system has to have action, movement, and empathic projection. For, according to Perlsian theory, only by being (in the sense of acting vs. talking about) projected, alienated, or split-off self, demand-based resentments, etc., can one bodily, organismically, reclaim and assimilate them.

In another integrative stroke of genius, Perls sees that role-playing type therapy involves this whole-body, motoric involvement. But he also sees that his theoretical requirements are too stringent for role-playing as in psychodrama of the type made famous by Moreno, for three main reasons. First, Perls has theoretically defined the emotionally healthy person as one who has given up manipulation of the environment, and is self-supporting. Thus, it is theoretically inconsistent for the "actor" to have a "supporting cast." And secondly, and most basically, the therapist's interventions must be too frequent and too concerned with organismic minutiae for an orthodox psychodrama approach. In this connection, it is important to remember that the organismically presenting self is seen on a continuum of potential discrepancies noted in verbal-vocal-body-affect-content behaviors, and the required technique in making the patient aware of these discrepancies is three-fold: inquiry, frustration, and presentment. The therapist continually inquires into the patient's awareness of himself, and continually brings to his attention all observed attempts, emotionally or behaviorally, to attenuate his experience or to distance himself from his behavior. This continual three-fold procedure is not practical in ordinary psychodrama. And thirdly, the basic organismic, bodily movement necessary in being (acting out) projections, toxic introjections, etc. is not present if others play the roles, e.g., "the toxic mother."

This therapy, then, theoretically requires that a role-playing form of therapy be employed, and that the patient play all the roles. And that is precisely the final form Perls came to (1969a, 1969b, 1970). The emphasis on staying with here-and-now experience is so thorough that talking about is radically discouraged in favor of talking to, which is accomplished by experiential, fantasmal role-playing. Past incidents are dealt with, but always in the context of the present. Present tense language is required. Experiential encounters with significant others are first-person, present-tense, here-and-now, I-Thou (addressing, by name or descriptive) dialogues and/or physical encounters. "Transference" is dealt with primarily in this same fashion, the patient being all parts or roles. Thus, transference is both minimized and dealt with. Dreams are treated the same way, the patient being all parts (or symbols) of the dream in interaction with the other parts and/or himself.

EXISTENTIAL-GESTALT THERAPY: BODY WITH PARADOXICAL LIMBS

If all this be the early theorizing of Perls, and if what has been depicted here is the functional essence of Gestalt therapy, what is existential about it? And, especially, how is it, as Perls claimed (1969a), more existential than any other form of therapy? These questions require a fairly elaborate answer, which begins with a brief discussion of pre-Gestalt existential therapies, especially their aversion to techniques.

The "existential therapies" begin with *Daseinsanalyses* (existential analysis), founded by Ludwig Binswanger (1942, 1946, 1962) and co-developed by Medard Boss (1963), Eugene Minkowski (1962), and others. They held that the purpose of psychotherapy is analysis of "the structure of existence." This analysis, they held, is effected by phenomenological bracketing (suspending) theoretical systems of therapy and logico-categorical ways of viewing psychopathology, in order to attune to the patient's "being-in-the world," that is, to his idiographic, unique pathological pattern. However, when the patient's particularity as psychopathology was thus comprehended structurally, remedial measures consistent with or explicitly based on this way of comprehending the patient were not proposed. Psychoanalytic skills were retained as "the base upon which the analysis of the structure of existence rests." Thus, most American therapists readily dismissed or minimized early existential therapy as a meaningful body of theory and often disclaimed it as techniqueless.

Perhaps most prominent in bringing the thinking of these European existential psychiatrists to this country, and at the same time establishing a somewhat different and more complex view of existential therapy, has been Rollo May (1958, 1959, 1961). May sees existential therapy as defined not by anything the therapist does, but rather by an attitude, stance, or orientation that is more foundational than any technique. This "stance" is "more foundational" than the "doctor-patient" or "doctor-person" relationship. It is, in effect, a "person-person" relationship in which the person who also is a doctor brackets theoretical-clinical systems of "being with" in favor of person-to-person "being with."

This phenomenological "being with" may lie at the heart of the apparent hesitation of many existential therapists to develop techniques, and their often explicit wish not to advocate or identify with them. For a major tenet of existentialism is the scrupulous avoidance of the subject-object dichotomy in human relationships, the "I-it" (vs. the "I-Thou") relationship. And, indeed, whenever a therapist applies any technique, the person to whom it is applied becomes an object of that application, generically an "it."

This basic tenet, along with its presumed implications for the development of techniques in an existential approach to therapy, needs examination. As a sort of generic phobia of treating persons as objects, it is functionally fallacious. Experience-inducing techniques in general, and Gestalt therapy techniques in particular, can be shown to be benevolently paradoxical in the sense discussed above. That is, they specifically treat the patient as an "it" in a more thoroughgoing way, but precisely for the purpose of helping him reclaim, own, or integrate his disclaimed, alienated part-self, *his "it."*

This can easily be illustrated. A young, married male patient complains of "a deadened feeling . . . hardly any sensation" upon ejaculation. He does not use "I"; he has no complaint of himself or of his wife; he complains of his penis as an "it," disclaiming any responsibility for *its* functioning. The Gestalt therapist wishes to assist the patient to experience his body, including his penis, as subject rather than object that is had, possessed. But, paradoxically, he takes the patient at his word, that he has split-off or alienated his penis from his experiencing personhood (or *vice versa*). He treats the patient accordingly. Functionally, he asks the patient to split-off his penis, *and* to dialogue with it. If the patient protests that this is silly, makes no sense, is not what he really wants, etc., the therapist points out that he (the patient) is already splitting it off, separating it from the rest of his personhood, and that he (the therapist) is only asking him to do so more thoroughly in order to experience more fully how he is doing so. As technique, this functional splitting off of the penis takes the form of an experiential dialogue between the person-minus-penis and the split-off penis, the patient taking both roles experientially, verbally, and perhaps motorically. As is well known to experienced Gestalt therapists, the ultimate effect of such splitting off of body parts for such dialogues is not a further experiential distancing or alienation from them, but rather an experiential reclaiming or owning of them, a mind-body unification experience, or, in more existential-psychiatric language, an "I-as-body" experience. This illustration has already made indirectly a case that will presently be made in more detail, that such therapy is not only Gestalt, but existential-Gestalt, in this instance through or by virtue of its continual orientation to the existential position with respect to the body subject or lived-body.

Gestalt Therapy as Existential Therapy

Gestalt therapy has in recent years become quite popularized, and most of its advocates know that its founder finally (Perls, 1969a) designated it as an existential therapy, and, peculiarly, (I think) declared it to be, with the possible exception of Frankl's Logotherapy, the only truly existential therapy, being the only one that "stands on its own two feet." Perls (1969a) described these "two feet" (or legs) as primary biological phenomena (holistic organismic theory) and the principles of Gestalt psychology described earlier. He seems to have "forgotten" the sub-title of his own first book and all the ramifications described in the first part of this essay.

Be that as it may, and aside from *any* basis for examining the validity or invalidity of Perls' statement, he did not make this case for the exclusivity of Gestalt therapy as an existential therapy in his writings. While indeed it is easy to show that Gestalt therapy does rely *primarily* on the two legs or feet Perls mentions, he never showed in his writings any thorough examination of how it relies *secondarily* on several basic existential tenets, or at least operationalizes them thoroughly, whether or not it may be said to "rely" on them. Perls' dismissal of other existential therapies (1969a) as relying foundationally on Judaism, Protestantism, Socialism, etc., will not be discussed here. However, his dismissal of them as relying foundationally on psychoanalysis is absurd, since all therapies are so reliant. And his dismissal of them as relying foundationally on language is both very peculiar and intriguing. It is peculiar because it goes in the face of his own substantial contributions to language "games" (e.g., Levitsky and Perls, 1970). And it is intriguing because it suggests that Perls did not have full theoretical grasp of the contributions of European existential psychiatrists and psychologists to the phenomenology of language and body subject (or "lived-body"), a relationship I shall attempt shortly to explicate as making Gestalt therapy even more existential than Perls understood it to be.

As the second major thrust of this essay (the question of language temporarily aside), I shall attempt to show what Perls left implicit, that Gestalt therapy is the most existential form of therapy as yet developed, not by virtue of "standing on primary biological and Gestalt psychological feet," but by virtue of having yet another "leg to stand on"—being the most complete body of combined theory-technique which implements the major tenets of existentialism as they have application in the psychiatric situation. To do this somewhat systematically, I shall follow a three-step procedure. The first step is an explanation of the germane existential tenets and their implications for psychiatric endeavors. The second step is a summation of how each of these tenets is operationalized by the Gestalt therapy system. And, finally, an illustrative description of an ongoing therapy transaction will bring these points into concrete focus. The basic existential tenets to be so discussed are: a phenomenological ontology of awareness; choosing *Dasein* (being there); and lived-body, language, and awareness.

A Phenomenological Ontology of Awareness. Existentialism was born as a rebellious offspring of the main body of nineteenth century philosophy, which took a course through realistic dualism, logical analysis, linguistic analysis, and conceptual analysis, culminating around the turn of the century in logical positivism (Weitz, 1966). These logical positivists declared that ontology was meaningless and dead. This dictum, however, was taken less than seriously by Edmund Husserl, who developed phenomenology as the study of the primordial world of immediate experience. Phenomenology, then, is the method so born. But as soon as he had developed the system of the epoché, or bracketing, Husserl used it peculiarly to bracket experiencing man in order to study the world of concrete objects. Thus he developed a *transcendental* phenomenology. Among his pupils, however, were those who, not being drawn into this fallacy, retained experiencing man in a radically empirical and existential ontology which is founded in, and remains rooted in, a phenomenology of awareness (Wild, 1955).

But existentialism was born methodologically not only as a rebellious offspring of logical positivism, but also, in content, as a rebellious offspring of Hegelian idealism. In attacking the essentialism of Hegel, Kierkegaard, the "father of existentialism," employed and simultaneously established a descriptive phenomenology not just of awareness, but also of ethics. He described boredom, apathy, melancholy, and despair as aspects of a certain kind of dread. While thus phenomenologically asserting the primacy of existence over essence, at the same time he described the unique character and peculiar significance of dread in a new sense, as the possibility of freedom. And, as if this were not already a mammoth accomplishment, he also developed descriptive ethics, defining "good" and "evil" as existential categories, and ultimately describing "good" as authentic existence manifested in choosing (Wild, 1955).

Choosing Dasein (being-there). Out of the above-described Husserlian-Kierkegaardian method-content, as modified and supplemented by the efforts of Binswanger, Frankl, Heidegger, Jaspers, Marcel, Merleau-Ponty, Minkowski, Sartre, Straus, and others, have evolved numerous existential-psychiatric concepts with many implications for an existential form of therapy. Some of the more important of such concepts are: existential guilt; existential depression; existential anxiety; existential vacuum; and existential dread.

These concepts find expression in existential-psychiatric writings in language which is often enigmatic, such as: existential resignation; existential surrender to finitude; choosing authenticity; and the very important (generically) and little understood Heideggerian concept, "choosing *Dasein*." Describable in plain English under the general rubric, "inevitable pain of choice, action, and responsibility," they imply that only *some* anxiety, guilt, depression, boredom, alienation, frustration, and rage is clinically based, that is, can be ascribed to conditions about which persons can do anything, and is to be remedied by any psychotherapy. They also imply that part of what is ordinarily called "adjustment" means surrendering to one's existence as, in part, suffering, but that, paradoxically, a too total surrender to one's existence as given, denying choice, is existentially pathological. But much more importantly to therapists—who after all, are interested in helping persons in respect to projects that in principle can be realized—they imply, paradoxically, that only by fully being there (choosing *Dasein*) can one become more than one now is. In existential language as expressed more simply by Perls (1969a, 1970), this latter implication is that in chosen assumption of action and responsibility lies increased response-ability. As a conglomerate, these existential tenets and concepts implicitly constitute a paradoxical-maturational theory of change.

Lived-Body, Language, and Awareness. Existentialism was born not only as a corrective to logical positivism as a method and to Hegelian idealism as a content, but also as a corrective to the mind-body chasm wrought by Descartes, "cogito ergo sum," which defined the body as but an object-vehicle for the soul or spirit. This dualism has had an almost indelible impact on psychiatric endeavors and psychological theorizing.

Freud made a start toward functionalizing the reified self or mind, but fell short, reifying it again as "Ego." His effort toward explicating the experienced body fell even shorter, for here he reified impulses as "Id" or "Libido." Earlier in this essay I have shown how Perls made great strides toward functionalizing ego into organismically presenting self, what might have been called "body-self." And I have made a passing reference to Perls' attempt to relate language to this kind of self. His entrée was through Korzibski and other semanticists (Perls et al., 1951), but he apparently never grasped the significance of the pioneering efforts of Binswanger (1946, 1962) in transforming Heidegger's *Daseinsanalytik* into his own *Daseins-Analyses,* a translation downward from the ontological to the ontic, from language as Being to language as expression of man's particular form of being in the world. Perls' failure to grasp this may have been due to Binswanger's retention of psychoanalysis as a primary method or to his lifelong friendship with Freud, toward whom Perls' feelings were well known (e.g., "debunking the Freudian crap," 1969a). At any rate, Perls was apparently unfamiliar with Heidegger's later work, his heuristic "hermeneutic phenomenology of language" (Edie, 1962), and of the work done with these notions as extended and concretized by French phenomenological psychopathologists such as Merleau-Ponty and Ricoeur. And, perhaps as a result, while Perls certainly established even more clearly than had Reich the importance of language as resistance, defense, or avoidance (1947: Perls et al., 1951), and developed therapy methods involving language "games" designed to overcome these avoidances (Perls, 1969a, 1969b, 1970, Levitsky and Perls, 1970), he apparently never ·comprehended the experiential relationship between language and growth in the sense of disclosure of being as becoming. This "line" of existential thought, the relationship between language and the lived-body, comes from two of Husserl's philosophical protégés, Martin Heidegger and Gabriel Marcel, and finds unity via combination and concretization in the word of the philosophical psychologist, Maurice Merleau-Ponty (1962, 1964; Kwant, 1968).

Marcel developed the concept of the lived-body *(le corp vécu),* the experienced body, or man as body, which says that man not only has but also is his body (Wild, 1955). Merleau-Ponty (e.g., 1962) extended this thought into the field of perceptual-cognitive psychology and philosophy. Consciousness, superimposed on a world that is radically primary, is not primary, but rather is secondary to the instructing spontaneity of the body. Similarly, the spoken word is schematic, giving form to one's signifying intention when he is about to speak. Words and speech have ceased to be merely *designata* for things or thought, and have become the presence of both thing and thought in the phenomenal world, as projected body.

In his last, unfinished book, *The Visible and The Invisible* (see Kwant,

1968), Merleau-Ponty describes the body as the self-awareness of Being. Though this, at this level, has a metaphysical background, Merleau-Ponty's phenomenological analysis itself is of concrete reflexivity in the body. It involves repeated phenomenological demonstrations that man as body is a perceiving percept who conditions his own perceptibility via his interactions with his environment, and that what has been called soul, spirit, mind, or ego can be described as the "back side" of the body, as yet not fully explicated but explicable through increased levels of awareness of the body, these levels of awareness can be achieved via Merleau-Ponty's particular form of the phenomenological reduction, which he called "radical reflexion" (Kwant, 1968). In short, Merleau-Ponty held that there is a pre-reflective, pre-objective unity of all the forms of corporal awareness, and that this unity supports and makes possible "superior, thinking consciousness."

This is another way of saying that man as body can raise the level of his awareness of body to an extent necessary to raise perceptible reality to a new level, that of abstract meanings and ideal significations. It says that in a continuing ontogenesis man as lived-body raises the level of his awareness. In practical psychiatric terms, this means that man, as, in, and through speech, written language, and behavior, projects his lived-body into the world, both empathically and psychopathologically. This implies that a phenomenology of language combined with a phenomenology of the experienced body demonstrates the absolute inseparable unity of thought, speech, experience of the body (whether or not in awareness), and behavior. Psychologically, it implies that a thoroughgoing combination of language and the experienced body, if phenomenologically integrated into a psychotherapy system, yields powerful results in terms of unifying the experientially split patient.

Implications of Tenets for Therapy System. These tenets have several pervasive implications for any therapy system purporting to operationalize them.

First, such a therapy system must be radically phenomenological, and this phenomenological effort must be in an attempt to develop an ontology of awareness, that is, awareness of way of being and of the volitional aspects of that way of being, and of change. As has been said and is repeated here only for continuity of thought, Gestalt therapy is radically phenomenological, and its primary aim is increased awareness of self. It is a pointing to that which is manifest concretely by and in the human organism as verbal-vocal-body-affect-content continuum. The method is a pointing to the resistances and avoidances employed.

Secondly, such a therapy system will less directly, if at all, focus on changing the patient in the sense of helping him to change from how he is to some other way of being. Rather it will focus on making him more aware of how he is. Such a psychotherapeutic system, then, must operationalize the tenet that awareness itself is a potential change agent, and that once full awareness is developed, choice is left to the patient. It will limit itself to a phenomenology of making available to the patient awareness of how he is, with the assumption that, paradoxically, this changes him, *and* that if with this awareness he does not change, then he chooses pathology as part of his life-style.

Just such a paradoxical-maturational theory of change is a core concept of Gestalt therapy theory (Beisser, 1970). Gestalt therapists frustrate the patient into staying with his experience on an awareness continuum arising out of the here and now. That is, they assist the patient, paradoxically, to be more fully where (how) he is, in order to develop organismic, bodily-experienced awareness. If I may take some liberty with the usual existential meaning of the term, I would say that the constant goal of the Gestalt therapist is to assist the patient to experience organismic being-there, that is, "organismic *Dasein*."

Thirdly, in an *ontology* of awareness, the patient must own, claim, take responsibility. This is persistent in the Gestalt therapy system (Perls, 1969a). The "it," the "this," the "that," the "relationship," the "impulse," the "problem," the "unconscious impulse," all are owned, via language, and via structured experiential dialogues. Projections are owned by being them, acting them out, as are toxic introjections, dream symbols, etc.

And finally, such a system of therapy must continually assist the patient as body subject or lived-body to *be his body*, rather than having it. The Gestalt therapy system is thoroughgoing in this respect. Perls' (1969a, 1970) work with patients as their hands, in right-left, should-want struggles, for example, is now famous in Gestalt circles. In examining scomatizations, retroflections, projections, introjections, and desensitizations, the Gestalt therapist not only is ever mindful of the patient's body, he is especially attuned to the person as lived-body.

Illustrative Example. The operationalization of the existential tenets discussed above can readily be seen in the following *verbatim* transcript of an in-therapy transaction. The patient, who will be called Tom, is a 21-year-old senior college student majoring in psychology. Some three weeks before this interchange, he had entered a psychiatric hospital in a paranoid state. At this moment he has claimed the "hotseat" (one of two facing chairs in the center of the group therapy room).

Th: Tom, what are you experiencing now?
Pt: Anger.
Th: Where do you feel this anger?
Pt: (Indicating chest) Here, and (indicating hands) here.
Th: Just stay with the feeling, and let it increase. And you may get more in touch with it if you breathe deeply, in your abdomen, and let a sound come out when you exhale.
Pt: What sound?
Th: Whatever sound you feel.
Pt: (Breathes abdominally, and, on exhalation, makes sighing breath sound).
Th: Just continue, and let that sound become more of a vocal sound and less of a breath sound.
Pt: (Breathing abdominally) ooooh! ooooh! ooooh!
Th: What is that experience?
Pt: Anger, resentment.
Th: Will you address that resentment to somebody?
Pt: Mother, I resent you . . . everything about you.
Th: Specify your resentment.
Pt: I . . . I resent you for making me dependent on you.
Th: Tom, how is your voice?
Pt: It's . . . it's a whine.
Th: Will you own your voice? Take responsibility?
Pt: I . . . I'm whining . . . I'm whining.
Th: Do that. Whine to your mother, and experience yourself doing that.
Pt: (Whining voice; reaching out with hands) Mother . . . Please . . . please let me go . . . please turn me loose.
Th: Tom, how are your hands?
Pt: What do you mean?
Th: As you whine to your mother again, try to develop an awareness of what you experience as your hands.
Pt: (Hands are retroflected claws; implores) Mother, please let me go . . . please . . . please!
Th: Be your hands. Give your hands a voice and speak to her.
Pt: (Leaves left hand palm up; turns right hand over in claw-like deportment; looks at hands) Mother . . . I'm . . . I need you and I resent you (begins, on own, clawing movements with right hand).
Th: Speak as your experience of your hands, and frame a statement of your existence.
Pt: (Continues with left hand palm up, right hand in clawing motions) Mother . . . I . . . I need and want support and control from you, but I resent you, and I'm clawing you.
Th: Tom, I don't hear you in your words. Will you change "but" to "and"?
Pt: (With some more affect) Mother, I need you *and* I *resent* you,

and I'm clawing you (feet squirm nervously on floor; tears come to eyes).

Th: And will you continue to be where you are with your mother, adding after each statement, "and this is my existence now"?

Pt: (Angrily, to therapist) But I don't *want* to be *there*. You damned well should *know that*. (Face red with anger) Why don't you help me!?

Th: Tom, you "don't want" to be there, and you *are* there. Will you continue to experience your existence now?

Pt: (Left hand in seeking attitude; right hand clawing) Mother . . . (a sob) . . . Mother . . . I need you (bursts into tears and sobs) . . . and I (screams) *resent* you!!

Th: Will you begin to specify your resentment?

Pt: (With appropriate affect, begins enumerating resentments, appreciations, and regrets—the Gestalt "goodbye" paradigm).

To sum up, as this young male patient attempts to express resentments to his mother, he is in fact whining and begging. The therapist sees this as, at first, retroflected anger, and assists the patient to develop an awareness of the whine in his voice, then to own the whine. As the patient does so, the therapist notices that both hands are retroflected claws. Without interpreting, he assists the patient in becoming aware of his organismic self, his lived-body. In doing so, the patient develops an awareness of his conflict between dependence on and anger toward his mother, but he affectively attenuates his experience of the conflict by an avoidant use of language. The therapist asks him to frame a statement of his existence which is descriptive, direct, unattenuated, and to be there organismically by speaking as his experienced hands. In the face of this request, the patient removes himself further from the experience of the dialogue by angrily protesting that the therapist is not helping him. The therapist, interpreting the protest as avoidance, encourages the patient, paradoxically, to be where he is rather than focus on change. As the patient then speaks the statement of his existence now, and as he simultaneously experiences his conflict and ambivalence at a bodily level (by begging with one hand and clawing with the other), he bursts into tears and great bodily shudders, and begins to "get into" the dialogue experientially.

This is not only Gestalt therapy. This case may be described in strictly Gestalt terms finishing the unfinished situation with mother by expressing the previously retroflected resentment. Or it may also be described in existential-Gestalt terms, as a radical phenomenological ontology of awareness assisting the patient to be there fully in an organismic sense, dependent and angry, and to experience his existence (choose *Dasein*) as body subject or lived-body, owning how he is, left with the choice of changing or remaining there. This latter formulation is seemingly a more complete description, whether or not Perls would so describe this therapy interaction.

PERLS-ISM

If what was depicted in an earlier part of this essay is the functional essence of Gestalt therapy, and if what was described at length in the middle part is existential-Gestalt therapy, what, then, is "Perls-ism"? In preliminary summary form, it is all that Perls as a person, personality, and informal philosopher brought to the system he founded and popularized. But that, as Perls might say, needs specification. It involves a particular linguistic-interactive style (that, too, needs specification), and a personal-philosophical style (likewise too generally stated). To "bring off" being a "Perlsian," one needs certain personal and philosophical requisites, and needs to show them regularly not only as a person, but in therapy as therapist. Some of these I shall try to explicate, hopefully at the same time catching some of the flavor of Perls as supportive evidence. And, beyond this linguistic-interactive-philosophical style, there *are* some areas of content which theoretically are not logically necessary to the skeletal essence of Gestalt therapy, and which are Perlsian. Some of these, too, I shall attempt to describe, demonstrate and discuss critically.

Perls is a peculiar kind of existentialist, what I would call a hedonistic, biologically grounded, philosophically naive one. I have already shown that in "repudiating" other forms of existential therapy, he was logically inconsistent, in one case logically vicious to himself, and intellectually unknowledgeable (so far as his writings show). He wanted, and held, Gestalt therapy to be a form of existentialism (operationalized) that did not rely on any other bodies of thought (philosophy, language, religion), but stood purely on a functional, organismic basis. Definitionally, of course, no philosophy (and, by inference, no therapy system operationalizing one) can so stand. But that is what Perls called "existential." It is true that perhaps the most basic (Sartrian) tenet of existentialism is that man is his own essence by determining it, that existence is prior to essence in that sense. Perls apparently used this line of thought to rebuke other therapy forms that relied foundationally on any body of knowledge other than the principles of biological hedonism. Perls' kind of existentialism, then, *if it is existentialism*, is biological-hedonistic existentialism.

This kind of existentialism, if taken seriously by a person interested in authentic, open, honest being-style, has severe implications for whatever that person's professional endeavor—in Perls' case, the development, description and demonstration of a therapy system. The first, and perhaps most obvious, place where this is evident is in Perls' formulation of maturity. Perls (1969a) defined maturity as transcending efforts to manipulate support from the environment, becoming radically self-supporting. There is, to me, a terrible, agonizing aloneness to that, which I think shows itself most clearly in what Perls finally formulates as "The Gestalt Prayer," but which, as I see it, should have been called, "The Hedonistic-Biological Existentialist's Lament":

> I do my thing and you do your thing.
> I am not in this world to live up to your expectations,
> And you are not in this world to live up to mine.
> You are you and I am I;
> If by chance we find each other, *it's* beautiful.
> If not, *it can't be helped. (Italics mine)*

Perhaps we can allow Perls these two "its," for if he had substituted "I," as he always exhorted others to do, the implications for him might have been beautifully horrendous. He might have realized what Tubbs (1972) points out in his revision of this statement, which he calls, "beyond Perls":

> If I just do my thing and you do yours,
> We stand in danger of losing each other
> And ourselves.
> I am not in this world to live up to your expectations;
> But I am in this world to confirm you
> As a unique human being,
> And to be confirmed by you.
> We are fully ourselves only in relation to each other;
> The I detached from a Thou
> Disintegrates.
> I do not find you by chance;
> I find you by an active life
> Of reaching out.
> Rather than passively letting things happen to me,
> I can intentionally make them happen.
> I must begin with myself, true;
> But I must not end with myself:
> The truth begins with two.

Now this is a beautiful Buberian I-Thou statement. But, for the moment, as devil's advocate for Perls, I must take exception to Tubbs' conclusion, *or* his *wording* of it. The "truth" of a hedonistic-biological existentialism is precisely what Perls says it is. However, the "truth" as the essence of caring love does begin with two. The "I-thou-ness" brought to Gestalt therapy by many therapists is not paradigmatically Perlsian. Thus, I can see an awful "truth," that the full implementation of maturity, by Perls' definition, is at least partly preclusive of a continuing, shared love, though it may permit, as he emphasizes and reemphasizes (1969a, 1969b, 1970), rhythmic, cyclic, transient, full here-and-nowness.

But I have become caught up in the beauty of these two pure-form ("hedonistic" and "altruistic") arguments. To continue with "Perls-ism," what are the implications, in instrumenting a therapy system, of this (Perls') kind of "existential now"? The therapist who is a "Perlsian" as well as a Gestaltist is almost utterly and consistently non-supportive. I hold that this, in extreme form, is not a necessary functional part of Gestalt therapy, and did not include it earlier in my "functional essence" presentation. But it *is* a part of "Perls-ism," and a part which has many and far-reaching implications. Perls is not merely a frustrator. He is a radical frustrator. He will not answer a question unless it is a how (for what purpose) question. He calls questions "hooks," alluding symbolically-literally to the fact that an inverted question mark resembles a fishhook, and to most questions being hooks on which the therapist should avoid being caught "helping" or "being helpful." This Perlsian position has perhaps been given its fullest expression by Resnick's (1970) description of the poisonous potential of "chicken soup."

Perls-ism is also a sort of anti-intellectualism. Perls does not merely minimize or deemphasize intellectual processes, but "outlaws" them from his kind of Gestalt therapy as "mind-fucking," his term for computing, intellectualizing, rationalizing, compartmentalizing, and a host of other intellect-based ego defensive operations (1969a, 1970). But careful examination of Perls' statement shows that he not only applies the term "mind-fucking" to these defensive operations, but also to operations which are ordinarily describable as discussing, cognitively consolidating, etc.

There is, to Perls-ism, also a certain antisocial aspect. Perls despises phoniness, game-playing, etc. But he carries this spite out of the realm of his own interactions and into Gestalt therapy. He, like his theoretical system, is orally aggressive. Thus he pejoratively describes virtually all social-interpersonal amenities as "chickenshit," ordinary interpersonal-intellectual pursuits as "bullshit," and high-powered intellectual-theoretical pursuits (such as his own talks on therapy or this essay) as "elephantshit" (1969a, b).

Within the context of this framework or view, he "actualizes" himself so thoroughly that, after the first book *(Ego, Hunger and Aggression,* 1947), he manages only to share in the editorship of one more theoretical one *(Gestalt Therapy,* 1951), then relies on John Stevens to put together various talks, recorded seminars, etc. to form *Gestalt Therapy Verbatim* (1969a), and on Fagan and Shepherd (and other Gestalt-oriented therapists) to put together *Gestalt Therapy Now* (1970). In these later books Perls does no writing as such; his later thought is presented in informal talks or seminars.

The only other book he and he alone writes is his fascinating autobiography, *In and Out The Garbage Pail* (1969b). Even here, in what he obviously "knows" will be his last effort, he narcissistically "elephantshits," only bringing himself intermittently and tangentially to theoretical "elephantshit" for the benefit of those of us who wish to learn from him. He will not really set down in clear, expository form his evolution in theoretical thought and system development. And (damn him!) though he may not have been nice, he was in some respects radically correct. If I dig it out for myself, by such efforts as this essay, I have got to grow from the experience, become more self-confident and self-supportive, less inclined to try to wheedle support out of *him* as to how I "should be" as a therapist. Thus, Perls apparently wanted anyone who wants to to try become a Gestalt therapist, but did not advocate anyone else being, or trying to be, a "Perlsian." I am also told by some who knew him personally that this was Perls' explicit wish, that he sought to avoid there being established a Perlsian cult or school of psychotherapy, that he realized that what he as person brought to the system, if imitated, would detract from innovativeness.

I am finding it hard not to digress. But to return, once again, to "Perlsism" in (and apart from and beyond) Gestalt therapy, another implication of the biological-hedonistic existentialism I have alluded to is a willingness to "therapize" a patient away from as well as toward societal norms or societal adjustment. Of course other existential therapists espouse this principle, but find it hard to live up to, being inclined (at least implicitly) to sway the patient away from societal norms (à la Ronald Laing's notions) or subtly toward them (in much existential therapy). Thus, another component of "Perls-ism" is not just not being helpful to an extent sufficient to avoid being caught up in the patient's manipulative efforts to get you to "take care of," "cure," or "take responsibility for" him (a principle all good therapists who are not father-figures in a psychoanalytic sense attempt to follow). It is radically, almost absolutely, not being "helpful." To the extent that a Gestalt therapist is a "Perlsian," his *only* function is to make the patient aware of how he is. Any change is strictly up to the patient.

A tremendous practical implication of this position, if truly held, can be seen in the fact that Perls discontinued conjoint marital therapy altogether (1969a, 1970), saying that virtually nobody wishes to be married to a real person rather than to an ideal-image they can shape, control, etc. And a radical "Perlsian" must find conjoint marital therapy a misnomer, and very trying to continue to try. For "Perls-ism" really has virtually no "shoulds"; it is not merely a system which says that. Being hedonistic-biological existentialism, it is almost totally nihilistic. It is certainly not altruistic.

The "Perlsian" is not only honest, open, and authentic in relationship to patients, as all existential therapists strive to be. He is this way to such an extent that he is virtually never protective of a patient, and may be extremely confrontative. Perls in his workshops, dream seminars, etc., was famous for catching "bear trappers" (those persons wishing not to work but to show him up as a therapist), and for dumping them out of the "hotseat" in no uncertain terms. Now this is certainly not a necessary part of Gestalt therapy, and if applied systematically in dealing with persons whose pathology runs much deeper than in those who attended Perls' workshops, has major consequences. A true "Perlsian" tells the person who calls him on the phone to threaten suicide, "I take *no* responsibility for you; if you do that, I will never see you alive again," . . . and hangs up the phone. Not long ago I worked for three years in a private psychiatric hospital setting using Gestalt, and, to some extent, "Perlsian" therapy. Had I been a radical "Perlsian," I would never have intervened with physicians in an effort to hold a patient in the hospital (against his will and occasionally, perhaps, in violation of his civil liberties), even when he obviously and desperately needed more psychotherapeutic effort. (Parenthetically, I might say that I was enough of a "Perlsian" to find that kind of a setting progressively more intolerable, though a fascinating opportunity to be confronted over and over again with the limits of caring for others versus being not only personally but theoretically authentic).

Again I personalize, though hopefully in a way relevant to this attempted analysis. There are other basic aspects to "Perls-ism" which are by no means a necessary part of Gestalt therapy. One of the most important of these is the one with which I began this essay eons ago, and which apparently overwhelmed Alan Stone (1972) in his review of Fagan and Shepherd's (1970) book. I am referring to "play" or "playfulness."

Paradoxically, as every *serious* student of psychological theory knows, play is creative of growth, development, and creativity itself. And adult play, which we euphemistically call "recreation," if right for the particular adult, is just that, re-creation. And while all work and no play makes Johnny a dull boy, all play and no work makes him a pretty poor existentialist—unless he happens to be a hedonistic-biological existentialist, in which case, virtually all work in which he engages *is* play.

Now that is a strange situation, one which pushes and pulls, strains, and tests language and logic as we have thus far conceptualized language and logic. Thus, some people (apparently Stone among them) get pretty frustrated in that situation. Those, like myself, whose "shoulds" still far outweigh their "wants," whose "top-dog" is essentially in control of their "under-dog," have much trouble "play-working" or "work-playing," being inclined to try to do one at the time. But not Perls, and not real "Perlsians." While there are degrees of work inherent in a role-playing model of therapy, there is never the absence of play in a "role-working" model of therapy. Perls had patients "play" their mothers, concrete blocks, whatever. And his wording was not an accidental choice, for a playful experimentation pervaded his style as therapist. And, much more seriously with and for the patient, I saw *"be* your mother; *be* a concrete block," etc. I am an existential-Gestalt therapist who, in this respect, is a poor "Perlsian," for I have patients *work* out an existential statement of their existence (e.g., "For and against you, mother, I will not be anything, and I am no thing, and I resent you treating me as your thing, and this is my existence"). Now there are compensations for being such a workday type existential-Gestalt therapist rather than a "playful Perlsian." For I am a "better" (harder working, harder writing) existentialist, and a thousand-fold more altruistic one, than was Perls. I get to help more people in a way that *they recognize as* helpful. This means, though, that as experiential-existentialist, I am still somewhat phoney, inauthentic, unactualized. The Devil Perls must have his due!

Another significant part of "Perls-ism" is his structural personality theory. Though I can see no way in which this personality theory helps one to be a Gestalt therapist, or is in any sense necessary to being a Gestalt therapist, it became a hallmark of Perls, particularly connoting his way of talking about persons. Being a functionalist genius, Perls was a "delayed" structuralist, and probably gained little if anything for his theory or system of therapy by his simplistic structural theory of personality. Of course, persons play "as if" in the "Eric Berne" or "Sigmund Freud," outer, phoney "layers" of themselves; and if and when they get "beneath" this "layer," get to the "phobic-neurotic" "layer" and hit their "sick point" or "impasse"; and if they get "beneath" that, implode and feel dead, empty, stuck; and if they get "beneath" or "through" that, "explode" into orgasm, joy, grief, rage, *or whatever*. (Parenthetically, I can't or won't understand Perls' never-explained, apparently arbitrary selection of these four explosions. My best effort to understand what must otherwise seem like arbitrary dimensional limitations is that these were probably Perls' own kind of explosions. They are, of course, explosions with strong physiological concomitants. Why not, for example, creativity?)

So people work through these "layers." So what? Does all this add anything to the functional process they undergo? Well, it's a way of talking to and explaining to people who really need something structural as part of their conceptual system. It's "Perls-ism," but not really. That Perls did this so late, cursorily, tangentially, and incompletely attests to how little it is really "Perlsian." It is Perls as teacher, not as creative therapist.

Then there is Perls' dream theory and "the Gestalt" (his?) technique for working on dreams. Now here again I believe that in my phenomenological analysis I have bracketed-out, then let back in, then bracketed-out Perls. I might say that in this instance, perhaps, Perls has overowned the it, or owned too much of it, by calling it "I." Perls says that all symbols in a dream are part-self, as part of an existential message from the dreamer to the dreamer (1969a, 1970). Now I cannot say about *his* dreams. Remembering that he was hedonistically and biologically existential, perhaps he was given to a strictly intra-organismic message system. But I have Gestalted my own dreams. And they contain not just part-self messages. They also contain, or I also am, self-other messages and mandates, frights and flights, approaches and trysts, even rendezvous. My messages are not only from me to me about me, but also are from me to me about me and being with others, and even about *their*, the others', messages to me about me and me, and about me and being with them. This does not invalidate the "Perlsian" technique of being (acting-out) all the symbols as if they were exclusively part-me. From that, I gain experiential insight, organismic knowledge whether or not I deny the strictly part-self Persian interpretation.

The "Perlsian" method is the most powerful method of my acquaintance for bodily, experientially working dreams through and out, of "getting the message." The *next* most powerful method I know for doing so is the Gestalt way of dealing with dreams (not necessarily based on the

Perlsian theory) which is having the patient be all the symbols of a dream, even how he experiences them in relationship one to the other *while being the dream.* Perls' theoretical thinking here, that every dream symbol is part-self, must take second seat to that of Jung, Binswanger, Boss, and others who first conceptualized (re-conceptualized, after Freud's mess) dream as existential, teleological messages depicting the ongoing growth or individuation process that is present in self.

Despite this theoretical oversimplification, the Gestalt method of being dreams is the most powerful experience-inducing *technique.* And despite this theoretical oversimplification, Perls (1969a, 1970) adds another dimension to dream work which does relate importantly to his functional theory of personality development. I refer to his "filling in the holes," or "being and finishing the avoidance of awareness." This is a "Perlsian" aspect of Gestalt therapy which goes above and beyond what can properly be defined as a Gestalt way of working with dreams. That is, rather than asking the patient to be all parts of the dream (which can be very tiresome) with verbal, imaginative persons, a Gestalt therapist who is also a "Perlsian" can work with parts of dreams or "holes in them" in an especially productive way.

By analogy to "filling in the holes" of a dream, it is natural to proceed to another Perlsian convention which is not logically necessary to a Gestalt therapy system but is brilliantly Perlsian *and* based on Gestalt principles —"filling in the hole" in a person as personality. Perls' "diagnostic acumen" in this sense became famous. In a few minutes with a person in the hot seat he could say, "You've got no feet, no genitals, no taste buds, etc., astutely describing the missing part (function) of the person which, if present, would make him functionally more whole, more of a completed or formed Gestalt.

My phenomenological-existential "criticism" of "Perls-ism" has but one more, though I believe very important, major point of issue. Being a hedonistic-biological existentialist, Perls never understood (or never "bought"?) certain existential concepts which less hedonistic and less biologically-based existentialists consider crucial and a necessary part of any therapy system which calls itself both existential and Gestalt. Illustrative of these concepts are existential dread, existential anxiety, existential depression, void or vacuum, and existential guilt (all opposed to their clinical-pathological counterparts or brethren). Not understanding or not subscribing to these notions, Perls regards all feelings of helplessness, aloneness, and alienation as reducing essentially to an infantilism, the "cure" for which is further frustration to assist the organism to stand on its own two feet.

Again (damn him again!), he is partially correct . . . *to the extent that there is a "cure"* for any such condition. But here he is a naive existentialist. He has made a subject-object dichotomy unacceptable to any more sophisticated kind of existentialism, and has, to an extent, missed the concrete phenomenon with which he as phenomenologist has to deal. He has placed a part of personhood under a biological-maturational rubric which will not quite hold it. Again, though, his system, and the Gestalt system, even if not "Perlsian," is tailor-made for sorting out those feelings which *are* infantile efforts not to assume responsibility for self-in-situation from those aspects of self-in-situation about which nobody can do anything and which lead to despair, anguish, or Kierkegaard's "suffering unto death." To say that these notions are "elephantshit" can itself only be one way of avoiding fully experiencing them in-situation. Perls' failure to grasp or buy the concept of existential guilt (hence existential depression vs. clinical depression) is less serious, for by means of his system, or the Gestalt system which is not "Perlsian," one can quickly discover how much of such guilt and depression is really unexpressed "existential-resentment" arising out of the other existential conditions described just above.

This whole area of discussion—the extent to which Perls-ism is "beyond" Gestalt therapy as such—begs for further explication. But for now, though I still have a feeling of incompleteness with this Gestalt, I am organismically aware of being "finished." So I commend this partial Gestalt to you, however incomplete. I suspect that the whole Gestalt of Perls and of Gestalt therapy, which is only to an extent "Perlsian," which only to an extent contains "Perls-ism," is just beginning to be formed. I further suspect that when it is more nearly formed, Gestalt therapy, all forms of experiential therapy, and many forms of existential therapy will be much further along than they now are, but, and still . . . becoming.

REFERENCES

BEISSER, A.: The paradoxical theory of change. In J. Fagan and I. L. Shepherd (Eds.), *Gestalt Therapy Now*. New York: Science and Behavior Books, 1970. Pp. 77-80.

BINSWANGER, L.: *Grundformen und Erkenntnis Daseins*. Zurich: Max Niehaus, 1942.

BINSWANGER, L.: Existential analysis and psychotherapy. In H. M. Ruitenbeek (Ed.), *Psychoanalysis and Existential Philosophy*. New York: Dutton, 1962. Pp. 17-23.

BINSWANGER, L.: Ueber die daseinsanalytische Forschungerichtung in der Psychiatrie. *Schweizer Archiv für Neurologie und Psychiatrie*. 57:209-225, 1946.

Boss, M.: *Psychoanalysis and Daseinsanalysis*. Trans. by L. B. Lefebre. New York: Basic Books, 1963. Pp. 2-285.

EDIE, J. M. (Ed.): *What Is Phenomenology? and Other Essays by Pierre Thevenaz.* Chicago: Quadrangle, 1962. Pp. 37-92.

ENRIGHT, J. B.: An introduction to Gestalt techniques. In J. Fagan and I. L. Shepherd (Eds.), *Gestalt Therapy Now.* New York: Science and Behavior Books, 1970. Pp. 107-124.

FAGAN, J., and SHEPHERD, I. L. (Eds.): *Gestalt Therapy Now.* New York: Science and Behavior Books, 1970.

KWANT, R.: The human body as the self-awareness of Being (An inquiry into the last phase of Merleau-Ponty's philosophical life. *Rev. Existential Psychol.,* 8: 117-134, 1968.

LEVITSKY, A., and PERLS, F. S.: The rules and games of Gestalt therapy. In J. Fagan and I. L. Shepherd (Eds.), *Gestalt Therapy Now.* New York: Science and Behavior Books, 1970. Pp. 140-149.

MAY, R., ANGEL, E., and ELLENBERGER, H. F. (Eds.): *Existence: A New Dimension in Psychiatry and Psychology.* New York: Basic Books, 1958.

MAY, R.: *Existential Psychology.* New York: Random House, 1961.

MAY, R.: The existential approach. In S. Arieti (Ed.), *American Handbook of Psychiatry.* New York: Basic Books, 1959. Pp. 1348-1359.

MERLEAU-PONTY, M.: *The Phenomenology of Perception.* London: Routledge & Kegan Paul, 1962.

MERLEAU-PONTY, M.: *The Primacy of Perception.* Evanston, Ill.: Northwestern U. Press, 1964.

MINKOWSKI, E.: Approches phénoménologiques de l'existence. *L'Evolution Psychiatrique,* 4:433-458, 1962.

PERLS, F. S.: *Ego, Hunger and Aggression: A Revision of Freud's Theory and Method.* London: Allen & Unwin, 1947.

PERLS, F. S.: Four lectures. In J. Fagan and I. L. Shepherd (Eds.), *Gestalt Therapy Now.* New York: Science and Behavior Books, 1970. Pp. 14-38.

PERLS, F. S.: *Gestalt Therapy Verbatim.* Ed. by J. Stevens. Lafayette, Cal.: Real People Press, 1969. (a)

PERLS, F. S.: *In and Out the Garbage Pail.* Lafayette, Cal.: Real People Press, 1969. (b)

PERLS, F. S., HEFFERLINE, R., and GOODMAN, P.: *Gestalt Therapy: Excitement and Growth in the Human Personality.* New York: Julian Press, 1951.

RESNICK, R. W.: Chicken soup is poison. *Voices: The Art and Science of Psychotherapy,* 6:75-78, 1970.

STONE, A.: Play: The "now" therapy. *Psychother. and Soc. Sci. Rev.,* 6:24-28, 1972.

TUBBS, W.: Beyond Perls. *J. Humanistic Psychol.,* 12:5, 1972.

WEITZ, M. (Ed.): *Twentieth-Century Philosophy: The Analytic Tradition.* New York: The Free Press, 1966.

WILD, J.: *The Challenge of Existentialism.* Bloomington, Ind.: Indiana U. Press, 1955.

11

The Gestalt Thematic Approach

BRUCE DERMAN, Ph.D.

Gestalt therapy is an educational and therapeutic approach developed by Fritz Perls, and, as with any approach, it has its own characteristics of both theory and style. This distinction is of vital importance since theory and style are separate entities. While most Gestalt therapists value similar principles and concepts, the method or style in which the theory is applied can vary markedly. The predominant style among Gestalt therapists reflects Perls' orientation of working with one member at a time in a group setting. Using this style, the therapist emerges as the distinctly dominant force.

This paper proposes an alternative style of Gestalt therapy that is relevant to me and possibly is more suited to other group leaders than the Perlsian style. I have labeled this method, in which the group is of primary importance, the Gestalt-thematic approach. The description and goals of this model, along with the methods employed and their implications, are presented in this paper.

Although the group can be a potentially powerful force, it is my contention that this potential has not been fully realized in actual practice. In many of the current therapy approaches, the group's interactions range from superfluous to overbearing.

I will briefly explain the types of interaction in five therapy approaches. 1) *Perls' Gestalt therapy:* Although the group interaction is often non-existent, when the members do participate it generally consists of put-downs, random, disconnected comments (I'm bored, frustrated, resentful), laughter, or after-the-fact feedback. Little focus is directed on the group process or the themes emerging within the group. 2) *Encounter groups:* The group is active and participation is emphasized. However, the members are often preoccupied with moving a person from where he is to where they think he ought to be. 3) *Synanon:* The group is primarily used as an attacking force, which seems to be extremely one-sided. 4) *Analytic groups:* The impact of the group appears muted by the proliferation of questions, story telling, and verbiage. 5) *Structured groups:* These groups stress group involvement but frequently disregard the specific individual. There is often a lack of continuity and integration of the various structured experiences.

I propose an approach that concentrates on the group, and is also extremely sensitive to the individual. Within the group, then, there is more feeling of involvement, less sense of passive observation, and thus a greater feeling of importance. This is accomplished by paying close attention to the themes most apparent within the group and involving the group in those themes. A theme can be any emotion or behavior that typifies one's existence at a given moment. The theme or atmosphere is constantly changing both within the individual and the group. One moment boredom and frustration might be in the foreground; thus, a feeling of frustration would be apparent in the room. Within a period of time a theme might shift to sex, distrust, helplessness, indecisiveness, power, or warmth. There is no limit to the number of themes or atmospheres within a group of people.

For a period in my own development, I focused my attention on how to create themes, taking most of the responsibility for the group's direction. I would decide on a theme (e.g., trust) and then gear all the group experiences toward facilitating a greater awareness of that theme. The group members were to become aware of their relationship within a particular theme. Although this format can be beneficial as it stimulates the group and draws out many feelings, it basically ignores the Gestalt principles of staying with "what is." Thus, while the group had become more active and responsible, the therapist still had control over the theme and its direction.

In contrast, the Gestalt-thematic approach seeks themes from within the group, rather than from the leader or an outside source. At all times, the atmosphere within a group consists of one or several themes. Whether the group and leader desire to face or avoid a particular theme is the question. Many groups work feverishly to avoid an existing atmosphere. For example, when the group discovers there is a feeling of coldness in the room, the leader and members may try various exercises to promote closeness and warmth. For a brief period the group may seem to have resolved the coldness. However, they have actually ignored it.

As in Perlsian gestalt therapy, the emphasis of the gestalt-thematic method is on "what is" in the here-and-now. Recognizing and becoming aware of what is foreground at a given moment is central to this approach. The individual then is responsible for deciding what he wants in relation to the theme. He can choose to move further into or away from it, to accept or reject it, or ignore it totally. Thus, the theme is not being forced on him, and he can stop the experience if he chooses to. The group and the therapist are accommodators rather than prodders or pushers.

Once a theme is brought into awareness, it is then the task of the group and the leader to expand the theme so that it is actually experienced in the room. Essentially, this idea is an expansion of the Gestalt theory of change: that change occurs by going with the behavior and not by opposing it. Thus, pain is not changed by tightening up, but rather by giving into the pain. A member in a group of mine expressed a fear of being vague and unstructured. In an effort to get her in touch with the experience of vagueness, the entire group expanded the theme and became vague. The group continually answered all questions with "I don't know" responses, began sentences without completing them, and left every situation or dialogue incomplete, indefinite and vague. The patient gradually was able to experience her fear and to accept her own vagueness. In summary, the Gestalt-thematic method allows the individual or group to fully experience a particular theme by creating the entire atmosphere of that emotion or behavior.

Themes can be further described by dividing them into two parts: thematic content and thematic process. Typically the content describes "what" the vehicle is and the process characterizes "how" that vehicle is used. Thus, sex might be the thematic content and how sex is used (e.g. as a smoke screen) would be the thematic process. While in most instances the content and the process are present, the process is paramount and central. If the group fails to tune into the process, and pays attention only to the content, the experience can become frustrating, remaining only on a superficial level.

The following illustrates in detail the distinction between content and process. In response to the question, "Where are you?", a man reported that he was somewhere off in a fantasy. After further questioning he revealed that he often finds ways to stay away from where he is in the here-and-now. Sometimes he tortures himself with the past, and on other occasions he loses himself in different fantasies, imagining himself a sports hero or a martyr. Thus, the content varies among heroic and martyr fantasy. The process, however, is distraction. All these contents are merely vehicles of distraction, some of which work more effectively than others. My goal as therapist was to allow him to feel the impact of his distraction by creating a thematic atmosphere. I asked several members to play his fantasy distractions: career torturer, sportsman, martyr, and hero. Anytime he became aware of himself or got in touch with his feelings, we would distract him from being aware. We followed his typical pattern of avoiding himself. In a short time he began genuinely to dislike his distractions. When his wife joined in with another distraction of warmth and affection, he became angry and stopped letting us distract him. At the moment he stopped allowing himself to be distracted, his face contorted and he experienced his fear of the present. This time he did not distract himself from his fear and chose to stay with it. In time he became more relaxed and gradually less afraid.

METHOD

Essential to a Gestalt-thematic approach and primary to the development of any theme is the method of accommodation. Pesso (1969) defines accommodation as the structured response of the group or individuals. Accommodation is accomplished by having the group member or members play a role or exaggerate a particular behavior in hopes of provoking an emotional response, thus creating an atmosphere for emotional movement. The emotional movement is assisted by the groups' assuming different gestures, sounds, and expressions. For example, by having someone express pain in response to an individual's physical aggression, the person experiences the effects of his aggression.

We create our own universe through our senses. Similarly, the group can create a variety of atmospheres by using its senses in accommodating different themes. Primarily, I have worked with sound, sight, and touch. As yet, I have not utilized taste and smell, but that by no means rules them out for the future. What follows is an elaboration of the uses of the three primary senses in accommodating a theme.

Sound can reach an individual's core, in many instances making an impact where words have failed. The key in using sound as a facilitative force is in finding the individual's rhythm. Rhythm reflects in sound how the person relates to the world. By becoming aware of an individual's sound pattern, intensity, and tone, a group can share with an individual its conceptions of his style of interaction. As an example, a sucking sound might typify the rhythm of the person who continually attempts to trap and "suck in" others. Telling the person he is sucking in others lacks the impact of the actual sucking sound. Another example is the person who continually complains in group. By having the group pick up the sound of his complaining, in possibly a whiney, baby sound, the individual may hear himself for the first time. The essential thing is to sense the person's behavior pattern and direct the sound to that. By having several members or the entire group make that sound, the entire room can become an individual's sound rhythm.

Visual images are another primary mode in creating an atmosphere. Through physical movement, facial expressions, and the use of different props, (such as pillows), a visual scene can come alive for everyone in the room. Perhaps distrust is the apparent theme in the group. To create an atmosphere of distrust, the participants can move through the group with extreme caution, apprehension, suspicion, and avoidance, imagining the group to be hostile, unpredictable, and threatening. Each member then can fully experience the distrust that previously was beneath the surface and avoided.

There are many possible ways in which touch can bring a theme to the foreground. Pulling, picking, pushing, hitting, stroking, rubbing, squeezing, and supporting are all elements of touch. To illustrate, a group member mentioned that he continually felt picked on by people. He related this in a whiney, complaining way, with little impact in his words. By having the group members physically pick on him with their fingers, a "poor me" situation turned into a powerful experience. In another example, a woman was talking in an emotionless manner about being pushed around. I asked two of the members to push her back and forth between them. At first they were too gentle for her to connect this experience with her feelings of being pushed and shoved. However, when they really started pushing her, she went into deep, convulsive sobs. She was then able to feel the true impact of her words and make the connection of this experience and the pushing in her life.

Any behavior that disrupts the impact of the theme is definitely contrary to the principal of accommodation. Actions not timed properly to the behavior of the person being accommodated can decrease the intensity of the individual's responses and cause frustration. Thus, if the theme is being silly, any incidental serious discussion will disrupt the tone in the room.

A clear illustration follows of the effect of good and poor accommodation. A young woman was seeking to get in touch with the non-sexual goal of childlike playfulness. She wanted someone to touch her and play with her like a child would. The two people who were accommodating her did not receive her message and attempted to relate to her as an adult woman. She felt frustrated and complained that their behavior was not relevant to her fantasy. Sensing her desire, I proceeded to roll on the floor, laughing and playing with her as a child. She repeatedly said, "That's my fantasy."

In summary, accommodation can be looked upon as an emotional facilitator and the accommodators as partners in the facilitation. The people are fully aware of the process. The more relevant is the accommodation to the person, the greater is the depth of the experience.

Types of Accommodation

There are three types of accommodation: 1) "isness" identification, 2) polarity identification, and 3) reaction related identification. The three types relate to the emphasis within the person or group. In the first type of accommodation, "isness" identification, the emphasis is to stay with, or join, the individual's experience. If he feels helpless, the focus would be his helplessness. "Isness" is being with the individual wherever he may be at the moment. In polarity identification the emphasis is on the extremes or poles in behavior—the disparity between where an individual is and what he avoids. For example, if an individual is presently very passive and submissive, attention would be given to this aspect of his behavior as well as to the opposite, more active, aggressive behavior. In the third type, reaction related identification, the emphasis is on the results of an individual's behavior or responses. Thus, in this mode the group accommodates an individual's behavior, whether it be anger, sadness, nagging, or playfulness. The accommodating behavior is directly related to the stimulus provided by the group member.

Gestalt-Thematic Approaches

There are three different ways that a theme approach can be used in a group setting, corresponding to the three types of accommodation described. The choice is left to the judgment of the leader. Using the first method, involving "isness" identification, the leader would determine if there is any theme that generally reflects the group at any given moment. Possibly by asking each member what he is aware of, it becomes obvious that most of the individuals are frightened. The leader might then decide to develop this theme by suggesting that the entire group exaggerate its fright. They can imagine the room and the people in it as very frightening, with each movement and expression reflecting that fright. If the theme mirrors what is going on, the members will easily join the theme at some level.

Another aspect of the first method is to have each member of the group join in and become an individual's theme. This approach is especially beneficial for the member who wants to work, but resists feeling the true impact of his experience. For instance, one group member had difficulty tolerating his own stupidity, awkwardness, and silliness. Thus, I had the entire group accommodate his stupidness so he could truly see himself. Upon experiencing and seeing the group as silly and stupid, he became much more tolerant of his own silliness and was able to accept his behavior. Although not overtly active, physically and verbally, the individual focused on is very much involved emotionally. He is receiving the group's total attention at all times and it is his behavior that is being mirrored.

In the second method, polarity identification, the person in question is more overtly active. He takes one side of his theme and the group takes the opposite position. Thus, in the stupidness theme the group could be stupid and the focal person could be the proper, should person who never makes mistakes. In this method a dialogue is possible. The person can then switch and take the stupidness side, with the group as the proper person.

The third method involves the reactive mode of accommodation. The goal here is to provide the person with experiences in which his emotional expression produces an effective response. While hitting a pillow is an important therapeutic technique, a pillow doesn't react. This void can affect the experience. By having another group member react to the angry, striking person as if he is being hit, the individual feels more effective and the experience more closely resembles reality. Other reactions might include falling down, groaning in pain, or expressions of agony. On other occasions, group members might accommodate expressions of love, power, criticism, and sexual feelings. The more relevant the reactive movement and expression, the greater the impact this method will have. To illustrate, suppose an individual is working on his ability to stand up for himself. The group can key itself on the strength of the individual's verbal signals and push against him in relation to that strength. When his voice is soft and almost inaudible, the group will push him firmly, and when his voice becomes loud and forceful, the group will only lightly touch him. The individual has direct control of the group's reactions.

Training Experiences in Accommodation

It is essential to the Gestalt-thematic approach that the members be comfortable and free in accommodating. Some training is definitely necessary to learn how to accommodate. I have developed some experiences that allow the individuals to learn accommodation as a developing process. The experiences also serve as a warmup for the group, which is important in creating a free atmosphere. The following three experiences relate to the mode of accommodation described earlier as "isness" identification. The first two concentrate on the development of specific senses.

—Ask the group to focus on the sound of a particular group member, being aware of the rhythm, tone, and intensity of that person. Allow that sound to develop among the members. One person's rhythm might sound like an itsy bitsy baby—Na Na Na Na. Repeat the experience with each person until each member feels the impact of his own behavioral sound.

—Now concentrate on sight or vision and have the group develop an image for each member. For a member who is seen as a clown, constantly joking, the entire group will joke and clown around. The group serves as a mirror for that person. The experience can be repeated with each member.

The last experience involves all the senses.

—Ask a member for a one-word theme to describe himself in the here-and-now. (i.e. frightened). Then have the group become that theme. The member being focused on absorbs the experience of seeing and hearing himself frightened. He provides the group with feedback to assure the relevancy of the theme. Then he shares the feelings he experienced as the group accommodated his one-word theme.

The next experience deals with polarity identification.

—Ask the group members to pair off. Then suggest several polarities for the members to experiment with, such as power-dependency, love-hate, passive-assertive, order-disorder, trust-distrust. Thus, the members learn to accommodate being the pole or opposite of their partner. It is essential that each person totally give in to being the extreme of each continuum.

The last experience relates to the mode of accommodation described as reaction related identification.

—Again the group members pair off. One member becomes the active participant and the other takes the reactive role. The pairs experiment with sound, sight, and touch. With each sense, the reactive member responds in relation to that stimulus. For example, if the active person makes a screeching sound, the reactive partner might behave in a scared manner. During the touch sequence, members have more freedom without fear of injury if they do not actually touch. In this way, they pretend to kick, push, and hit, and the partner reacts as if contact were actually made.

IMPLICATIONS

In this section I will discuss the implications of a Gestalt-thematic approach with groups, couples, and families. Although this method is limited by the therapist's level of commitment and his skill in accommodating, it is free to be used with any type of group or population. A good example of the flexibility of this method can be seen in a poorly motivated and resistant group, typified by a probation referred group. Here the therapeutic movement is often slow and infrequent. The therapist who tries to move this group in a positive direction, or in opposition to the flow, quickly becomes frustrated in his attempt to increase the members' motivation. The usual theme in these groups is "I don't care to be here" or "I don't give a shit."

To emphasize where the group members are at the moment, the Gestalt-thematic method encourages the members to exaggerate their resistance, distrustfulness, and hostility. The therapist then reinforces any of their natural, "I don't give a shit" behavior. If an individual expresses his dislike of the group or his unwillingness to come to group, the therapist strongly supports this position. Using this approach, it is possible for a leader to give an instruction that is totally in tune with a poorly motivated group. It also provides the members the opportunity to truly face the impact of their behavior. Thus, by telling a group of probation referred adolescents not to care about anything and by supporting that position, the leader is in congruence with the group. Since these adolescents depend on being opposed, the experience becomes a unique one. As the therapist continues with this approach and the dissonance increases, two alternatives generally become apparent to the members: to quit or to move in another direction.

Often, with couples and families an enormous amount of time is spent on meaningless content, that is used merely as a vehicle to disguise the essential process that is going on between man and wife or within the family. The theme approach can quickly cut through the content in an effort to discover the process. Suppose it becomes evident in the family structure that at one time or another the members are saying "I am right" regardless of the content. Pointing out this behavior will many times fall on deaf ears. By having the entire family purposely express the theme "I am right," both verbally and nonverbally, the impact of their lifestyle can actually come into the foreground.

REFERENCE

PESSO, A.: *Movement in Psychotherapy.* New York: New York U. Press, 1969.

12

Gestalt Therapy and the Core Conditions of Communication Facilitation: A Synergistic Approach

CHARLTON S. STANLEY, Ph.D. and PHILIP G. COOKER, Ph.D.

Two theoretical structures have appeared in recent years which have exerted an unusual amount of influence on dynamic counseling and psychotherapy. One of these has been the concept of *core conditions* in the helping relationship. Rogers (1957) postulated that there are several basic conditions which must exist before therapy can take place. Researchers have examined Rogers' hypothesis, and have confirmed that there are indeed about eight conditions which must be present in order for therapy to be effective (Truax, 1966; Truax & Carkhuff, 1967; Carkhuff, 1969a, b). The other of these dynamic concepts is Gestalt therapy, developed by the late Fritz Perls (Perls, 1969a, b, c; Perls, Hefferline, and Goodman, 1951).

We are very encouraged that research in both counseling and psychotherapy (Martin and Gazda, 1970), as well as education (Shaddock, 1972) supports the claims of proponents of systematic training in the core conditions of communication facilitation. Similarly, Gestalt therapy promises much for both the therapist (Fagan and Shepherd, 1970) and the professional educator (Passons, 1972; Brown, 1971).

Our concern is that both these systems have been misunderstood and consequently misused. This is unfortunate, because we suspect that both these systems have been rejected outright by persons who have attempted to use them without adequate preparation. In our conversations with a few of those who "tried it but didn't like it," we have found several common misconceptions.

160

One such misconception is that there seems to be a belief that training in the core conditions of communication facilitation alone is the same as training to be a counselor or therapist. The implication is that if one is trained and skilled in the core conditions, then it is not necessary to have an understanding of personality dynamics. Neither, we have been told, is it necessary to identify with a "school" or system of counseling or psychotherapy. Among some who call themselves "purists" in the use of the core dimensions, we find this rejection even extending to psychological testing. One question we have heard several times is, "Why do you need to know that kind of stuff anyway? You can't do brain surgery." To us this seems incredibly naive. As in the well known case of the late composer George Gershwin, psychotherapy never cured a brain tumor!

There also seem to be many misconceptions about Gestalt therapy as well. Many persons who claim to be using Gestalt therapy appear to us to have acquired a repertoire of games, techniques, and gimmicks. At the same time, their understanding of the foundation of the system is virtually nonexistent. After hearing a lecture, seeing a film or demonstration, and perhaps reading an article on Gestalt therapy, they then attempt to try it out. Upon using this approach, they get the results that one of our students reported: "I tried to do some Gestalt with him, and he told me he thought I was crazier than hell."

In this article, we will discuss the core conditions of the helping relationship, and some of the basic assumptions of Gestalt therapy. We will then attempt to achieve a synthesis of the two in order to answer some of the criticisms that have been leveled against both systems. For instance, Patterson (1973, p. 375) comments that Gestalt therapy has never been adequately evaluated. Of particular importance, says Patterson, is whether it is useful for clients from populations other than those demonstrated via film and typescript by Perls and his associates. We will attempt to respond to this and similar questions, and explain how we are using these concepts in our own work. In keeping with our overall philosophy of the equality of interpersonal relationships, we will use an *I-Thou* approach to pronouns, trying as much as possible to avoid assignment of gender.

THE CORE CONDITIONS

Carkhuff (1969, a, b) has identified seven counselor-directed behaviors or dimensions. They are: (1) empathy, (2) respect, (3) genuineness, (4) personally relevant concreteness or specificity of expression, (5) counselor self-disclosure, (6) confrontation, and (7) immediacy. The primary client-centered scale describes the degree of self-exploration taking place at any given time in the interview. These eight factors make up the conditions that must be present for any helping relationship to occur. Carkhuff describes these dimensions in behavioral terms and assigns a quantitative value to the degree that the behavior is present. The scales range from a low of 1.0 where the activity is totally absent, to 5.0 where the behavior has reached a maximum level of depth and intensity. Although the scales describe some personal qualities of both the helper and helpee, they are basically behaviors, and behaviors can be observed and noted. Furthermore, given an adequately intelligent and motivated subject, these behaviors can be taught.

It is our opinion that the development of the concept of the core dimensions has been one of the major breakthroughs in the teaching and evaluation of counseling and therapy. On the other hand, we are concerned that these dimensions are being taken as a school of thought, a system of therapy, or as a repertoire of techniques that can be used in therapy. We don't see them that way. Briefly, let us describe what the core dimensions mean to us.

Empathy means trying to put myself, the helper, in your position. I misuse empathy when I repeat what you say word-for-word. Restatement of the *content* of what you say is to deal only with the intellectual side of you. Empathy is when I can get past your words and put myself into your feelings and let you know it. I do this with a word, a sentence, or a nonverbal cue. Often, my response will not even resemble the content of what you have said. The content itself is relatively unimportant, and in fact may even be a denial of the truth. Instead, I as a helper am interested in what you, the helpee, are really feeling at this moment in time—or the lack of feeling if that is what's happening. The key to empathy is understanding, but understanding alone is not enough. My understanding of your experience must be communicated to you. Otherwise, I am in my world, you are in yours, and neither of us touches the other.

Respect is present when I am able to take you for who and what you are. I may not like your behavior, but your behavior is less important than my appreciation of your individual worth. In behavioral terms, I will probably be rather selective with regard to reinforcing socially appropriate behaviors. At the same time I will not judge you, or offer to take responsibility for your decisions. Ways I can disrespect you are to try to give you advice, or to explain to you *why* you are doing or feeling something. I am respecting you only when I restrain my own impulses enough to allow you to discover things for yourself. I communicate respect by trusting you. If you view me as an authority, one who is going to set you straight, then poor results can be expected, at least until you disabuse yourself of this notion. There is nothing wrong with your seeing and experiencing me as a resource person with skills which can facilitate learning; however, if I communicate to you that I am going to "help" or "change" you, then I become a seducer. Seducers are not helpers, because they are more interested in meeting some need of their own than they are in the other person.

Genuineness is a function of being real, of not being phony. Basically, the genuine person is an *honest* person. Verbal and nonverbal cues must communicate the same message to the other person. Genuineness is absent if you sense, either consciously or unconsciously, that I have a hidden agenda different from the ostensible reason for the meeting. If you are getting a mixed message, then I will be seen as untrustworthy, and you will be justified in remaining guarded. Genuineness requires that I be attuned to my own visceral cues, and that I be willing and able to share them with you. A practicum student will often say, "Oh, I couldn't say *that* to a client could I?" At this point in the relationship the most important thing happening may very well be the student's very real fear of the client. Thus the fear itself, the way the student perceives the relationship, becomes the most important information to be shared. Genuineness requires that two things be present. First, I must be aware of my own feelings. Second, I must be willing to share my feelings with you.

Empathy, respect, and genuineness are the *passive* elements of the helping relationship. No less important are the *action* dimensions. These action oriented behaviors are: concreteness, helper self-disclosure, confrontation, and immediacy.

Personally relevant concreteness or specificity of expression requires that the helper not deal in abstractions. Nothing will happen in the relationship as long as you and I discuss generalities at the intellectual level. While such a discussion may be intellectually stimulating, no counseling or therapy will occur. Therapeutic movement requires that I focus on you. Your resistance to this is expected, since you will be more comfortable talking about the *there and then* than the *here and now*. This will be particularly true if the topic concerns what is happening to you personally, right now. Even when you talk about your past, your future, or your present, concreteness requires that you talk about these events in terms of specific behaviors and emotions, and how they are affecting you right now.

Helper self-disclosure means that I am willing and able to let you know what I am thinking and feeling, even though I may be uncomfortable in telling you. At these times I am being "transparent" (Jourard, 1964). Behaviorally, what I am doing is modeling self-exploratory behavior. Clients tend to be sensitive to what is expected of them, and as a result pick up behavioral cues rather quickly. Early in my career as a helper, as an unskilled beginner, I thought self-disclosure meant that I should relate back-home stories of the, "Something like that happened to me once . . ." variety. Self-disclosure is actually more closely related to genuineness. I communicate to you that I am not holding back or censoring personally relevant information. In summary, self-disclosure may be described as a sort of bridge between genuineness and immediacy in interpersonal relationships.

Immediacy is a direct function of the I-Thou relationship in counseling and therapy. When you make a statement, *any* statement, it must stimulate both cognitive and affective components in me. This is particularly true when your comment involves me directly. In our culture, the usual way to deal with any kind of talk is to focus on the content, the words, the cognitive material. The affect, or feeling, involved is not listened for, or if heard is not dealt with. Feelings seem to stimulate embarrassment or other discomfort in the listener. As a helper, I must deal with your feelings, especially when those feelings involve me personally. For example: "I like you." "You scare me." "I want you to tell me what to do." "You are no help to me at all." "Why are you looking at me like that?" When you say these things to me, I can reduce or kill the immediacy of our relationship if I choose to ignore or turn aside your statements. By not dealing with you at these points, I am preventing any kind of psychological contact from taking place. And if I reduced immediacy in this manner, I would be seen as cold and distant.

Another way I can reduce immediacy is to dilute it with interpretations and explanations, such as explaining to you that your liking for me is only a function of normal transference. I can increase immediacy by responding to you directly: When you say, "I like you," I will tell you how you are making me feel at the moment as well as how your remark affects me. I may like you, I may dislike you, but whatever it is I will share it with you. What is of primary importance here is that I take responsibility for my feelings, and communicate this responsibility to you. There are very few relationships that are more personal and intimate than counseling and therapy. Immediacy promotes intimacy.

Confrontation is seen as one of the most profoundly important dimensions of the helping relationship. It is also the most likely to produce anxiety in both of us. Many counselors, especially those lacking in self-confidence, are actually afraid to confront even the most inappropriate statements and behaviors. Even more often, the low-functioning counselor operates out of a framework of self-reference. If I devote most of my attention to myself, I will be oblivious to all but your most blatant inconsistencies. Confrontation requires two basic qualities in the helper. First, I must be observant of your verbal and nonverbal behavior. Second, I must be able to state my observations out loud. Things I may be able to confront you on may be: a statement of fact or feeling that does not fit in with previous statements; a statement of feeling that does not fit in with observed behavior; or when you engage in projection by attributing your disowned feelings or attitudes to me. Doubtless, additional examples could be developed. The point of all this is that I must actively encounter you any time you become inconsistent or inappropriate. In confrontation, both verbal and nonverbal behavior becomes grist for our therapeutic mill.

Helpee self-exploration is the degree of willingness you have for talking about yourself. The resounding failures in therapy take place when there is no self-exploration on the part of the helpee. There are two basic reasons you may find self-exploration difficult. One reason is that it is too painful, too distressing. The other is that I may be so inept that any attempts you make to engage in self-exploration are thwarted by me. In the latter category there are so many ways I can destroy your morale that they are almost too numerous to mention. When the discussion centers on me, or on outside topics such as the weather, or on other people in your life, no counseling or therapy can take place. Your self-exploration will probably be rather low early in the session, moving to a greater depth as you continue to talk. The most significantly successful sessions will be those where you are willing to face even the most painful and uncomfortable material. Even though in obvious distress, you will continue to talk about your thoughts, feelings, and behavior.

GESTALT THERAPY

Gestalt therapy, as conceived and developed by the late Frederick S. (Fritz) Perls, seems to provide one of the simplest, and at the same time, most elegant personality theories available. We want to make one thing clear at the outset: While Gestalt therapy *has* rules and games (Fagan and Shepherd, 1970), it *is not* just a set of rules and games. More than anything else, Gestalt therapy is an existential explanation of human behavior, a marriage of behaviorism and phenomenology. And in the Gestalt way, the weaknesses of both are overcome in such a way that their strengths are thereby increased manyfold.

What we can see, touch, hear, smell, or taste can be described empirically and verified by others. Often it can be recorded electronically or chemically. These are our behaviors. If I touch a hot stove, I will jerk my hand away. This is an observable act of fairly large magnitude. Most human behavior, or at least the behaviors we are interested in in counseling and therapy, is much more subtle. Gestalt therapy provides a system for utilizing these subtle behaviors in the helping process. Let's look at an example. As we talk, I observe you to repeatedly gaze out the window. Now, most systems of therapy have no way of dealing with this behavior, so the behavior would go ignored. Furthermore, ignoring your behavior makes me feel safer because you will probably think me an idiot for making a big thing out of such a small behavior. If this is the case, we will probably have a conflict about it, and I would be most uncomfortable. On the other hand, your window-gazing behavior could be very important to the purpose which brought you into therapy in the first place. Even after I decide to deal with your behavior, there is still room for me to be inept.

Upon noticing that you are looking out the window, I could place an interpretation on your action: "You wish you were outside." As a Gestaltist I have just made a major mistake. What happened was that I put my own fantasy, that I wish *I* were outside, off on you. Whether my interpretation was accurate or not is immaterial. I have engaged in projection.

Another way of dealing with the same sample of behavior is for me to ask you *why* you are gazing out the window. This is about the least important thing I could have asked. By asking you why you are doing something, I have implied that your behavior is questionable at best. In reply, you will more than likely become defensive, since *why* questions are often perceived as an attack. The counselor or therapist who asks a lot of *why* questions generally has a lot of evasive and defensive clients. Besides, even if you tell me why you are window-gazing, what can I do with the information that will be useful to the therapy?

The Gestalt way of dealing with your window-gazing activity is simply to observe it and report to you what I am observing: "I notice that as we talk you are looking out the window." From the purely behavioral *what*, we are now ready to move into the phenomenological *how*.

Phenomenology refers to the subjective field of experience. Kepner and

Brien (1970) describe it as all that goes on inside a person, that is, his experiencing.

As behavior therapists move away from public to private events, they describe *covert* behavior (Cautela, 1970). Homme (1965) coined the term *coverant* as a contraction of covert-operant. Despite the diversity of terminology, all these terms refer to *how* the individual processes external environmental events. Obviously, then, it is the business of therapy to examine the client's private events as a behavior paradigm. The primary problem is that we are forced to deal with a behavior pattern of such low intensity that it is below the awareness of the client. Obviously, if one were completely aware of all the *whats* and *hows* of one's life therapy would no longer be needed.

Let's go back to our example of window-gazing. Working backwards, we have an observable behavior, or *response R*. By simply making you aware of *R*, the fact that you are gazing out the window, I will try to get at the *covert stimulus s*. To do this I ask, "What are you getting out of window-gazing?" This should result in your spontaneous discovery of both *s*, and it's antecedent *covert response r*. As he know, any response must come as a result of a stimulus, in this case *stimulus S*. What you have re-discovered (not discovered) is that my dull speech *S* triggered your response *r*, boredom. You were then stimulated *s* by the attractive view out the window (remember the Premack Principle?) which elicited the overt response *R*. As the full sequence or chain *S-r-s-R* emerges into your awareness as a Gestalt, we have achieved a moment of therapeutic insight —in the language of Gestalt therapy, the "aha" or mini-satori. As Perls (1969b) said, "Awareness per se, by and of itself, is curative."

There is a missing step in the above argument. What if we find the sequence looking something like this: *S-r-X-s-R*, where *X* represents some as yet unknown contingencies that make the *S-r* portion of the chain unacceptable and therefore inaccessible? In real life, where few things are textbook simple, this is what we are more likely to get. In this event we will find that the client, rather than talking about the observed behavior *R*, will begin resisting. Resistance may be seen as anger, defensiveness, withdrawal, passive-aggressiveness, or even seductiveness. Anything to divert attention from the danger area. The alert therapist will realize that the stimulus of the therapist's voiced observation has elicited a whole new *S-r-s-R*, with the new *R* being the defensive behavior. If the therapist is a good Gestaltist, then the new flow of the situation must be attended to. In other words, I will follow your lead, and deal with your new behavior rather than try to resurrect the previous situation.

Perls called resistance one of the functions of neurosis. Drive-reduction theory gives us the mechanics of the approach-avoidance behavior of the neurotic. The Gestalt therapist describes the approach half of the neurotic behavior as "top-dog," while "under-dog" is the avoider. Encouraging the client to allow the top-dog and under-dog to carry on a dialogue will bring the neurotic conflict under conscious control.

All this brings us to the point of examining the levels or stages of the therapeutic process as seen by the Gestalt therapist.

Neurotics are in poor contact with both themselves and others. This poor contact is clearly seen in the manner by which they attempt to communicate. Although many neurotics *think* they are communicating, what we actually hear are *clichés*. Clichés are those verbal exchanges that require no thought and no self-reliance since others have already pre-digested the thought content. In interpersonal relationships we hear clichés such as inquiries about our health, the weather, and other nonsense. These verbal noises are just that—noises. The other person is not interested in our health, the weather, or whatever topic was mentioned. Instead they are turning away from any significant human contact. They appear to want closeness, but fear it at the same time.

Once we move past the obvious superficiality of clichés, we find people becoming more tricky. They want to play games with us. Here, people act *as-if* they were something they are not. They are nice—even if they feel unpleasant. They are tough—but feel weak. They are caring—but are secretly indifferent. This is nothing more than role-playing, or phoniness. In the phony layer of neurosis, we find the greatest discrepancies between verbal and nonverbal behavior. This is because verbal behavior is subject to a greater degree of conscious control than nonverbal activity. Consequently, we may see a person acting a certain way while verbally denying the message being sent by body movements and postural cues.

If the phoniness of the mixed message behavior of the client is confronted through one of the "games" of Gestalt therapy, panic or psychological shock will result. When we experience that our defenses of being phony have been taken away, our subjective experience is that of a void, nothingness, emptiness. Environmental support has been jerked away, and self-support has not appeared. At this point in therapy, we as clients are unaware that we are stuck, only that something is terribly wrong. We can no longer go back to the role-playing, but may still make some attempt to do so. This may appear as an attempt to belittle or laugh off the therapist's confrontation. The impasse is often marked by trembling, as if we were trying to move in all directions at once, with the result that we go nowhere. The immobility of the impasse will be escaped the moment we come to realize that we are stuck, because at that point we will also realize how we are hanging ourselves up. This understanding will usually be more at the visceral than the cognitive-intellectual level.

We have speculated that the phobic behavior surrounding the impasse comes at least partly as a result of unconscious awareness that the old environmentally dependent personality must "die" before any new personality can take its place. The consideration of death, even if only as a personality construct, can evoke terror in the most stable of us. Bad as it may have been, the old personality was at least familiar. The new, or restructured, personality is an unknown quantity. "What if people won't like me if I changed," is a typical catastrophic expectation. This appearance of "death or fear of death" (Perls, 1969b, p. 56) is the result of the paralysis of opposing forces. Hence the famous Perls quotation, "To suffer one's death and to be reborn is not easy."

Only if the client willingly gives up the fear and becomes self-sufficient enough to trust his own experience, no matter what the consequences, do we find the death layer turning into the release of an *explosion*. This comes with the re-integration of some disowned part of the personality— the moment in which this particular aspect of the personality forms a *Gestalt*. The client is free to experience the previously feared emotional state. Perls has identified four fundamental emotional states which seem to be appropriate for most occasions: joy, anger, grief, orgasm.

Let's look at this another way. The imploded energy of the neurotic as conflicting drive reduction needs is expressed by the death (or implosive) layer. There are two basic ways I can block my energy. The first is shown when I want to do two or more things and am unable to decide on one, expressed schematically as ←→. Secondly, I can block myself by being afraid to do anything and running from everything, expressed as →|←. In the first example I am tearing myself apart without really going anywhere. And in the second I am cowering—withdrawn and fearful—in my corner. Yet, once I become aware of how I am keeping myself blocked on dead center, then I am free to make an existential choice based on my personal preference and not on environmental support. The unblocking marks the achievement of the *explosive* layer, which is accompanied by a sudden clarity of vision and sharp release of the blocked energy. Our phenomenological experience is that we see things more clearly, colors seem brighter, our eyes focus better, and other people seem somehow to be more transparent in terms of feelings. Also, we feel more energetic and vigorous because we now have all our energy moving in the same direction. This then is the "aha" experience in Gestalt therapy—the "mini-satori."

What is the end result of our efforts as Gestalt therapists? Our goal is threefold. We are interested in developing an awareness of where our energies are and how they are being used. If, through awareness, we find that our constructive energies are being blocked in any way, we take *responsibility* for what we are doing to ourselves—that is, no one can block my energy but myself. By knowing that we are doing something to ourselves, we can either take the responsibility for continuing to do it or we can stop and do something else. Either way, we all make our own choices. Finally, the ability to release blocked energies allows us to experience the *excitement* of living.

Our goal is not to achieve either behavior change or attitude change in the usual sense of the terms. Instead we desire awareness. We assume that once the client is aware of what is going on, behavior change becomes the client's choice, not ours. We refuse to make decisions for our clients, and by refusing we place them in a position whereby they must become self-reliant and responsible for their own decisions. We tell our clients that because we are responsible *to* them, we cannot be responsible *for* them.

The goals of Gestalt therapy are not attained with a few emotionally charged and dramatic sessions. There seems to be a popular myth about this, which is fed by the several very dramatic training films made by Fritz Perls, and by the verbatim transcripts of some of his sessions (Perls, 1969b). As Perls himself emphasized repeatedly (but who listened?), one must keep chipping away at the neurotic's elaborate defense system. Only through repeated experiences of awareness, little by little, does the client move from relying on external support to self-sufficiency.

RELATIONSHIPS AND APPLICATIONS

That we must be warm and empathic is a given in Gestalt therapy. But beyond this, we have discovered that our understanding of the basic postulates of Gestalt therapy not only allows us to understand how a person is feeling, but aids us in identifying where that person is in the hierarchy of neurotic layers, or, to put it in a more positive sense, where the person is in Maslow's hierarchy of needs. Gestalt therapy, with its emphasis on awareness and observations, tends to facilitate high levels of empathy.

Gestalt therapy holds that interpretations and explanation are therapeutic errors. By explaining, you are denying the other person his own experience. In short, explaining is equivalent to disrespect. In order to explain, or interpret, the would-be helper must engage in projection. No matter how much empathy is present, no one can get inside another's head. Projection is just a fancy word for judging another person. And when we judge, we set ourselves up as an authority on what is best for another. Since it follows that authorities encourage dependency relationships by discouraging independent thinking, then the authoritative explainer or interpreter is disrespecting the other person by "helping" him. The Gestalt therapist respects his clients enough to frustrate them by not solving their problems for them. Only in this way, through frustration, do we develop the internal resources for solving our own problems.

We believe that a person cannot be a Gestalt therapist unless he has broken through his own impasse. We have found that the more we take responsibility for ourselves, the more effectively we are able to deal with our own clients and patients. By being aware, we find that there are fewer discrepancies between our verbal and nonverbal behavior. We are also told by those around us that we are seen as being more self-confident and honest. All this is a function of genuineness, and is definitely a part of our work as Gestaltists.

Because we use only those things about our clients which we can observe without projecting, we become more specific. We operate from the assumption that experience and awareness will be manifested as behaviors. A Rorschach test is not needed to see you fidgeting in your chair and watching the clock. I do not know for sure what it means, but I will point out to you what I see you doing. This is about as specific and concrete as we can get. At another level, Gestalt therapy postulates that it does not matter whether you are talking about the past, present, or future. Your experience of those events is taking place in your mind right here and now. Again, your behavior will reveal what you are feeling deeply about those events, and if I am functioning at a high level of concreteness and specificity, your behaviors will be pointed out to you. In this way, we both become aware of the obvious. Consciously striving to stay in the here and now makes it much easier to be concrete and specific.

Self-disclosure is one of the more important elements of Gestalt therapy. The game of *making the rounds* is an example. In this exercise, everyone in the group, one by one, shares his own feeling about a given event. This sharing will often reveal the deepest and most significant emotional material, material that would not be shared except under the most unusual circumstances. Yet this sharing has a very powerful therapeutic value.

We are of the opinion that Gestalt therapy could not exist without the core condition of immediacy. The core of Gestalt therapy is *I and thou in the here and now.* The two of us are separate; you are you, and I am I. The term *we* is to be avoided. If we use *we* in the therapeutic relationship, one of us may include the other in something the other does not wish to be identified with. To avoid talking about our relationship is to deny a very important portion of the therapeutic encounter. We must affirm the validity of our relationship even though talking about it is uncomfortable for both of us.

The Gestalt therapist is confrontive. Even the most minor inconsistencies must be dealt with, because a small behavior may lead to a major breakthrough in awareness. I do not save my confrontation for the so-called "important" issues, while you engage in all sorts of minor inconsistencies. Confrontation is vigorous and continuous. We are shaping up the client's internal behavioral pattern to help him become more aware of what he is doing, how he is doing it, what he is getting out of it. By confronting you with the unimportant minor features of your existence, I am training you to deal better with the more serious problem areas that might be uncovered later. In effect, I am heading off some of the resistance I might otherwise encounter if suddenly confronted material that is very painful to you.

Gestalt therapy seems to get client self-disclosure better than any system we have tried or know about. There is none of the "gradual" moving from the there-and-then to the here-and-now that Carl Rogers talks about. The Gestaltist *demands* that the client stay in the present; by talking about the present only, we are dealing with behaviors that we can see for ourselves. Clients are not permitted to avoid self-disclosure by telling long-winded circumstantial stories. In such cases, the avoidance behavior itself, and not the substance of the story, becomes the focus. The overall philosophy of Gestalt therapy provides some very powerful techniques for the facilitation of client self-exploration. The ultimate goal of self-exploration is self-awareness. To us, self-exploration refers to the examination of the emotional interface between ourselves and our environment. We must do this in order to maintain a healthy, unhampered contact with the environment—to be continuously and freely aware of what is going on both internally and externally.

Both of the authors are using the philosophy and techniques of Gestalt therapy in our own work. The concept of the core dimensions provides us with a measuring tool so that we can examine our effectiveness—or lack of effectiveness. This synthesis works for us synergistically. It is our firmly held belief that if we were trained only in one area and not the other, we would not be nearly so effective. We have some research data to support this view (Stanley, 1972). We have outlined below how we have incorporated both Gestalt therapy and the concept of the core conditions of therapy in our own lives.

CHUCK STANLEY: As a Staff Psychologist in a large state hospital, I have been doing group therapy with a patient population. I do not use individual therapy as a general rule, because of the greater efficiency of the group. By using the Gestalt approach, however, I am doing what amounts to individual therapy in a group setting. My normal meeting time for a therapy group is twice a week, for two hours at each session. The groups are open-ended, which means that new patients are coming in all the time while old patients are being discharged. Each patient has a regular attending physician, and if the physician thinks the patient would benefit from therapy, he is referred to the group. Unlike most patients of other Gestaltists I have talked to, many of my referrals are psychotically decompensated. This is in addition to the usual quota of neurotic persons. In some cases, an affective disorder will be overlaid by brain damage, or possibly alcohol or drug addiction.

Despite the fact that many patients seem to have such a discouraging potential, I find myself able to use my understanding of Gestalt therapy in conjunction with the core conditions of communication facilitation. I must remember that the goal is not to be a Gestalt purist, but to do whatever is necessary for getting the patient to engage in self-exploration. So far, the results have been most encouraging. Progress is often slow, and occasionally marred by regression; however, progress does take place which cannot be accounted for by organic (drug) therapy. Which brings up another point. I have found that drug therapy is a great help in getting the patient calm enough to work with. As Rogers (1967) observed, the first condition of the helping relationship is that the helper and client must be in psychological contact. Ideally, of course, the ultimate desirable goal would be to get the patients to the point where they would be so healthy and self-sufficient that they no longer need the kind of environmental support that drugs provide. In reality, I do not see the patients long enough to bring them to this point, and I doubt that any therapist working exclusively in a hospital setting would be able to do so. As soon as the patients are able to function at a level where they can live in society with a minimum of distress to themselves and their family, they are sent home.

Most of the usual games and gimmicks of Gestalt therapy are not applicable when working with hospitalized patients. For one thing, many, if not most, hospital patients are from a different sort of patient sample than Perls used in his demonstrations (Patterson, 1973, p. 375). They tend to be culturally and educationally impoverished in many cases. Most are not used to verbal expressions of their feelings, and many simply do not have the words in their vocabulary to describe feelings. Psychological confusion is common. For these reasons, the empty chair technique is quite difficult. Dreamwork is also remarkably difficult. The dream material is frequently too bizarre and frightening for them to deal with. In addition, I have observed that, as a general rule, most patients are much less spontaneous and more inhibited than the general population, although some of this may be due to the peculiar nature of the open-ended group. By this I mean that the trust level in the group seems to vary in direct proportion to the ratio of old and new members present.

The hospitalized patients are walking a psychological tightrope. On one side, they see an environment that is trying to do them in (projection), and on the other there are all sorts of internalized horrors (introjection). And throughout all this, they are helpless to do anything about their situation (retroflection). In this condition the patients are terrible fragile. They are unable to maintain a good defense system due to the breakdown of both conscious and unconscious control. Their thoughts become flights of ideas. A major onslaught by the therapist would be destructive at this point. Rather than being in the "role-playing" layer of neurosis, they are stuck in the impasse. Environmental support is gone, but since thay are unable to rely on themselves, they cannot move. Stuck, phobic, they find themselves very vulnerable, and have poor ego strength.

Interestingly enough, when the hotseat is used, the more seriously disturbed patient is more likely to volunteer to work than the neurotic ones. This is only up to a point, however. If the psychological disturbance is really severe, I find it almost impossible to budge the patients from their chairs. Indeed, it is hard to get them to come to the group at all.

Although I do use the hotseat technique, I have had only fair success with the "empty chair." This added element seems to be too confusing to most patients, and creates unnecessary resistance. The best way I have found to overcome this problem is to ask them to close their eyes if they wish, and then carry on a dialogue with whatever disowned part of themselves they are currently working on.

Because of the open-ended format, the here-and-now emphasis of Gestalt therapy has been a definite benefit. I do not have to depend upon an unchanging membership for continuity from session to session. The importance of time becomes more apparent when we consider that some patients may get to come to the group only once or twice. On the other hand, several members have attended for many months before being discharged.

One important point should be reemphasized. A frequently neglected fact of any therapy is that we must keep coming back and going over the same ground repeatedly. A spectacular emotional breakthrough, with all the drama associated with powerful insights, does *not* constitute the finish of therapy. True, it may be an important turning point in the individual's progress, but most people will still have many areas of unfinished business. I think it is important to assist the patients after they have developed an awareness of what they are doing and how they are doing it. The choice to change one's own behavior must be that person's own individual choice; however, he may not have sufficient information available to him to enable him to select alternative behaviors. At this point in our relationship, the communication facilitation model states that it is entirely appropriate for me to assist the other person in setting up a different behavior. This is described by Carkhuff and Berenson (1967) as "phase two" of the helping relationship.

During the second phase of the helping relationship, I become very action-oriented. If the patient has actually made an existential choice as to what he wants to do, based on some new awareness, then I may use such behavioral techniques as contingency contracting, assertiveness training, and other assignments he can do on his own after leaving the group.

PHIL COOKER: The principles of Gestalt therapy and the core conditions of communication facilitation are central to my function as a counselor educator, group leader, and therapist.

Training counselors, especially within the individual practicum experience, almost always involves significant behavior change for the trainee. This means that the student must drop all stereotypes of what counseling, therapy, and helping are supposed to be. During the initial stages of training, novice counselors are encouraged to view the core conditions as a means of *evaluating* their behavior. There is a tendency, at least during early sessions, to utilize the core conditions as a complete system of counseling—"from theory to practice in three easy steps!" Each student, however, is encouraged to develop a personalized system using the core conditions as a means of giving and receiving feedback related to the helping processes.

Throughout intermediate and later stages of training, some of the basic concepts inspired by Gestalt therapy are brought into use. These may include the "hotseat," role reversal, and "making the rounds." Awareness of the here-and-now during supervision is a primary focus. Trainees are required to tape interviews with clients to play back later for the supervision group. The here-and-now seems to be more appropriate for gaining a realistic reaction to the supervised performance, e.g., "How do you feel about that response to your client *now?*" This is a more accurate and better learning experience than if my question had been, "How did you feel when you made that response?" My goal is to give the trainee an awareness of the relationship between feeling and behavior, and the implications this has for effective counseling and therapy.

The trainee is asked to present a dialogue between the "top-dog" and "under-dog" whenever an internal conflict appears to be interfering with the progress of therapeutic movement during supervision. A typical example may sound like this:

PHIL: "What kept you from confronting the client's behavior at this point?"

TRAINEE: "I couldn't do that!"

PHIL: "That wasn't my question. I didn't ask if you *could* do it, but rather what are you telling yourself that results in your not doing it?"

TRAINEE: "They might get mad at me." (Or other catastrophic expectation.)

At this point, the trainee is asked to begin a dialogue with the "client" centering upon this particular projection. My goal is to heighten the trainee's awareness of his or her own motivations, anxieties, strengths, and weaknesses. I believe that in this instance the principles of Gestalt therapy can be used creatively, probably as Perls intended them to be. The belief that "therapy is too good to be used only with the sick" is borne out in this application.

My work with Gestalt therapy and the core conditions at the University of Mississippi is with a non-clinical population. Although Maslow's (1968) referral to the *psychopathology* of the *average* indicates that most of us operate at relatively low levels in terms of human potential, the clientele that compose my groups are essentially coping successfully with situations in daily living. Such is not the situation with inpatient groups where the individuals are simply trying to develop minimal levels of coping behavior.

Just as therapy was previously described as having two phases (three if you consider an intermediate phase), I find it helpful to view the processes of the intensive group as having similar phases. Rogers (1967) refers to the stages evolving through the group experience based on participants' behavior. According to Rogers, members react to the unstructured format by "milling around" as they look for direction. Next, negative feelings are usually expressed by a number of participants, probably as a defense against or resistance to revealing personally relevant material. Finally, positive feelings are dealt with while the members become less defensive and more open with each other.

Knowledge of these stages is reassuring, yet this does not provide an action model for the leader to follow. Utilizing the concept of an *exploratory* (initial and downward) phase preceding an *action* (later and upward) phase does provide the facilitator with such a model. Again you can conceive of a *transitory* (intermediate) phase coming between the exploratory and action phases. The task of the facilitator during the initial stage is enhanced by modeling the conditions of *empathy, respect,* and *concreteness,* and encouraging the group members to respond to each other in terms of these conditions.

After the group members develop an understanding of their motives and goals (individual and collective), they can then move into the action phase. Interpersonal learning and growth takes place as the action conditions of *confrontation, immediacy,* and *self-disclosure* are developed and utilized. What makes sense about this particular strategy is that in order to effectively produce movement in light of group goals and objectives, there first needs to be solid understanding of where each participant is and where each intends to go. This understanding can be accomplished through the initial, exploratory phase. The later, action phase provides conditions and opportunities for dealing with and maximizing learning from the personalized interactions that had beginnings in the early stages of group communication. The core dimension of *genuineness* has a place throughout the group process. Just as with helping on a one-to-one basis, the emphasis at first is on not being phony and on accentuating the positive when making statements and giving feedback. Later, when the group has attained a relatively high level of trust, being real is just as important as before. This is especially true in the case of negative material.

Gestalt therapy obviously provides a number of techniques for me as a leader to utilize throughout the group experience. Implementing techniques alone, as we have previously stated, does not comprise Gestalt therapy. Instead, an understanding of the theory as a *system* for precipitating change in individuals is of primary importance. Seeing the growth (therapy) process as the bringing together of polarized elements (disowned parts) is basic to making sense of the techniques and games of Gestalt therapy.

REFERENCES

BROWN, G. I.: *Human Teaching for Human Learning: An Introduction to Confluent Education.* New York: Viking Press, 1971.

CARKHUFF, R. R.: *Helping and Human Relations.* Volume I. *Selection and Training.* New York: Holt, Rinehart & Winston, 1969. (a)

CARKHUFF, R. R.: *Helping and Human Relations.* Volume II. *Practice and Research.* New York: Holt, Rinehart & Winston, 1969. (b)

CARKHUFF, R. R., and BERENSON, B.: *Beyond Counseling and Therapy.* New York: Holt, Rinehart & Winston, 1967.

CAUTELA, J.: Covert reinforcement. *Behavior Therapy,* 1:33-50, 1970.

FAGAN, J., and SHEPHERD, I. L. (Eds.): *Gestalt Therapy Now: Theory, Techniques, Applications.* Palo Alto: Science and Behavior Books, 1970.

HOMME, L. E.: Perspectives in psychology: XXIV, Control of coverants, the operants of the mind. *Psychological Record,* 15:501-511, 1965.

KEPNER, E., and BRIEN, L.: Gestalt therapy: A behavioristic phenomenology. In J. Fagen and I. L. Shepherd (Eds.), *Gestalt Therapy Now: Theory, Techniques, Applications*. Palo Alto: Science and Behavior Books, 1970.

JOURARD, S.: *The Transparent Self*. New York: Van Nostrand, 1964.

MARTIN, D. G., and GAZDA, G. M.: A method of self-evaluation for counselor education utilizing the measurement of facilitative conditions. *Counselor Education and Supervision*, 9:87-92, 1970.

MASLOW, A. H.: *Toward a Psychology of Being* (2nd Edition). Princeton, N. J.: Van Nostrand, 1968.

PASSONS, W. R.: Gestalt therapy interventions for group counseling. *The Personnel and Guidance Journal*, 51:183-189, 1972.

PATTERSON, C. H.: *Theories of Counseling and Psychotherapy*. New York: Harper and Row, 1973.

PERLS, F. S.: *Ego, Hunger and Aggression*. New York: Random House, 1969. (a)

PERLS, F. S.: *Gestalt Therapy Verbatim*. Lafayette, Cal.: Real People Press, 1969. (b)

PERLS, F. S.: *In and Out the Garbage Pail*. Lafayette, Cal.: Real People Press, 1969. (c)

PERLS, F. S., HEFFERLINE, R. F., and GOODMAN, P.: *Gestalt Therapy: Excitement and Growth in the Human Personality*. New York: Dell Publishing Company, 1951.

ROGERS, C. R.: The necessary and sufficient conditions of therapeutic personality change. *Journal of Consulting Psychology*, 21:95-103, 1957.

ROGERS, C. R.: The process of the basic encounter group. In J. F. T. Bugental (Ed.), *Challenges of Humanistic Psychology*. New York: McGraw-Hill, 1967.

SHADDOCK, J. D.: Relative effectiveness of two communication training models on student teacher classroom behavior. Unpublished doctoral dissertation, University of Mississippi, 1972.

SKINNER, B. F.: Behaviorism at fifty. In T. W. Wann (Ed.), *Behaviorism and Phenomenology*. Chicago: University of Chicago Press, 1964.

STANLEY, C. S.: The relative effects of encounter groups on interpersonal and communication skill. Unpublished doctoral dissertation, University of Mississippi, 1972.

TRUAX, C. B.: *Counseling and Psychotherapy: Process and Outcome*. Fayetteville: University of Arkansas Rehabilitation Research and Training Center, 1966.

TRUAX, C. B. and CARKHUFF, R. R.: *Toward Effective Counseling and Psychotherapy: Training and Practice*. Chicago: Aldine, 1967.

Part V

GESTALT THERAPY AND
EASTERN PHILOSOPHY

This section is concerned with Eastern philosophy as it continues to influence the evolution of the Gestalt approach. In Part I we saw the influences of Eastern philosophy on the development of Perls' position. Here, in Part V, is the continuation of that influence as it provides a growing edge.

George Greaves skillfully flows between pointing out philosophical parallels between Tantric and Zen Buddhism and the Gestalt approach and the practical use of Tantric and Zen techniques in psychotherapy. His philosophical discussion allows an understanding, and his clear examples of practice serve as guides for the therapist who wishes to stretch in the direction of the East.

James Stallone has written about the current popularity in the United States of Gestalt psychotherapy, Zen Buddhism and Transcendental Meditation. In his discussion of these three movements he makes a case that in terms of goals there are more similarities than differences among them.

The final chapter in this section concentrates on Taoism and Gestalt therapy. In this chapter Charles Gagarin presents the philosophical points of compatibility between the two, as well as an outline for a practical integration.

13

Gestalt Therapy, Tantric Buddhism and the Way of Zen

GEORGE B. GREAVES, Ph.D.

In an earlier article (Greaves, 1972), I have shown how the use of meditation and Gestalt methods may be used to supplement one another. Being surprised at the widespread curiosity evoked by the article and my growing success with the combination of these two methods, I have found myself combining various Eastern teaching methods and philosophies in an ever-growing manner in my practice of psychotherapy. In particular, I have found valuable the methods of Zen teaching, and the meditation and meditative aids of Tantric Buddhism.

The potential use of Eastern mysticism as a vehicle for promoting healthy psychological-spiritual development within the Western psychological tradition was first envisioned by William James (1907). Writing in *The Varieties of Religious Experience*, James argues that the experiencing and practicing of religion is mankind's most important function and that "personal religious experience has its root and centre in mystical states of consciousness . . ." (p. 299). He proceeds to praise the richness of Eastern methods of attaining mystical states, while pointing to the comparative paucity of such methodology in the West. However, with the subsequent burial of Jamesian phenomenology in favor of behavioristic psychology, it remained for the wide-ranging interests of psychoanalyst-scholar Erich Fromm to reiterate the practical interplay of Eastern and Western approaches to human growth, in this case, that of *Zen Buddhism and Psychoanalysis* (Fromm, Suzuki & De Martino, 1960). However, that book was

---

This chapter is dedicated affectionately to Lucinda Boster whose journey frequently leads her along the Path of Zen.

written a decade before its time and produced little more than a few ripples on the water.

In Japan, in the meantime, particularly at the Jikeikai School of Medicine in Tokyo, in conjunction with Kyoto University, Zen techniques had been refined by the 1950's into a formal treatment method known as *Morita* treatment. Its principal use has been in the treatment of obsessive-compulsive states. However, with the social revolution initiated in the United States by the "flower children" of the mid and late 1960's characterized by their turning away from materialistic, object-oriented values toward spiritualistic, inward-oriented values, tens of thousands of late teenagers and young adults began turning their attention to the religions of the East, which had cultivated the "inward life" for tens of centuries. Thousands began seeking treatment for numerous neurotic and existential ills, or simply to extend their self awareness, through the medium of Transcendental Meditation, the Hare Krishna Meditation Society, and Hatha yoga. Finally, with such innovative works appearing as drug-researcher Robert DeRopp's *The Master Game* (1968), psychotherapist Sheldon Kopp's *Guru* (1971) and *If You See the Buddha on the Road, Kill Him!* (1972), and with numerous articles appearing in the provocative psychotherapy journal, *Voices*, alluding to the integration of various Eastern concepts, viewpoints and methods into the practice of psychotherapy, many therapists began making use of Eastern ways of growth.

My basic contention in this present contribution it that there are many important similarities between the Ways of Zen and Tantric Buddhism and the goals of Gestalt therapy. Given these similarities, it is reasonable to assume, and it bears out, that certain methods of learning the Way of Zen and Tantrism* are applicable to Gestalt therapy, thus enlarging and complementing the various methods traditionally employed by Gestalt therapists.

I am not simply interested in drawing an "academic" picture of the similarities and differences between the Way of Zen, Tantric Buddhism and Gestalt therapy. The intent of the present chapter, rather, is to comment on the practical aspects of the use of Zen and Tantric methods in the practice of Gestalt therapy, and to provide illustrations, guidelines and rationales pertaining to the use of these methods.

In the service of this aim, I will note the sometimes striking similarities of Tantrism, the Way of Zen and the goals of Gestalt therapy. Secondly,

---

* For literary ease I will use the word "Tantrism" interchangeably with "Tantric Buddhism."

I will show the *criteria of the application* of Zen and Tantric teaching methods, based on my experience in using them. Thirdly, I will address myself to the issue of specific Zen and Tantric *methods* of growth, including certain similarities between them and methods of Gestalt therapy. Finally, I will share some of my *case experiences* with the use of these methods, so that the reader may gain some insight as to how I conduct therapy sessions within the context of the use of Zen and Tantric methods.

First of all, however, probably owing to my background in philosophy, I feel a need to set the Way of Zen and Tantrism in their historical perspectives. My treatment of such perspective will be concise, and to some, perhaps a bit breezy. For those with an in-depth interest in tracing the intricate history of Eastern thought, I am yet to find a more readable work than Nancy Wilson Ross's *Three Ways of Asian Wisdom* (1966). For those interested in the history and practice of Tantric Buddhism (the most important direction that Tantrism has taken), I commend the reader to *The Tantric Mysticism of Tibet* by Blofeld (1974). For those interested in the history of Zen, there are excellent works by Chang Chung-Yuan, *Original Teachings of Ch'an Buddhism* (1969), and *The Way of Zen* (1957) by Alan Watts. As to the practice of Zen, Philip Kapleau's *The Three Pillars of Zen* (1967) makes for fascinating reading. And I hasten to introduce anyone interested in any aspect of Zen to Nancy Wilson Ross's *The World of Zen* (1960), a well-balanced anthology of the wide range of materials and activities associated with the Way of Zen, ranging from poetry to *koans** to Zen archery to Zen teachings to commentaries on the Zen way of life.

The Historical Perspective

When the Buddha died in 483 B.C., he charged his disciples with seeing that his teachings became a growing and living thing, and that they not be dogmatized. Despite this, the disciples memorized the teachings of the Buddha in great detail, passed them down by word of mouth for several centuries, as was the Asian tradition of teaching, and finally meticulously recorded the teaching of the former Prince during the first century, A. D. These *Sutras* became the written canon of Buddhism (Ross, 1966). The dogmatization of the teachings of the Buddha prevailed for some 13 centuries until a series of generations of Chinese Buddhists instigated the practice of Ch'an Buddhism, during the eighth through twelfth centuries (Chung-Yuan, 1969).

---

* This and other technical terms will be defined later in the chapter.

Ch'an Buddhism had strong ties with one of China's two major religious philosophies of the time, Taoism (see Lao Tsu, 1972) and Confucianism. Confucianism was and is primarily a pragmatic and ethical religion concerning the proper way of conducting oneself in day to day affairs. Taoism, on the other hand, has been from its outset highly concerned with the spiritual nature of man, particularly the mystical spiritualism alluded to earlier by James (1907). The result of combining the Way of Tao with traditional Buddhism was to ultimately bring about the "purification" of Buddhism, once again emphasizing the growth aspect of human beings and tending strongly to de-dogmatize traditional Buddhism, as was the Buddha's original intent.* The traditional founder of Ch'an Buddhism was Ma-tsu (709-788 A. D.), though, as in the case of virtually all founders of any school of thought or religion, he built upon the foundations laid down by others. During the height of Ch'an Buddhism in China, there were five different sects of the evolving Taoist-Buddhist philosophy-religion.

By the twelfth century, however, Ch'an Buddhism faded rapidly in China, for complex reasons too extensive to relate here, yet the teachings had been picked up by visiting Japanese Buddhists who, in turn, implanted Ch'an Buddhism in their homeland. Ch'an Buddhism has flourished in Japan since the twelfth century under its Japanese name of Zen. Of the five original Chinese schools of Ch'an Buddhism, two were transported to Japan, both of which have survived to the present day. The first and largest of these is the *soto* school, which places heavy emphasis on *zazen*, i.e., the complete emptying of all contents of the mind while in the sitting position (Kapleau, 1967). The second surviving school of Ch'an Buddhism is the *rinzai* school, which favors a more active method of attaining Enlightenment, largely replacing *zazen* with *koan contemplation*.** Thus, the goal of attaining Enlightenment or perfect Self Awareness is the same for both schools, though arrived at in a different manner.

---

* In addition to Taoism, a second factor contributed greatly to the rise of Ch'an Buddhism. Some of the *Sutras* or teachings of Shakyamuni Buddha (the original Buddha) were considered more important than others. In the beginning the Lankavatara Sutra was considered to be the key to Buddhahood. However, those who were to develop the Ch'an sect of Buddhism turned instead to the Pragnaparamita Sutra. *Pragnaparamita* literally means "non-dual knowledge," and was felt to be arrived at through the process of *Madhyamika*, or the dialectic process of negation leading to *sunyata*, *or* Emptiness (Chung-Yuan, 1969, pp. 3-4). The modern Zen expression of *sunyata* or Emptiness is the Void.
** A third very small and minimally influential sect was introduced in Japan much later than the *soto* and *rinzai* schools. This is the *obaku* sect whose connections with the original five schools of Ch'an Buddhism are uncertain (Kapleau, 1967).

In either case, it often seems paradoxical to "action-oriented" Westerners that the road to becoming most fully human can be found in nonaction and silent contemplation. What Westerners fail to see is that meditation is a method which facilitates the *process* of shifting one's awareness from his outer-directed ego to his inner-directed *self* or *being*, seen by many Western therapists as a necessary condition for attaining humanness and centeredness, with the oft sought for serenity which accompanies such centering and awareness. I will speak more of this issue later.

The history of Tantrism follows a somewhat different course. Tantrism, like Buddhism, has its foundations in India, but, unlike traditional Buddhism, Tantrism has been a highly mystical, if not magical, religious sect. The most important expression of the Tantric mysticism of India, however, has become that of Tantric Buddhism, originally found only in Tibet and the Himalayas, forming a unique religion and world-view, with considerable emphasis being placed on the employment of elaborate rites and rituals as aids to meditation and the attainment of Enlightenment. The practice of Tibetan *lamanism*, the direct outgrowth of Tantric Buddhism, is still practiced today despite the invasion and occupation of Tibet by China in the 1950's. The most visible and influential settlements of Tibetan Buddhists are now in California with the largest *lamasery*, the Tibetan Nyinga Center, being located in Berkeley. The specific application of Tantric Buddhism and the Way of Zen to Gestalt therapy will be treated in a later section.

Gestalt Therapy, Tantrism and Zen

While there is not a total overlap between the goals of Gestalt therapy, Tantrism and Zen, there are a number of important similarities which these approaches to human growth and development share and which make possible the sharing of certain growth modalities between them. Among these are the following:

1. They all share a strong "here and now" orientation.
2. They seek to resolve perceived polar opposites and polar conflicts through the process of centering.
3. They view integration of the person, both within himself and within his life space, as a major goal (Baba Ram Dass, 1971, refers to this process as *re-membering*, i.e., putting oneself back together again).*

---

* Baba Ram Dass received his training and Enlightenment in India from teachers of *yoga;* thus, it may seem odd to quote him in the context of Buddhism. However, no student of far Eastern philosophy-religions can help but be impressed by the widespread trading around of ideas among them, nor help but be impressed by the all-encompassing views of Hinduism.

4. They place heavy emphasis on the process of continued growth. Zen writings, in particular, are replete with examples of Zen masters continuing to be taught by their disciples to the point of their death, as well as continuing the uninterrupted practice of the Way.

5. They place heavy emphasis on the existence of awareness systems other than thinking as modalities of knowing the world, stressing that the intellect is a highly incomplete system of knowing and experiencing the world. Each approach would easily agree with Carl Jung's (1971) concept of the "four mental functions" of *thinking, feeling, sensing,* and *intuiting* as equally valuable modalities of knowing the world, and could also readily agree with Jung that a balance among the four mental functions, or a centering among the four mental functions, would be the ideal state of knowing the world.

6. They all stress the value and ultimate necessity of self-realization, self-reliance, and ultimately self-actualization.*

7. They involve a *focusing of awareness* in the here and now.

8. They are strongly oriented toward the *accepting* of experiences as opposed to the *analysis* of experiences. Put another way, Gestalt therapy, Tantrism and Zen are all non-analytical in nature.

9. They lay emphasis on developing a maximally-functioning (or as Rogers, 1961, would say, "a fully-functioning") person, or, alternatively, an "ultimately human" being. This striving for humanness is an obvious antidote to neurotic functioning so eloquently described by Horney (1937), particularly in regards to her discussion of the neurotic person's highly overdeveloped and impossible to attain ego-ideal.

An apparent discrepancy between the Gestalt approach to human growth and that of Tantrism and Zen is Gestalt's comparative lack of emphasis on the development and awareness of one's personal spirituality and spiritual essence. While this is not an explicit goal of Gestalt therapy, per se, most Gestalt therapists I have encountered tend strongly to develop the spiritual aspect of man, considered so psychologically crucial by James (1907), Jung (e.g., 1957) and Fromm (e.g., 1947, 1955)—whether this spiritual awakening be secular or religious in character. (I am not sure that it is possible for a "spiritual awakening" to occur in the absence of

---

* As in the case of Jungian psychology (1971), a strong distinction is drawn in Tantrism and Zen between ego-identity and self-identity. Fromm (1947) and Maslow (1961) draw a similar distinction between ego-identity and being-identity. Thus, when Zen and Tantrism speak of the goal of "no ego" there is no intent to seek the denial of self. Rather, it is held that only through giving up of one's ego can one become Enlightened, Self-Realized or Self-Actualized.

some form of religiosity. Thus, my use of the words "secular" and "religious" above may be what William James calls "a difference without a distinction." Furthermore, allusions to such spirituality are easily found in Gestalt writings, such as Fritz Perls' famous understatement: "To suffer one's death and to be reborn is not easy" (1969a). I submit, therefore, that Gestalt therapy, Tantrism and Zen converge even at the crucial juncture of personal spirituality.)

Criteria of Patient Selection

As in the case of most eclectic practitioners of psychotherapy, I strive to match my abilities and treatment strategies to the presenting problems of the patients I see. Therefore, I am quite aware that there is no method of psychotherapy which is a panacea which will resolve all psychological-emotional dysfunctioning any more than there is a single medicine which is a panacea for all medical ills. Therefore, I wish to share what I have found in working with Tantrism and Zen, particularly in terms of those persons who do and do not seem to profit from such methods.

A prime group with whom to employ the methods I will be discussing in the next section are those persons who are severely divided within themselves intellectually (are of several minds about things), suffer misery and depression growing out of their ambivalence, indecision and never-ceasing obsessiveness, and lead the major portion of their lives "in their head," i.e., are fixated upon their intellect as their primary means of interacting with the world. We (many of us) commonly refer to such persons in our technical jargon as "obsessive-compulsives."

A second group who respond well to certain Tantric and Zen growth methods are those persons who are "fragmented," in Gestalt terminology, i.e., those persons whose thoughts, behavior and actions are at odds with one another and need "integrating."

Another group who respond well to the methods I will be discussing are those persons suffering from identity crises (see Erikson, 1950).

Four other groups who seem to respond exceptionally well to this approach are persons who are already basically healthy and who are seeking additional growth as human beings (the best candidates of all); those persons suffering from "existential anguish" (see Kierkegaard, 1946); aimless persons lacking any apparent meaning in life (see Frankl, 1955; and May, 1953); and, in general, *any* persons seeking more out of life, or to maximize life (including me).

Persons with whom I personally have had little success with either Gestalt, Tantric or Zen methods are:

1. Persons whose thought processes are highly "diffuse" (usually psychotic persons with an hysterical personality structure);

2. Persons with whom I cannot build rapport (in which case all therapy fails with the possible exception of behavior modification);

3. Persons who have "given up" the growth process (the "existentially dead");

4. Persons who are extremely "outer oriented" and tend to strongly resist introspection and contemplation ("psychopathic," "sociopathic," "characterologically disturbed," "strongly hysterical," "massively repressive" persons);

5. Persons whose presenting psychological problems are secondary to organic disturbances; and,

6. Persons of subnormal intelligence.

The Methods of Gestalt, Tantrism and Zen

Those of us who are schooled and trained in Gestalt methods are already familiar with various Gestalt techniques such as *focusing, role playing,* teaching individuals to personalize their use of language (an example of owning) rather than using impersonal constructions (e.g., "I feel uncomfortable in this situation" instead of saying "*It* feels uncomfortable here" or even "This place feels uncomfortable"), dialoguing between "top-dog" and "under-dog," and so on. For those relatively unfamiliar with Gestalt procedures, there are many excellent books readily available (e.g., Fagan and Shepherd, 1970; Perls, 1969a, 1969b, 1969c; Perls, Hefferline and Goodman, 1950; Polster and Polster, 1973), as well as the present book. Therefore, I will not expand on those methods here.

I wish instead to speak here of the major methods of Zen and Tantric teaching, and how I employ them. Of Zen methods there are mainly three.*

The first of these methods is that of *koan, (kung-an* in Chinese). Generally speaking, a *koan* is a statement or question which seems to, and often does, defy all the laws of logic, the solution to which requires an unusual response or fresh way of viewing the world, which tends to

---

* Two other methods are mentioned in the Ch'an literature: that of *Ho!,* a sudden loud, unexpected shout designed to provoke surprise and insight; and *striking,* the administration of certain number of blows with a flailing stick, designed to increase a person's concentration (Chung-Yuan, 1969).

loosen the intellect from its usual rigid patterns of functioning. One famous *koan* which illustrates this point very well goes as follows:

> A Zen *roshi* or master, carrying a flailing stick in his hand, approaches one of his students with the following problem. "Observe what I am holding in my hand," begins the master. "If you tell me it is a stick I will strike you with it. If you tell me it is not a stick I will strike you with it. If you fail to respond promptly with an answer, I will strike you with it. Now, I ask you, what is this that I am holding in my hand?"

Most Westerners (or most Easterners for that matter), being accustomed to confronting such situations by seeking to discover appropriate verbalizations would in all likelihood wind up with a good whack. The solution to the *koan*, of course, is not to respond verbally at all, but rather to seize the flailing stick from the master.

In addition to provoking persons to new responses, it is also the purpose of the *koan* to frustrate the intellect, and by such frustration to point out the inadequacy and incompleteness of the intellect in knowing the world (Chung-Yuan, 1969). Or, as Professor D. T. Suzuki so eloquently puts it:

> The *koan* . . . has a most definite objective, the arousing of doubt and pushing it to its furthest limit. A statement built upon a logical basis is approachable through its rationality; whatever doubt or difficulty we may have had about it dissolves itself by pursuing the natural current of ideas. All rivers are sure to pour into the ocean; but the *koan* is an iron wall standing in the way and threatening to overcome one's every intellectual effort to pass. When Joshu says, "the cypress-tree in the courtyard" or when Haquin puts out his one hand, there is no logical way to get around it. You feel as if your march of thought had suddenly been cut short. You hesitate, you doubt, you are troubled and agitated, not knowing how to break through the wall which seems altogether impassable. When this climax is reached, your whole personality, your inmost will, your deepest nature, determined to bring the situation to an issue, throws itself with no thought of self or no-self, of this or that, directly and unreservedly against the iron wall of the *koan*. This throwing your entire being against the *koan* unexpectedly opens up a hitherto unknown region of the mind. Intellectually, this is the transcending of the limits of logical dualism, but at the same time it is a regeneration, the awakening of an inner sense which enables one to look into the actual working of things. For the first time, the meaning of the *koan* becomes clear and in the same way that one knows that ice is cold and freezing. The eye sees, the ear hears, to be sure, but it is the mind as a whole that has satori; it is an act of perception, no doubt, but it is a perception of the highest order. Here lies the value of the Zen

discipline, as it gives birth to the unshakable conviction that there is something indeed going beyond mere intellection (Suzuki, 1949).

The second major method of learning the Way of Zen is through the process of *zazen*. The object of *zazen* is, through the process of intense concentration, to empty one's mind of all thoughts, ideas, images, and so on, leaving nothing but the concentration itself. Or, put in psychological jargon, to create a blank phenomenal field. The ultimate object of practicing *zazen* is that of achieving *satori* or profound insight and Enlightenment. The highest form of *zazen*, that of *schikan-taza* (or "just sitting") is very difficult to master, and is usually attempted only after one has mastered lower forms of *zazen*, that is, those requiring aids to concentration, such as through counting one's breath or being aware of one's breathing. Technically, neither seeking the solution to a *koan* nor engaging in *zazen* is "meditation" in the usual sense of the word, since there is no specific thought or object to be meditated upon (Kapleau, 1967).

The third major method of Zen teaching is that of *mondo (wen-ta* in Ch'an Buddhism). Mondo consists of a conversation between a master and student. Generally, the student asks certain questions of the master who in turn replies (or fails to reply) in such a way that the student must somehow find the solution to his own question, aided by the master's often baffling response. An entertaining and typical example of the art of *mondo* is the following, quoted from Kapleau (1967):*

> One day a man of the people said to Zen Master Ikkyu: "Master, will you please write for me some maxims of the highest wisdom?" Ikkyu immediately took his brush and wrote the word "Attention." "Is that all?" asked the man. "Will you not add something more?" Ikkyu then wrote twice running: "Attention. Attention." "Well," remarked the man rather irritably, "I really don't see much depth or subtlety in what you have just written."
>
> Then Ikkyu wrote the same word three times running: "Attention. Attention. Attention."
>
> Half-angered, the man demanded: "What does that word 'Attention' mean anyway?"
>
> And Ikkyu answered gently: "Attention means attention."

While it is comparatively easy, even if frustrating, to lead persons into *koan* contemplation and *mondo* interaction, many persons find *zazen* to be extremely difficult. When this situation arises, as it commonly does, I

---

* Who in turn quotes from Matsuo, K. and Steinilber-Oberlin, *Zonso Mondo.* No publisher or date given.

introduce suitable persons to Tantric technique of meditation. As Blofeld (1974, p. 31) puts it:

> Despite enormous external differences, [Tantric Buddhism] is essentially close to Zen. Its goal is the same—Enlightenment *here* and *now*—and its approach is no less direct; but, unlike Zen, it relies on an abundance of aids. For the many people who, not being spiritual giants, conscientiously practise Zen or some other austere form of mysticism over the years without notable results, meditation becomes more of a burden than a joy. Some of these may be glad to attempt the cloud-girt peak again with skillful devices to help them. They may at first be troubled by Tantric Buddhism's lavish use of rites and symbols; but once it is understood how far the sublime purpose of the rituals is removed from mere liturgical pomp, they will perceive their value and perhaps welcome them. Then the [Tantric way] will awaken a deep response and lead to the achievement of results that eluded them before. The point is not that [Tantrism] is superior to Zen; no one intimately acquainted with Zen could doubt the excellence of its methods; what is more doubtful is the ability of most of us to employ them successfully.

Unlike Zen, then, Tantric Buddhism relies heavily on *meditation* as the road to Enlightenment. There are basically three primary aids to meditation found in the Tantric method. These are the use of *mantras*, *yantras* or *mandalas*, and *mudras*. *Mantras* are sacred sounds or words to be meditated upon or used in chanting. The most potent *mantra* in existence is felt to be *Om* (pronounced a-ou-oo-mm).* The most popular, best known, and probably the most sacred mantra used in Tantric chanting is *Om Mani Padme Hum* ("Behold the Heart of the Lotus!"). A *yantra* is a relatively simple symmetrical design which is constructed dynamically toward the pulling of one's attention to a central point in the design. A *mandala* is also a design to be meditated upon, but much more complex than a *yantra*. Mandalas are usually four-sided, symmetrical figures surrounding a central core.**

Mudras are symbolic gestures of the hands and the fingers which are an aid to attaining certain inner states. In the West we are more accustomed to using gestures of the hands and fingers to evoke responses

---

* *A as* in father, *ou* as in ouch!, *oo* as in food, and *mm* as in humming—a complex diphthong in which all the sounds are uttered in an uninterrupted flow.

** The specific structure of Tantric Buddhist's mandalas is closely tied to Buddhist's doctrine, which I largely avoid in the employment of Tantric techniques. Nevertheless, there is a fascinating account of the rationale of the construction of such *mandalas* in Blofeld's (1974) book.

in others. We are familiar, however, with the act of folding our hands in prayer—a form of *mudra*. Other aids to Tantric meditation include the use of flowers, incense, lights, water, musical instruments and grain.

Case Excerpts

I hasten to point out that neither the methods of Zen or Tantric practice involve the use of *introspection* or *retroflection*. The methods can, instead, be summarized as *contemplation, shikan-taza* and *meditation*. Introspection and retroflection place undue emphasis on intellectual activity and tend to foster analysis. Zen, Tantrism, and Gestalt all see undue intellection and analysis as enemies of human growth. I often have the charge thrown at me that my views are "anti-intellectual." To this I respond by asking how, if I am "anti-intellectual," it is possible that I hold a Ph.D., have read countless books, and publish so extensively. To label Zen, Tantrism, Gestalt or my own conglomeration of viewpoints as anti-intellectual is to miss the whole point. Intellection, I freely acknowledge, is *one* valid way of knowing the world, although, as Polanyi (1967) so brilliantly argues, it is categorically impossible for a person to possess knowledge of *anything* independently of such irrational functions as *intuition* and *belief*. My personal philosophical conviction, then, is not one of anti-intellectualism, but one of *trans-intellectualism*. Intellection is incomplete; it needs complementing. In this section I hope to share with the reader how I help to develop trans-intellectual functioning with some of my clients.

First I will speak of my use of *koan* and *mondo*. These methods I employ extensively, though I do not label them as such.

In the administration of a *koan* during the course of psychotherapy, it is essential that the koan produce a *felt* confusion. To clarify, I have observed basically three kinds of confusion which people exhibit. The first of these is the confusion of the psychotic person or the person in the throes of an acute or chronic brain syndrome who simply, for whatever reasons, is disoriented and seemingly unable to get a "handle" on anything. The second kind of confusion is the confusion generated out of neurotic or other internal conflicts which is used as a defensive tactic against receiving or understanding threatening material. The third kind of confusion, the *felt* or *genuine* confusion is that which occurs when a person both acts upon and feels the weight of a paradox or illogical statement put to him, but is unable, at least at the moment, to discover its meaning.

It is this third kind of confusion which is of maximum importance in the application of the *koan* or paradox within the context of Gestalt therapy, because it takes advantage of the Gestalt process itself, that is, the need for *closure*. If the *koan* or paradox is keenly felt, it remains with the person far beyond the therapy session. It may endure for weeks, sometimes even months, nagging at the person, plaguing the person, demanding resolution (as described so vividly by Professor Suzuki above).

I rarely give classical *koans* to any patient without considerable preparation before. If done without preparation, it is often seen as irrelevant, a game, or a "trip" laid on the person by a perceived authority. This only breeds resentment and rarely generates felt confusion.

My favorite manner of introducing persons to *koans* is one in which we both participate from the onset. An example of this occurred in the following segment:

> I had been interviewing a young man in his early 20's whose presenting problem was depression. By the end of the third session I had a pretty clear picture of the young man as being highly rigid, dogmatic, opinionated, whose stance of moral superiority over his peers and professors had successfully alienated them. The young man was lonely and alone. He lived in a black-white, right-wrong, yes-no world in which there were no shades of gray. I decided to attempt to force his thinking patterns into superordinate categories (Harvey, Hunt & Shroder, 1961) through the use of *koans*.

To our next session I brought two dried four leaf clovers and a razor blade. After our opening amenities I said:

> Me: "Ronnie, there's something here I'd like you to see." I produced the first of the two clovers from my desk. As soon as he recognized it as a four leaf clover, I promptly pulled off one of the leaves. Holding out the stem and remaining three leaves to him, I asked,
>
> Me: "What is this?"
>
> He: "A four leaf clover with one leaf missing," was his prompt reply.
>
> Me: "Given the choice of calling this a three leaf clover or a four leaf clover, which would you do?"
>
> He: "I would have to call it a four leaf clover."
>
> Me: "But it has only three leaves."
>
> He: "But it had four leaves."
>
> Me: "All right." I proceeded to tear off a second leaf. "Now, given the choice, would you call this a two leaf, three leaf, or four leaf clover?"
>
> He: "I would still have to call it a four leaf clover, although I would prefer to call it a four leaf clover with two leaves missing."
> I then proceeded to pull off another leaf.

Me: "Still a four leaf clover?"

He: "Yes."

I pulled off the final leaf and held up the stem.

Me: "Given the choice of a one, two, three or four leaf clover, what is this I am holding?"

He: (Confused.) "I have difficulty seeing it as any of those."

Me: "Your logic is inconsistent. From the beginning you called what I held in my left hand a four leaf clover, no matter how many leaves it had on it. Now that there are no leaves, why should it be different?"

He: (Long pause.) "I . . . suppose . . . that it still must be a four leaf clover, though it doesn't seem right."

Me: "Then if this is a four leaf clover," I said, holding forth my left hand, "then what are these?" I opened my right hand producing the torn off leaves. He appeared very confused. I sat for a moment while he said nothing, then arose from my chair and went back to my desk.

Me: "Look." I produced the second four leaf clover from my desk along with the razor blade. When he had recognized it as a four leaf clover, I placed the clover on top of a tablet on my desk and carefully cut the stem into two pieces. I then held one piece in each hand. Ronnie watched me attentively.

Me: "Which one of these is the original four leaf clover?"

He: (Slowly.) "They both are."

Me: "Have I in my hands two things or one?"

He: "Two."

Me: "And can each survive or be destroyed independently of the other?"

He: "Yes . . ."

Me: "And can either destroy the other?"

He: "I don't see how."

Me: "Then tell me—how can two things be the same thing and at the same time be independent of one another?"

The young man was very puzzled.

Me: "That is your problem for next week."

He: (Questioning look.) "Why are we doing this?"

Me: "The only answer to be found to that question is in the doing of it."

The key to introducing a *koan* in this manner, especially to a relatively new client, is that it was something that *we* did. We did it together. We shared it. The problem was felt, yet I didn't simply dump it on him.

Sometimes a *koan* occurs incidentally in a session, with very important results, as in the following example.

I had been seeing a Vietnam veteran in his mid 20's who was feeling extremely guilty for "fragging"* one of his officers during the war while on patrol. He had been feeling extremely suicidal, and was caught in the bind of wishing to take his life in repentance while at the same time not wishing to promote further hurt to his wife and young daughter. (They had suffered from his long absence and subsequent depression.) Nevertheless, he was suffering from profound nightmares arising from the fragging incident and other aspects of the war, along with acute insomnia and depression, was unable to perform the duties of his job because of "nervous tension," and had obtained a medical leave of absence from his job. His physician, in turn, referred the young man to me for treatment. I might also add that this was a very passive person who was looking for a doctor or particular kind of medicine which would lift his burden of guilt and depression from him. He was highly dysphoric and an excellent candidate for drug addition (see Greaves, 1974). He had used several kinds of opiates during the war and had acquired some since. Over a period of time we developed a very intense relationship, and I was determined that I would use every province of my skills to keep him both from suiciding and becoming an addict.

On one occasion of our frequent meetings the following occurred:

He: "I did what you said."
Me: "Yes, and what happened?"
He: (Shifting in chair.) "Well, I didn't think it would work, but it did."
Me: "Tell me about it. First of all did you try to catch the trout with your hands."
He: "Well, I honestly don't think there are any trout in that stream."
Me: "That doesn't matter. The point is did you *try?*"
He: (Somewhat to my surprise.) "Well, there were some fish there . . . they weren't very big . . . I don't think they were trout. More like fingerlings."
Me: "What size trout did I ask for?"
He: "You didn't say."
Me: "So what happened?"
He: "Well . . . at first I felt foolish. I was afraid someone would see me and would ask me to explain what I was doing. So what could I do? Tell them I was dipping into the stream with my bare hands out in the middle of the rain trying to catch trout that probably didn't exist because my shrink told me to?"
Me: "Oh, it was raining. That's excellent. Go on."
He: "Then it happened. Some kind of change came over me. I

---

* "Fragging," which was apparently very common in the Vietnamese Conflict, was the art of killing one's superior officer in such a manner that it looked as if the death were due to enemy action.

suddenly came to realize where I was. I was alone, outdoors in the wilderness. And there was the sound of the rain (tearfully) and the trees were very green, and the water was cold on my hands, and my body felt wet all over (voice breaking; long silence) . . . and I stayed there for what seemed like several hours and I was amazed at how wise you were to have prescribed this seemingly pointless act which I first resented you for."

Me: "You see me as *wise?*"

He: "Yes."

Me: "Then you must kill me."

An astonished face. Pause. A look of great hurt.

He: "Kill you? Why would I want to do a thing like that?"

Me: "Only because you must. There is nothing more I have to say about it."

The ancient Zen *koan*, "If you meet a Buddha on the road, kill him!" (or "proverb" to those who have begun to understand the Way of Zen), flowed easily from my lips. Nevertheless, I saw immediately the hurt, the wound, the confusion, the feeling of betrayal. In the middle of the next session, after some considerable "mindfucking," to use Fritz's term, the following interchange occurred, "out of the blue," as it were. This interchange serves as an example of *mondo* growing out of a *koan*.

He: "Why did you tell me to kill you during my last visit?"

Me: (Pause) "Let's see if I can put it in a way that you can understand it. Since you've been coming here, you've been seeking answers to your questions. But you keep asking the wrong questions. What you need are the right questions and your answer to them, not my best answers to your wrong questions."

He: (Long silence; Confusion) "What's that got to do with me killing you?"

Me: "All that I've said is the same."

From the preceding segment it should be obvious that *koan* and *mondo* are complementary. Both approaches present a seeker with a puzzle rather than an answer. The main difference between *koan* and *mondo*, as I see it, is in the more formal, systematized nature of *koans*, and the wider range and relative spontaneity of *mondo*. Nevertheless, the questions which clients raise are often so similar that I have developed a virtual repository of *mondo* interactions, while, to my delight, many of my clients push me to *de nouveau* responses, whereby I am forced to grow.

Some of my repository of *mondo* includes the following:

Pt: I feel lost. I don't know who I am. How do I find myself?

Me: By not looking.

Pt: But if I don't look for myself how am I going to find me?
Me: That is something you will come to know only in the not-looking.

Pt: Everything I touch turns rotten. Every person I approach flees from me. How can I get what I want?
Me: Most important things in life can be gained only if you do not pursue them.
Pt: But if I don't go after what I want, how can I possibly get it?
Me: Only by not going after it.

Pt: I often ask myself "Why am I here? Will it do me any good?"
Me: I often ask myself "Why am I here? Will it do me any good?"
Pt: Do you think it will do me any good?
Me: Do you think it will do me any good?
Pt: Why should it do you any good?
Me: If our relationship serves me no good, how could it possibly serve you good?

Pt: You couldn't possibly be interested in me. You are only listening to me because it is your job.
Me: I have no job.
Pt: What do you mean you have no job? Doesn't someone pay you to sit here and listen to people like me?
Me: No. No one has the power to force me to sit and listen to anyone I don't want to listen to.
Pt: But don't you have a professional obligation to listen to me?
Me: I have no obligations; only choices. When I choose to be somewhere or with someone I try my best to honor that choice. When I choose not to be somewhere or with someone, I try my best to honor that choice, also. Your choices are no different than mine.
Pt: Then I don't bore you?
Me: If I allow myself to bore myself with you, that's my decision, not yours. If I decide to exceed the speed limit on the highways, that is my decision and not yours. If I decide to play the guitar in my own miserable way while watching the national news, that is my decision and not yours. The point is: I choose to be here now.
Pt: I can't believe what you say.
Me: I can't command or control your beliefs even if I kill you, send you to prison, or to a state hospital. I desire only to fight for my own integrity. You, as I, have the choice of being here or not being here, and that choice is modifiable at any moment. So leave, stay, or do neither; just as I will. Choice is the only mystery of life as great as being.

Of the three major approaches to the Way of Zen, I rarely use *zazen* or *schikan-taza*. I am not an adept of *schikan-taza*, and, since I am not turned on to a direct knowledge of the significance of *schikan-taza*, I tend to transmit my doubts to those who are possibly prepared for its discipline. I do, however, make use of deep relaxation techniques, and, from a procedural standpoint, at least, these are often indistinguishable from the lower forms of *zazen*.

But now my thoughts turn abruptly to Tantrism, though I may sound like a commercial—"I use Tantrism less than Zen, but enjoy it more." Let me cite some examples. As in the case of Zen methods, I do not simply instruct my client on what to do (though I used to). I instead demonstrate and instruct him or her on how to proceed. Such instruction is usually given in the presence of incense, a single soft fluorescent light, and often in the semi-lotus position on the carpet in my office. At this point I am also beginning to use select recorded sounds. I often encounter resistance to the introduction of *mantras* and *mandalas* (I don't even attempt to introduce *mudras* until the former have been accepted), because of the strangeness and newness of what they are encountering. However, I have found that resistance is usually overcome by the introduction of two mantras and two mandalas at any given time rather than just one. After gently persuading the person to gaze at the center of one mandala for five minutes, then the other, then back to the first, and so on, I then asked the person if he has a preference between the two. Almost invariably he or she does. I then go on to question about the differences in subjective experiences stimulated by the *mandala*. Persons will say various things about this: that one or the other makes them feel more relaxed, strange, confused, disorganized, etc. And some say they experience no difference between the two at all. In that case I give them the homework assignment of discovering the subjective differences generated by the respective *mandalas*.

I do essentially the same thing with *mantras*. I may introduce *hum* and *vum* at the same time, or, perhaps, *vum* and *yum*. The reason persons are able to accept *mantras* and *mandalas* presented in this way, I perceive, is that it gives them an opportunity to engage in more familiar behavior such as intellectualizing, analyzing, comparing and contrasting. This is, of course, exactly what the process of meditation is trying to avoid. This inconsistency is only apparent, however, for what I have described is the way I prepare people for Tantric meditation; it is not meditation itself. It is a way of setting their fears at ease with a new experience. Once the actual process of meditation is begun, I instruct the person to meditate no more than fifteen minutes a day, at least at first. (This, admittedly, is reminiscent of Tom Sawyer whitewashing the fence, but, once stimulated to meditate, most persons find it far more of a pleasure than a chore.)

I also encourage persons, when possible, to make use of candles, and a wide variety of scents, selected sounds, and even water (applied to forehead, fingertips, lips, etc.) in the course of their meditating. These, then, become, in effect, conditioned stimuli which aid in the attainment and maintenance of deep meditative states. In introducing a person to *mudras*, we begin by playing with our hands. We look at them, explore them, focus on them, play with them, and experiment with them. We experience how it feels to hold our hands in various positions, both apart and together. There are a number of traditional *mudras* with specific names, but I tend to avoid these because they are often tied to specific points in Buddhist doctrine which I avoid altogether. Except for two or three classical *mudras*, which I do introduce, I encourage persons to search for and discover hand positions they find most pleasing in their meditation. What I ultimately aim for in introducing Tantric meditation is a state commonly called "walking meditation." This is the ability to carry on one's daily affairs in a serene, meditative state. It could, of course, be argued that unless my ultimate goal is to help persons attain Enlightenment or Oneness or a lasting state of *satori* through the use of these methods, then I am misusing them altogether. To this I would reply that there are generally many steps on the journey to Enlightenment, and, historically, few have achieved it, though many have sought it. Thus, with the use of these methods I send my clients upon an uncertain journey. If they achieve Enlightenment or perfect Self Awareness, then I rejoice. If they take the journey and do not find Enlightenment, I also rejoice, for the fulfillment and justification of the journey is the journey itself. For those who never journey. . . .

Epilogue

As I stated in my article on meditation and psychotherapy mentioned earlier, it takes no expert on Asiatic religions to apply the methods discussed above. I am neither *guru* nor *roshi* nor *lama*, nor do I represent myself as such. Basically, the mastery of these methods, or at least the educated and productive employment of them, requires familiarity with their precepts, commitment to and feel for their mystical and intuitional aspects, including their largely trans-intellectual bias, experimentation with their use such that one comes to understand their impact (or lack of it), plus considerable sensitivity and intuition as a therapist in knowing when such methods may be optimally applied. This also includes the learning and ability to deal with the feelings of the individual client in this form of treatment, either within or without the context of Gestalt therapy (see Fagan, 1971; Shepherd, 1971).

REFERENCES

BABA RAM DASS: *Be Here Now.* Albuquerque: Lama Foundation, 1971.
BLOFELD, J.: *The Tantric Mysticism of Tibet.* New York: Causeway, 1974.
CHUNG-YUAN, C.: *Original Teachings of Ch'an Buddhism.* New York: Pantheon, 1969.
DeROPP, R.: *The Master Game.* New York: Dell, 1968.
ERIKSON, E.: *Childhood and Society.* New York: Norton, 1950.
FAGAN, J., and SHEPHERD, I.: *Gestalt Therapy Now.* Palo Alto: Science and Behavior Books, 1970; New York: Harper & Row, 1971.
FAGAN, J.: The tasks of the therapist. In J. Fagan and I. Shepherd (Eds.), *Gestalt Therapy Now.* Palo Alto: Science and Behavior Books, 1970; New York: Harper & Row, 1971. Pp. 88-106.
FRANKL, V.: *The Doctor and the Soul.* New York: Knopf, 1955.
FROMM, E.: *Man for Himself.* New York: Holt, Rinehart & Winston, 1947.
FROMM, E.: *The Sane Society.* New York: Holt, Rinehart & Winston, 1955.
FROMM, E., SUZUKI, D. T., DE MARTINO, R.: *Zen Buddhism and Psychoanalysis.* New York: Grove Press, 1960.
GREAVES, G.: Meditation as an adjunct to psychotherapy. *Voices: The Art and Science of Psychotherapy,* 8:50-52, 1972.
GREAVES, G.: Toward an existential theory of drug dependence. *J. Nerv. and Ment. Dis.,* 1974, 159,1,263-274.
HARVEY, O. J., HUNT, H., and SHRODER, H.: *Conceptual Systems and Personality Organization.* New York: Wiley, 1961.
HORNEY, K.: *The Neurotic Personality of Our Time.* New York: Norton, 1937.
JAMES, W.: *The Varieties of Religious Experience.* London: Longmans Green, 1907; New York: Collier, 1961. (Contemporary edition.)
JUNG, C. G.: *The Undiscovered Self.* New York: New American Library, 1957.
JUNG, C. G.: *The Portable Jung,* Edited by J. Campbell. New York: Viking, 1971.
KAPLEAU, P.: *The Three Pillars of Zen.* Boston: Beacon Press, 1967.
KELLY, G.: *The Psychology of Personal Constructs.* New York: Norton, 1955.
KIERKEGAARD, S.: *A Kierkegaard Anthology,* Edited by R. Brettall. Princeton: Princeton U. Press, 1946.
KOPP, S.: *Guru.* Palo Alto. Science and Behavior Books, 1971.
KOPP, S.: *If You See the Buddha on the Road, Kill Him!* Palo Alto: Science and Behavior Books, 1972.
LAO TSU: *Tao te ching.* Trans. by Gio-fu Feng and J. English. New York: Random House, 1972.
MASLOW, A.: *Toward a Psychology of Being.* New York: Van Nostrand, 1961.
MAY, R.: *Man's Search for Himself.* New York: Norton, 1953.
PERLS, F., HEFFERLINE, R., and GOODMAN, P.: *Gestalt Therapy.* New York: Dell, 1951.
PERLS, F.: *Ego, Hunger and Aggression.* New York: Random House, 1969. (a)

PERLS, F.: *Gestalt Therapy Verbatim.* Moab, Utah: Real People Press, 1969 (b).

PERLS, F.: *In and Out the Garbage Pail.* Moab, Utah: Real People Press, 1969. (c)

POLSTER, E., and POLSTER, M.: *Gestalt Therapy Integrated.* New York: Brunner/ Mazel, 1973.

POLANYI, M.: *Personal Knowledge: Towards a Post-Critical Philosophy.* New York: Harper & Row, 1967.

ROGERS, C.: *On Becoming a Person.* New York: Houghton-Mifflin, 1961.

ROSS, N. W.: *The World of Zen.* New York: Knopf/Random House, 1960.

ROSS, N. W.: *Three Ways of Asian Wisdom.* New York: Simon and Schuster, 1966.

SHEPHERD, I.: *Limitations and Cautions in the Gestalt Approach.* Palo Alto: Science and Behavior Books, 1971. Pp. 234-238.

SUZUKI, D. T.: *An Introduction to Zen Buddhism.* London: Rider, 1949.

WATTS, A.: *The Way of Zen.* New York: Pantheon, 1957.

14

Gestalt Psychotherapy, Zen Buddhism and Transcendental Meditation

JAMES A. STALLONE, Ph.D.

For as many growth or spiritual movements as are underway in America today, there are as many individuals saying that practically every movement is *meaning* the same thing but *saying* it in different words. My purpose here will be to bring to light some commonalities and differences present in three major contemporary movements across the land today: Gestalt Psychotherapy, Zen Buddhism and Transcendental Meditation, in order to show that the paths are many but the goal is the same. Call that goal by any name: *Awareness, Now, Enlightenment, Nirvana, Bliss Consciousness, Ultimate Union,* or no name at all—it is the same. The differences lie on the path level. Thus, many paths, but one goal. Fortunately, as we will see, there seem to be more commonalities than differences on the paths as well.

What a melting pot we are in America even when it comes to achieving life's most ultimate experiences! Germany puts in Gestalt, Japan puts in Zen, and India, Transcendental Meditation. Such a situation is at once a blessing and a possible source of confusion. It is a blessing because it affords us an opportunity to bring together into one, grand synthesis the various orientations of the family of man. And it is a source of confusion because if we try to follow several paths at once, most of us run into the same difficulty as a tourist in a strange town following the advice of several different but well meaning guides—we get lost. The sage conclusion we can draw from this is that it is best to pick one path and follow it—unless, of course, one is already a highly evolved person with a most

202

discriminating intellect. Of course, we may highly recommend our path to others, but whatever we do we don't have to take the responsibility of selection because we couldn't if we wanted to, and if we do try hard enough, we might wind up in another Holy Inquisition with an army of fanatics bent on saving the world through destroying it.

What is Gestalt? What is Zen? What is Transcendental Meditation? One Gestalt story is that someone once asked an accomplished Gestaltist, "What is Gestalt?" and received as an answer "When I didn't know, I couldn't tell you; now that I know, I can't tell you." Another story, this time bearing on Zen, relates that a novice approached the master or roshi and asked, "What is the experience of Zen?" only to receive a slap in the face. Maharishi Mahesh Yogi, in one of his lectures, was describing the ultimate experience of Transcendental Meditation and stated that he could summarize the description he had given in one word, "indescribable." This writer, too, is stuck to describe the indescribable experience, and can only state modestly that Gestalt, Zen and Transcendental Meditation are practical approaches to the experience of "Reality."

One development shared by all three movements is the recent rapid growth of each. Gestalt has blossomed into a major therapeutic approach likely to equal or better the popularity of psychoanalysis. Gestalt Institutes offering a variety of programs are popping up, and one need only scan recent psychological meeting/workshop agendas to find evidence of its popularity. While the introduction of Zen in America occurred a good many years ago, its popularity is recent. There currently exist several Zen centers and numerous teachers, both Japanese and American. Popular literature and television (Kung Fu) have also contributed their share to bringing Buddhist concepts to the American eye. The Transcendental Meditation movement now claims close to half a million meditators and thousands of teachers in the United States alone, and an ambitious "world plan" is already well off the ground. Obviously, the growth of all three is part of a greater spiritual movement currently underway in America, particularly among young people. This movement includes encounter-growth groups, peace movements, shared communities, religious-spiritual groups of all types, and "back to nature" movements, to name a few.

The distillation of the Gestalt psychology into a psychotherapeutic medium is principally the work of Ferderick S. Perls (1947, 1969 a, b; Perls et al., 1951), the founder of the Gestalt Institute in America, and himself a practitioner and exemplar of his theory. His wife and co-founder, Laura Perls (1968), has added publications, and a more recent book edited by Joen Fagan and Irma Shepherd (1970) presents a fairly complete body of literature.

Perhaps knowledge of Zen in America has come more from books than from oral teachings. One prominent name comes to mind, that of Daisetz Teitaro Suzuki, an extensively published Japanese (1949, 1959, 1960, 1962) whose works far exceed those cited here. Suzuki has been widely recognized as not only a writer but a living embodiment of Zen. Two students of his, the Englishman, Christmas Humphreys (1949, 1962), and the American, Alan Watts (1957, 1958), have also made significant contributions to the understanding of Zen in America. Other writers include Isshu Miura and Ruth Fuller Sasaki (1965), Phillip Kapleau (1965), an American roshi, and the Japanese, Shindai Sekiguchi (1970).

Clearly, the knowledge of Transcendental Meditation in America has come from the spoken and written words of Maharishi Mahesh Yogi (1963, 1969). Maharishi is always careful, however, to emphasize that this knowledge in its pure form comes from the ancient and long line of Vedic masters in India and, as such, is not new, only re-introduced. Another book, by Forem (1973), discusses the history of the movement, basic principles and some firsthand experiences, while many leading periodicals (Wallace and Benson, 1972; Levine, 1972) have recognized weighty experimental research evidence and educational support. A systematic theory called the Science of Creative Intelligence, which puts the practice of Transcendental Meditation into a more universal perspective, is also the subject of a course popular on many leading college and university campuses.

The convergence/concordance of all three movements is seen vividly in their emphasis on the present or "now" experience. Gestaltists constantly stress the point by claiming that we can only live in the now. Perls (1970) has stated: *"To me, nothing exists except the now. Now = experience = awareness = reality. The past is no more, the future not yet."* If we try to live in the future, that distance between now and the future is filled by anxiety or restlessness, and if we try to live in the past, the distance between past and now is taken up by guilt or idle remembrances. Indeed, practically all verbal interchange in Gestalt psychotherapy is carried out in the present tense.

The Buddha himself preached the Eternal Now as the timeless still point and ever-present awareness in human consciousness. Zen crystallizes the notion most clearly in suddenness of the satori or Enlightenment experience, like hearing the resonance of a bell in the clear air. We cannot experience the bell as past or future. We can only think about it or talk about it (verbalized thought) as past or future. This "aboutness" is not Zen, since Zen is not here about, but right here and now as the bell resonates. Hence, the master's reply to the student's question *about* the meaning of Reality is simply pointing out the bamboo grove over yonder.

The emphasis in Transcendental Meditation is also on the present, and particularly the improvement of day-to-day life. There is little or no discussion about concerns tomorrow might bring, the life hereafter, or the "astral" world, and only the simple advice to "take it as it comes." In fact, Maharishi's (1963) advice to psychologists is that "*Analyzing an individual's way of thinking and bringing to the conscious level the buried misery of the past, even for the purpose of enabling him to see the cause of stress and suffering, is highly deplorable, since it helps to strengthen directly the impressions of the miserable past and serves to suppress his consciousness in the present.*"

One need only reflect (not for long, please) on the peak experiences of one's daily life to realize that such experiences take place in the now, not with preoccupation in past or future. Really seeing a beautiful flower, hearing music absorbedly, sexual lovemaking, and a unique insight into one's behavior are just a few examples of the complete presentness of Now behavior.

In Western civilization it would be an acceptable practice to hang up a sign which says "Think." A Zennist, Gestaltist or Transcendental Meditator meditating would most likely hang up a sign saying "No Thinking." The suspension of thought is a vital phenomenon in all approaches. Shikan-taza is a principal form of Zen meditation which is simply (in theory, but not in practice) the absence of thought. Creative awareness can only come out of the absence of memory which influences our thoughts with "pastness." What is creative is new, not old. Thus, when thought is suspended, then, and only then, is transformation possible. In like manner, if we compare Rodin's piece of sculpture, "The Thinker," a man with tightened muscles of body and head resting on fist, with that of the sitting Buddha, serenely smiling and composed, we see effort versus effortlessness. As long as thought continues, so do effort and striving. Effort and striving mean a goal not yet reached. A Zen koan or puzzle such as "Who is it that is thinking?" is often given to the aspirant for solution, thus putting him in the squirrel cage of thought and driving home the notion that thinking cannot solve the most basic problem of Existence. Gestalt psychotherapy, as well, considers thought as mere "mental rehearsal." How can we ever be really present in our "acting" if we continue to "rehearse?" The unconditioned aspect of human behavior cannot come out of the conditioned. When we stop the vicious circle of thought and talk, the moment of uncluttered awareness is reached. The practice of Transcendental Meditation also relegates thinking to a somewhat humbler level of consciousness, since to the question, "What is transcended in Transcendental Meditation?" comes the obvious answer, "thought." Thought itself is taken to subtler and subtler levels until the most refined thought is reached, transcended, and pure consciousness brought into being.

It must be cautioned, however, that none of the three movements is advocating that man's life must be "thoughtless," since productive thoughts aid our evolution, but only that it is necessary to bring thought to a restful standstill in order that it may come out with the qualities of power, clarity, pointedness and creativity, rather than weakness, confusion, circuitousness and destructiveness.

The directness, immediacy or timelessness of the awareness, satori or transcendental experience is another factor common to all three approaches. Teachers of Transcendental Meditation are quick to point out that transcending leads to bliss consciousness, and that experience is one which is infinite, timeless and boundless. The mind is conscious, but not of space or time, only of itself. Meditators often state after meditation that time seemed to stand still, but only after meditation, since analyzing time standing still while meditating is tantamount to being further trapped in the illusion of time. The direct experience of bliss consciousness, rather than merely reading about it, talking about it, or contemplating it, is felt to be essential in Transcendental Meditation. This timeless experience, along with the "suddenness" characteristic of peak experiences or satori, is shared by the other two approaches. The story of the Zen novice who became so weary of his time-consuming efforts at achieving satori is classic. He lit a stick of incense and held it in one hand while grasping a dagger in the other, and vowed to kill himself if the incense burnt down without his experiencing satori. As the glowing stick was about to burn his fingers, the block of ice shattered and his mind broke into awakening. This experience in its timeless occurrence is from "moment to moment" and typifies Zen awareness.

In Gestalt as well, we see the immediacy of experiencing. The early Gestalt experiments emphasized the "Aha!" nature of any authentic or creative learning experience. It was only when the disparate elements came together during the "thoughtless" incubation moment that real learning took place. Momentary and powerful transformation is an apparent and key element in the Gestalt psychotherapeutic happening.

Toward the end of his life, Perls began to refer to these experiences as "mini satoris," thus pointing to his recognition of the like occurrence in Zen. The question whether transformation takes place through one great immediate realization or through a gradual series of lesser realizations is one to which Zennists and Transcendental Meditators would most likely answer, "Both." Certainly, none would deny the necessity of the direct, immediate realization.

Unconscious processes are dealt with similarly in the three schools. While recognized, such processes are not intentionally analyzed or directly managed. During one's zazen (Zen meditation) practice there often occurs the welling up of unconscious forces in the form of fears, exhilarations, various sensory hallucinations, and bodily apparitions. Zen masters caution the aspirant against such occurrences and realize that this reservoir of repressed or inherited unconscious material must be brought to the surface only to be cleared away. Such material is looked upon as "makyo," or evil distractors whose importance is only secondary in one's practice. True awareness of reality is compared with grasping an iron bar with one's bare hands, without such "side trips" as hallucinations or delusions. Gestaltists as well would agree that their approach is one which stresses the "utmost surface" of consciousness, rather than the utmost depth as in psychoanalysis. The patient's or client's past history is not essential in Gestalt psychotherapy, since it begins where he is right now, not where he was. The integration of the past with the present is taken as a "fringe benefit" of the awareness experience. In Transcendental Meditation the word "unconscious" is scarcely to be found, since it is consciousness and not unconsciousness out of which creative intelligence springs, and when consciousness disappears (as in coma) or is overshadowed by stress, then the birthright of man is lost. The presence of deep seated stresses in the nervous system of man are looked at as blocks to fulfillment which need to be released but not dwelled on or analyzed, since dwelling on the stresses or analyzing them serves only to increase stress. The unconscious causes of behavior can best be dealt with by bringing the light of bliss consciousness where the darkness of stress exists. Thus, by gaining rest, deeper than sleep, in meditation, man releases his stresses physiologically, purifies his nervous system, and opens his creative intelligence to such an extent that further stresses are not taken on. Ultimately, distinctions between conscious and unconscious processes become unnecessary, since both are completely available to the man of Awareness. In this regard, the simplicity and practicality of Transcendental Meditation, Zen, and Gestalt stand in bas relief to the great complexity and theoretical exhortations of many philosophies, psychotherapies, and religions.

The subject of religion presents another similarity between the three movements. Gestalt and Transcendental Meditation are not thought of as religions, and Zen sometimes is and sometimes is not. Rather than belabor the definitions of "religion," it might serve to point out that none of the three has heralded any set of moral tenets, rights or wrongs, "shoulds" or "should nots" concerning personal and social behavior. Gestaltists are generally open to all sorts of different and experimental life-styles. It has been reported that Zen aspirants and the masters themselves have on occasion burned statues of the Buddha, tippled heavily, and engaged in various shocking behaviors. Transcendental Meditators are constantly encouraged to take it easy and enjoy life, since the problem is not desires but the inability to fulfill desires. Certainly, this doesn't mean that immortality is present or condoned. What it does mean is that the emphasis is on the "end" of Awareness, Enlightenment and Ultimate Union rather than on any "means" of moralizing, dictating rules and regulations, fault finding and squelching desire. The written or unwritten message of all three movements seems to be that on the path to the end, desires will not attach themselves to us, but increased awareness and natural intelligence puts us in tune with the wholesome evolution of all creation.

In terms of goals, then, we can see that Gestalt, Zen and Transcendental Meditation are similar. It is true that, in comparison, the stated goals of Gestalt such as growth, awareness, creativity and integration in human behavior are somewhat mild compared to the Zen goals of Buddha-mind, ken-chu-to (perfect inner freedom), and the Domain of Non-Form, or to the higher goals of Transcendental Meditation such as God-Consciousness and Unity-Consciousness. What can be said, however, is that as far as the basics of the goal are concerned, we find more similarities than differences among the three movements.

What are the differences on the path? Essentially, we find an emphasis on "technique" in Zen and Transcendental Meditation that is not found in Gestalt. In Transcendental Meditation, regular practice for 15 to 20 minutes morning and evening is a necessity. Only through the systematic alternation of deep rest and activity can the benefits accrue. One may skip the meditation occasionally or frequently and still evolve, since evolution is an ongoing natural phenomenon, but rapid strides in the evolution of consciousness come through regular practice. Meditators are also strongly urged to complement their meditation experiences with knowledge gained from books, video-tapes, meetings, residence course weekends, and the like. The knowledge is felt to be necessary for proper guidance and elimination of confusion along the path. Also it is essential that one receive an individualized "mantra" (thought-sound) for use in meditation and the technique itself from a specially trained teacher of Transcendental Meditation.

Many Zennists have emphasized that reliance on any technique would foster attachment and not the unattached demeanor so characteristic of an Enlightened person. There have emerged, however, certain methods or approaches which have been traditionally utilized. In Zen, meditation has been advocated most extensively, and the zendo or meditation hall is a familiar structure at most centers. Meditation usually proceeds from concentration on the counting of breaths, to watching the breath, to "thoughtless" attention and the concentration of one's efforts on "solving" a particular koan. Other Zen methods would include individual sessions (dokusan) with the master or roshi, chanting, manual labor, and an occasional discourse (teisho). Depending on the Zen school, these techniques are occasionally voluntary, but more often required.

In Gestalt, techniques are played down as "gimmicky" or "crutches." What is important is the process, rather than the content or technique. Although this is so, people consistently come for individual or group therapy and undergo the ritual of the "hotseat" and other techniques, such as speaking in the present tense: "Now I am aware of . . .," the alter ego or role play situation with an imaginary, significant other or phenomenal self, tuning into one's bodily feelings at the moment, and relating and experiencing dreams in the present tense. The techniques are there, but no Gestaltist says that they are necessary or required.

When it comes to "how long will it take," we find some difference among the three approaches. While none would deny that instant complete realizations is possible for some, they would not say it is likely for everyone. Gestalt and Transcendental Meditation people hold that thirteen years on the analyst's couch or in a monastery is not at all necessary, and that the process is a rapid, emerging and evolving one characterized by progressive growth and improvements. "Two steps forward and one step back" is a favorite byline with both. On the other hand, Zen stresses the necessity of satori and doesn't deny that indeed it might take thirteen years, with agony present right up to the last minute.

How much work or effort will it take? Despite an "effortless" goal, the literature of Zen is replete with admonitions to work harder on the path and to concentrate more and more on one's meditation. The severity of many Zen masters and the austerity of the Zen life is also well known.

As in Zen, Gestalt does not play down the presence of pain and suffering. Dramatic releases of pain and the struggle with one's own existence are common therapeutic occurrences. Quite the opposite is emphasized in Transcendental Meditation. The claim is that no man need suffer since the natural state of man is "joy." The meditation itself is widely reported to be an "easy," "natural," and "charming" process that any effort or concentration will spoil. Deep stresses are released naturally and gradually so as not to overwhelm the nervous system. Meditators agree that theirs is not the "only" way, just the "quickest" and "easiest."

Even with these differences along the path, we can still conclude that the three movements are more in agreement than disagreement. Fortunately for us, there is now something available for everyone, and the last thing we need is competition among growth or spiritual groups. If this day and age is really the dawning of the Age of Awareness for the family of man, as many believe, then we need all the help we can get— be it from Gestalt Psychotherapy, Zen Buddhism, or Transcendental Meditation.

REFERENCES

FAGAN, J., and SHEPHERD, I. (Eds.): *Gestalt Therapy Now*. Palo Alto: Science and Behavior Books, 1970.

FOREM, J.: *Transcendental Meditation: Maharishi Mahesh Yogi and the Science of Creative Intelligence*. New York: Dutton, 1973.

HUMPHREYS, C.: *Zen, A Way of Life*. New York: Emerson, 1962.

HUMPHREYS, C.: *Zen Buddhism*. New York: Macmillan, 1949.

KAPLEAU, P. (Ed.): *The Three Pillars of Zen*. New York: Harper & Row, 1965.

LEVINE, P.: Transcendental Meditation and Science of Creative Intelligence. *Phi Delta Kappan*, Dec. 1972.

MAHARISHI MAHESH YOGI: *Transcendental Meditation* (formerly titled *The Science of Being and the Art of Living*). New York: New American Library, 1963. P. 256.

MAHARISHI MAHESH YOGI: *Maharishi Mahesh Yogi on the Bhagavad-Gita: A New Translation and Commentary*. Baltimore: Penguin Books, 1969.

MIURA, I., and SASAKI, R. F.: *The Zen Koan*. New York: Harcourt Brace and World, 1965.

PERLS, F. S.: *Gestalt Therapy Verbatim*. Lafayette, Cal.: Real People Press, 1969. (a)

PERLS, F. S.: *In and Out the Garbage Pail*. Lafayette, Cal.: Real People Press, 1969. (b)

PERLS, F. S.: *Ego, Hunger and Aggression*. New York: Random House, 1947.

PERLS, F. S.: Four Lectures. In J. Fagan and I. Shepherd (Eds.), *Gestalt Therapy Now*. Palo Alto, Cal.: Science and Behavior Books, 1970. P. 14.

PERLS, F. S., GOODMAN, P., and HEFFERLINE, N.: *Gestalt Therapy: Excitement and Growth in Human Personality*. New York: Julian Press, 1951.

PERLS, L.: Two Instances of Gestalt Therapy and Notes on the Psychology of Give and Take. In P. Pursglove (Ed.), *Recognitions in Gestalt Therapy*. New York: Harper & Row, 1968.

SEKIGUCHI, S.: *Zen, A Manual for Westerners*. Tokyo and San Francisco: Japan Publications, 1970.

SUZUKI, D. T.: *Essays in Zen Buddhism*. New York: Grove, 1949.

SUZUKI, D. T.: *The Essentials of Zen Buddhism*. New York: Dutton, 1962.

SUZUKI, D. T.: *Zen and Japanese Culture*. New York: Pantheon, 1959.

SUZUKI, D. T.: *Manual of Zen Buddhism*. New York: Grove, 1960.

WALLACE, R., and BENSON, H.: The Physiology of Meditation. *Scientific American*, Feb. 1972.

WATTS, A.: *The Way of Zen*. New York: Pantheon, 1957.

WATTS, A.: *The Spirit of Zen*. New York: Grove, 1958.

15

Taoism and Gestalt Therapy

by CHARLES GAGARIN

Psychotherapy, though a relatively new science in the West, has been, for centuries, an essential part of many Eastern doctrines. The Taoists have always recognized that the individual must become integrated. His conflicting forces must be brought into balance and harmony. In other words, he must become centered. For the Taoist, to aim at spiritual development without the concomitant centering of the individual, would be like building the wheels of a cart and neglecting the cart's framework.

When Fritz Perls and others developed Gestalt therapy, they provided a form of psychotherapy that shares Taoism's directness and immediacy.

The nuts and bolts of Gestalt fit neatly into the philosophical framework of Taoism, and the two form an effective working combination. Taoist Gestalt provides an excellent path not only for centering, but also for spiritual growth.

What Is Taoism?

Taoism, with roots going back to the beginning of Chinese culture, is based on the Tao, the first cause and underlying essence of all. The Tao is invisible, yet through it the world is made manifest; formless, yet it permeates all forms. It is like a great cosmic river that flows through all things. It is the Way, the path, and the goal. It is the dynamic interaction of yin and yang, of positive and negative, of male and female. It is the mother of all things.

The Sage: With this construct, the Taoist writers Lao Tsu and Chaung Tsu describe the perfect man as the sage who learns to flow with the Tao. He is ego-free and at one with the world. With this total peace and harmony, he does not push, but lets the cosmic tide carry him. He is like a man who travels down a great river on a raft. He exerts no effort, yet he travels far. The Taoist sage practices effortless effort, and action through non-action. Like the man who has a hobby which later grows into a full-time business, he does his thing and gets paid for it, too.

Being Centered: The sage has no desires and no demanding ego. Things come easily to him. Being detached and content, he suffers no loss. Being centered and aware, he stays in the now.

> Thus the sage knows without traveling.
> He sees without looking.
> He works without doing.
> *(Lao Tsu—trans. Feng, 1972, chapter 47)*

Taoist sages have been called "Cloud Water People" because they float like clouds and flow like water. Chuang Tsu said of them,

> the true man of old slept without dreaming and woke without anxiety. His food was plain, and his breath was deep. Carefree he went. Carefree he came. That was all. He did not forget his beginning and did not seek his end. He accepted what was given with delight, and when it was gone, gave it no more thought.
> *(Chuang Tsu, trans, Feng, 1974, p. 114)*

The sage teaches by example. His gift to the world is the Tao, and the peace he brings by being in it. Chuang Tsu and Lao Tsu give many instructions on how to live, but both recognize the ultimate change as an internal one and a matter of consciousness. Though the Taoist may act paradoxically, he still remains within the flow. Whether he is a ruler, a hermit or a cook, he works in perfect rhythm and harmony.

COMMON GROUND

Taoism and Gestalt have much in common. Both aim at balancing the forces within the individual—reaching the zero-point or center. Both recognize that with this centering there is an improved perspective and increased awareness. Both believe in the wisdom of the organism, as opposed to rational intelligence. Both believe in being in the "here and now."

Growing Up: Good Gestalt helps the patient remove the blocks that keep him from standing on his own two feet. Fritz Perls viewed the mature person as one who does not need to manipulate others for support. Perls was fond of saying, "Gestalt therapy is wiping your own ass." Likewise, the Taoist has no need to manipulate others. He stands independent and alone.

Awareness: Understanding what is going on is essential to Gestalt therapy. The therapist must be centered, and have his inner static turned down, so he can be more aware of others. As he works with a patient, he helps that person become aware of the blocks and forces at work within him. Once this awareness is achieved, the patient can begin to complete the unfinished work, or "Gestalt." Awareness, then action, then a restoration of the balance. As in Taoism, an increased awareness in Gestalt helps the person become centered and grow in harmony with his environment.

Action Through Non-Action: The master Gestalt therapist lets the patient do the work. He observes, and brings awareness to the patient. Then, through the "hotseat" method, the patient helps himself by acting out the different aspects of his conflict. Fritz Perls often refused to answer questions such as, "May I sit down?", shifting the burden of responsibility back to the asker. If Perls wanted to arouse a patient or say he was bored, he would pretend to fall asleep (and sometimes did). This is Taoist action through non-action in the truest sense.

While both Taoism and Gestalt aim at centering the individual and bringing the forces within him to a balanced harmony, Taoism goes one step farther. For the Taoist, centering and awareness are essential, but beyond that comes the spiritual state of enlightenment—the unity with all things in which man flows with the Tao.

TAOIST GESTALT

The concept of Taoist Gestalt is no book-bound theory. It has been practiced many years by Gia-Fu-Feng at the Stillpoint Foundation, a Taoist meditation center in the mountains. Gia-Fu was present at the creation of Esalen, where he spent several years walking endless miles, meditating, and conducting workshops. There he got to know Fritz Perls and his technique. After he founded Stillpoint, Taoism and Gestalt therapy were to merge into a distinctive blend that was felt throughout the day's activities.

Though Stillpoint, like a living organism, is always changing, the following description is based upon the author's experience there in 1971.

Meditation and Chanting: Stillpoint's schedule was fixed around the rising and setting of the sun. An hour before sunrise, the Stillpointers, whose numbers ranged from about fifteen to thirty, got up to meditate together. Since the quieting of the mind and centering are both important factors in full human development, meditation was a useful tool towards such an end. At sunrise, the group began to chant "om." This varied in mood and texture according to the day. Sometimes it was smooth and peaceful; other times it was loud and cathartic. After meditation and chanting, the group generally sensed a great feeling of calm and togetherness.

The Daily Meeting: After breakfast, the gong was rung for the morning meeting. The meeting first dealt with any daily business or announcements of the community, and then developed into a Taoist encounter which will be discussed later. The meeting was the focus of the day.

Tai Chi: After the meeting, there were several hours of free time. Gia-Fu, who walked ten miles a day, encouraged others to do the same, and much walking-meditation resulted. At sunset the group met on a hill facing west and followed Gia-Fu in Tai Chi Chuan—a form of Chinese moving meditation in which one becomes more aware of his body and his "chi," the life energy which circulates through it.

After Tai Chi, the Stillpointers would eat, take saunas or baths, rap, and retire around nine o'clock.

Long-Term: Though there were always short-term visitors, most Stillpointers stayed for several months; some for years. Unlike most weekend workshops, the daily encounter sessions involved a community of people who lived, meditated, ate, and worked together. There was an easy-going mood without the fear of the unknown or the sense of urgency that often exists in short-term workshops. No one felt compelled to work out all his problems in a day. The tempo was slow, and the interaction flowed.

Chop Suey Therapy: The morning meetings varied according to the mood of the day, sometimes quiet and peaceful, sometimes loud and violent, but the presence of the leader, Gia-Fu-Feng, was always felt. He believed in a "chop suey" therapy: using all available methods including baths and walks. He used imagery, dreams, physical tremors, drama, or fantasy to express the Tao, to bring out the Tao in other people. Often "the hot-seat" was used to focus on a particular person, but the group was also involved, as Gia-Fu put it, "so the Tao becomes manifested—a group awareness."

Liberation: The modern Taoist views the three phases of life as first, the original nature of the child, second, the layers of society impressed upon the individual, and finally, when possible, liberation. With liberation, the individual returns to the original nature of the child, but brings with him an increased awareness. The Taoist Gestalt encounter tries to help the individual become centered so that he can more easily gain liberation.

Liberation entails being ego free—the state of "no me," or "Wu Wo" in Chinese. To accomplish this, one goes through a period of humbleness —"Little me" or "Hsiao Wo," and then boasting therapy—"Big me" or "Ta Wo." Often, at Stillpoint, boasting therapy was employed. An individual could parade around saying, "I'm the greatest!" No blame.

Blithering: The master therapist merges his ego with the group, and his work becomes effortless effort. He lets the people come to him. He does not force anything out. When the group begins to become vocal, he observes, and provides feedback. The Taoist therapist encourages "blithering," like a "blithering idiot." To "blither" is to talk off the top of your head without stopping to think, and, therefore, without blocks. Blithering allows the essential nature of the person to come through.

Anger: As important as blithering is the release of anger or resentment (getting your shit out) similar to Janov's Primal Scream Therapy, though not necessarily as intense. Once the anger is released, the person can truly begin to function and live. "Getting the shit out" is especially important at a community where thirty people live at relatively close quarters. Tension builds like the electricity in the air before a storm. Only when the thunder and lightning of anger come and pass can peace be restored. By making anger socially acceptable, the explosions caused by interpersonal friction become small and harmless rather than large and damaging.

Stillpointers often let out their steam in the controlled environment of the meeting which often leads directly into a group therapy focus on one of the two involved. Many times the anger stems from an internal problem merely triggered by some small external event. Group living helps determine whether the cause is internal or external. For example, Sue vents her irritation in the meeting about something Joe has been doing. The other group members, who have also been living with Joe and Sue, give their own reactions. Sometimes the other members will add, "Yea, Joe, that's been bugging me, too." The focus moves to Joe. If, on the other hand, no one else is bothered by Joe's actions, the focus usually moves to Sue who could be projecting her problem onto Joe.

This group interaction facilitates the uncovering of the problem which then can begin to be worked out with Gestalt and other methods.

Master Therapist: The master therapist tries to reach the essential nature of the patient—the "suchness." Through meditation, walks, and the encounter sessions, the person begins to get a better idea of his true being. Also, the therapist, who must be detached and centered himself, helps others become aware of cosmic intelligence and organic wisdom (such as the body's powers to regulate itself). He avoids emphasis on human intelligence. Meditation is a great aid to such awareness.

The therapist gets his own therapy by giving therapy. He does what feels right at the moment. There are no rules, no gimmicks; he only follows the flow. He lets anything (short of violence) happen. If the meeting goes to hell, so what. There is no such thing as an unsuccessful meeting, no pattern each meeting has to fit in.

The therapist is quiet inside, so he can perceive others without distortion; he is at one with the patient, and even when he rages, there is love. As in Zen, he can shock a student out of his confusion by raging at him, or even by throwing him out of the meeting. Gia-Fu was once admonished that a cure would take a long time. "Bah," he replied, "does lightning take time?"

The Taoist lets the person get into the feeling. If the person is depressed, let him really feel depressed, let him cry and moan. Only when he becomes at one with the feeling will the feeling leave.

He can use "humor-healing." Most people have "buttons"—emotional sore spots to which they react quickly. The therapist can constantly "push" this button until the situation becomes humorous and the button disappears. For instance, if a person hates to have others put their hands on his shoulder, the therapist will do this at various times until the situation becomes humorous, and no longer a button to be pushed.

In conclusion, Taoism and Gestalt come together to form an effective, versatile form of therapy. The therapist in Taoist Gestalt is limited only by his imagination. The techniques of Gestalt fit well into the framework of Taoism, and Taoist thought likewise adds a solid philosophical base to Gestalt. Taoist Gestalt is dynamic and flexible, and, most important, it works.

REFERENCES

Chuang Tsu: *Inner Chapters.* Trans. by Gia-Fu-Feng and J. English. New York: Random House, 1974.
Lao Tsu: *Tao Teh Ching.* Trans. by Gia-Fu-Feng and J. English. New York: Random House, 1972.

Part VI

A SUMMING UP

To conclude this volume, Laura Perls has presented, in her typical, clearly stated style, what she sees as the essence of Gestalt therapy— the awareness continuum, the contact boundary, and support. She emphasizes that Gestalt therapy is a hypothesis, not a rigid Gestalt, and that each Gestalt therapist can bring with him whatever skills and knowledge he has in order to illuminate awareness, make contact, and, when appropriate, provide support.

16

Comments on the New Directions

LAURA PERLS, D.Sc.

The German word "Gestalt" is untranslatable into a single English term. It covers a multitude of related concepts like countenance, shape, form, figure, configuration, structural entity, a whole that is something more than, or different from, the sum of its parts. A Gestalt stands out from the background, it "exists," and the relationship of a figure to its ground is what we call "meaning." If this relationship is tenuous or non-existent, or if, for whatever reasons (cultural, educational), we are unable to recognize and understand it, we say: "It doesn't make sense." It is absurd, bizarre, meaningless.

Whatever exists is here and now. The past exists now as memory, nostalgia, regret, resentment, phantasy, legend, history. The future exists here and now in the actual present as anticipation, planning, rehearsal, expectation and hope, or dread and despair. Gestalt therapy takes its bearing from *what is* here and now, not from what *has been* or what *should be*. It is an existential-phenomenological approach, and as such it has to be experiential and experimental. Thus talking "about" Gestalt therapy is really quite contrary to the philosophy of Gestalt.

The *actual experience* of any present situation does not need to be explained or interpreted; it can be directly contacted, felt and described here and now. Gestalt therapy deals with the obvious, with what is *immediately* available to the awareness of client or therapist and can be shared and expanded in the actual ongoing communication. The aim of Gestalt therapy is the *awareness continuum*, the freely ongoing Gestalt formation where what is of greatest concern and interest to the organism, the relationship, the group or society becomes Gestalt, comes into the foreground where it can be fully experienced and coped with (acknowl-

221

edged, worked through, sorted out, changed, disposed of, etc.) so that then it can melt into the background (be forgotten or assimilated and integrated) and leave the foreground free for the next relevant Gestalt.

Any *fixed* Gestalt in time becomes a block. In psychoanalytic terms, one would speak of complexes, inhibitions, and resistances, and look for their origin and causes in past early experience. But the fixation is not *on* and *in* the *past;* it is right here and now in the still activated muscular tensions, the habitual and automatic behavior patterns and social attitudes which have become second nature. Automatisms save energy and are useful when they support the ongoing life process. In Gestalt therapy we work through the resistances by deautomatizing those behavior patterns which have become impediments by bringing them into the foreground where they can be experienced again as conscious activities that the patient can then take responsibility for: "This is what *I* am doing. What does that do for me? Do I want to do that now? What else could I do?" With the increasing awareness of *how? where? when? to what extent?,* the *why?* either becomes self-evident or unimportant. We can experiment with alternatives here and now, and change becomes possible.

The fixed Gestalt as a block applies not only in personal, social and scientific development. I see it also and particularly in the theories and practice of psychotherapy. I think of any theory (including Gestalt) not as holy script but rather as a working hypothesis, a serviceable device for the description, communication, and rationalization of our particular personal approach. And in practice I would rather speak of *style,* a unified integrated way of expression and communication, than of definite prescribed techniques. The experiments are not fixed constellations of technical steps, but invented ad hoc to facilitate awareness of *what is.* Fritz Perls—with a pre-psychiatry history of interest and active involvement in the theater—would use a psycho-dramatic approach. Other Gestalt therapists work with art, music, poetry, philosophy, meditation, yoga, and other body awareness methods like sensitivity training, modern dance, Alexander and Rolfing techniques, bio-energetics, Arica training, eye exercises and whatever else they have assimilated and integrated into their total functioning. So it is not Gestalt therapy *and* body awareness, or Gestalt therapy *and* art, or Gestalt therapy *and* something else, but Gestalt therapy in itself as a continually ongoing innovation and expansion in whatever direction is possible and with whatever means are available between therapist and patient in the actual therapeutic situation.

It is unfortunate that what has become very widely known and practiced as Gestalt therapy is only the method used by my late husband for demonstration workshops and films in the last three or four years of his life. The dramatization of dreams, identifying with and acting through every part of the dream, is an immensely impressive demonstration method, and Fritz Perls used it with a skill and sensitivity that was informed by 70 years of experience. Imitating his method as "the" therapeutic technique without full regard for the specific needs and limitations in the actual situation is superficial, simplistic, mechanical, manipulative, and inauthentic. A Gestalt therapist does not use techniques; he applies *himself in* and *to* a situation with whatever professional skill and life experience he has accumulated and integrated. There are as many styles as there are therapists and clients who discover themselves and each other and together invent their relationship.

In facilitating the awareness continuum, I find the experience and the concept of contact as the *boundary function* most useful, particularly in its application to education and child and family therapy. Contact is a boundary phenomenon between organism and environment. It is the acknowledgment of, and the coping with, the *other*, the not-me, the different, the strange. The boundary where I and the other meet is the locus of the ego functions of identification and alienation, the sphere of excitation, interest, concern, and curiosity, or of fear and hostility.

The *elasticity* of the boundary equals the awareness continuum. If there is no interference with the sensory and motoric functions, there is a ceaselessly ongoing exchange and growth on the boundary, the growing edge (as Carl Whitaker would call it), and a continuous expansion of the ground for communication.

A small child, before becoming socialized, lives on the boundary: looks at everything, touches everything, gets into everything. He discovers the world, expands his awareness and means of coping at his own pace: playfully serious or seriously playing, he makes an ongoingly creative adjustment to his own potential. We all know how in the usual upbringing of children the ongoing spontaneous development and growth are systematically interfered with: Don't do this, don't touch that, don't answer back, don't be a cry baby, pull yourself together, etc., etc. This results in *self-interference*, the muscular tensions and contractions which Wilhelm Reich recognized as the character armour, the fixed attitudes, habits, and principles that pervade our whole culture and confine and define the so-called *"normal,"* e.g. more or less obsessional, personality that is "well adjusted," lives rigidly and righteously by law and order, pride and prejudice, and remains ignorant of, hostile to, and isolated from anything and anyone beyond these fixed boundaries.

On the other hand, convention and conformity insist on a *confluent* attitude *within* the fixed boundaries, a taking for granted of sameness and agreement, of being *one*—a "we"-ness without the I and Thou—the acknowledgement of the other and oneself as separate individuals. This blurring and ignoring of boundaries apply not only to society at large and certain social, political, educational, and scientific or business organizations, but particularly to the interpersonal relationships in marriage and family. It is still largely taken for granted that husband and wife should be not only one flesh, but one mind and soul, they should have the same opinions, interests, involvements, friends. Differences are glossed over or ignored, and occasionally lead to a fight (where eventually they make *real contact*) in which the stronger partner usually asserts his (or her) superiority and restores the confluence. In confluence relationships the stronger partners have a greater chance to express their individuality. The weaker ones submit, hold back their disagreements and differences, and eventually become resentful and possibly spiteful, while the stronger partners become bored with the relationship, as no interesting stimulus or response can come from a partner who feels oppressed. Resentment and boredom are the very characteristics of the average marriage. Only when these couples are ready to split are the differences and recriminations finally expressed, often with great vindictiveness and violence.

The same difficulties apply, even to a greater extent, in the parent-child relationship. The embryo is *de facto* in complete organismic confluence with the mother. After birth, the infant breathes separately; but breathing is a primary automatism that the child remains unaware of. For nourishment and care the child remains confluent, e.g. experiences the mother and the caring environment not as separate but as an extension of himself. The contact functions like coping with solid food, orientation, and manipulation develop only slowly in accordance with the development of the cortex, the visual, tactual, and aural recognition of people and objects, the muscular co-ordination in handling objects and achieving upright posture and mobility.

On the other side, the *parents* tend to experience the child as an extension of themselves, the mother by maintaining the original confluence with the embryo and infant, both parents by investing in the child all their own unrealized desires, hopes and ambitions. The child "belongs" to the family; and belonging means to be owned, having no separate existence, but being confined within the same boundaries and, of course, also being protected by them as long as the child becomes and remains adjusted. But while animals stop nursing their young so that they will learn to find their own food; while birds push their young out of the nest so that they will fly; while Australian aborigines send their adolescent boys into the wilderness where they have to prove that they can survive on their own, we in our culture keep our children longer and longer dependent far beyond the age of actual physical and mental maturity and expect them to remain confluent with family, school, and social establishment. When we succeed, we produce the infantile hanger-on, the greedy introjector who swallows indiscriminately what is stuffed down his throat and who can't stand on his own feet. When we fail, we get the reaction formation, the spiteful brat who says "no" to everything, remains undernourished, and becomes progressively more alienated and isolated. But conforming or spite are both two sides of the same coin: dependence. True independence is possible only with the experience of separateness *and* the ability to make contact with what is different. Confluence (within the *same* boundary) or isolation (away from the boundary) are not contact which is *on* the boundary. "Good fences make good neighbors."

We talk about being or staying in contact, having erratic or indifferent contact, or being out of contact. Now contact is nothing one *has*, or *is* or *stays in* or *out* of. If we stay too long, we may end in confluence; if we withdraw too far, we end in isolation. It is not a state, but an activity with a certain rhythm of touching and letting go. We *make* contact by acknowledging and tackling the *other* and experiencing ourselves in doing so. It is a continuous shuttling or oscillating between *me* and the *other*, and no English or German or any other Caucasian language has an adequate word to describe it except the ancient Greek: *aisthesthai*—to be aware—is a medium form; grammatically it is passive, but it is used as an active verb. And, of course, full awareness implies the collaboration of all sensory and motoric functions.

Contact can be good and creative only to the extent that sufficient and adequate support for it is available. Any lack of essential support is experienced as anxiety. *Support* is everything that facilitates the ongoing assimilation and integration for a person, a relationship, or a society: primary physiology (like breathing and digestion), upright posture and coordination, sensitivity and mobility, language, habits and customs, social manners and relationships, and everything else that we have learned and experienced during our lifetime. In short, everything that we usually take for granted and rely on, even and particularly our hangups and resistances, the fixed ideas, ideals, and behavior patterns which have become second nature precisely because they were supportive at the time of their formation. When they have outlived their usefulness, they become blocks in the ongoing life process. We are stuck, in a bind, at an impasse.

In Gestalt therapy, we de-automatize these secondary automatisms by staying with the apparently insoluble conflict and exploring every available detail: the muscular tensions, the resulting desensitization, the rationalizations, the investment in the status quo, the introjections and projections, etc., etc. With increasing awareness and the concomitant insight, re-sensitization and re-mobilization *alternatives* become available and change becomes possible. The *impasse* turns into a *present problem* that we can cope with and take responsibility for here and now.

How we go about facilitating the awareness continuum and developing the support functions depends on what support we have in *ourselves* and on our awareness of what our client has available and what kind of support he is lacking. As I have said before, every Gestalt therapist develops his own style: I—with a background of music, eurythmics, modern dance, Eastern body approaches, and Eastern and Western existentialism, familiarity with several languages and their literature—work a lot with body awareness, with breathing, posture, coordination, continuity and fluidity in motion, with facial expression, gestures, voice. I work with speech patterns and the particular idiosyncratic uses of language. I work with dreams and fantasies to facilitate the identification with alienated or undeveloped parts of the personality. I'll quote from the Bible or Goethe, or tell a Zen story or a joke, if it will illuminate a dark corner in the patient's awareness. I'll work with a musician at his instrument and with a writer on his manuscript.

There are many more interesting and meaningful aspects of Gestalt therapy. Here and now I want to limit myself to the concepts and the experience of the awareness continuum, contact boundary, and support which—for me—form a coherent, very meaningful, strong Gestalt, the very essence of Gestalt therapy.

Biographical Sketches of the Contributors

PHILIP G. COOKER, Ph.D.

Philip Cooker is a counselor educator and Associate Professor at the University of Mississippi. He received the Doctor of Philosophy at the Florida State University in 1971. Work experience has been as a secondary school teacher, a counselor at elementary, junior high school and university settings, and a consultant in a program to establish programs of elementary school guidance and counseling in Florida and Georgia.

Current professional interests and activities include facilitating small group experiences for personal and professional growth and effectiveness, training peer group counselors to function in school drug education programs, and working with teachers and educators toward humanizing the learning process in schools.

BRUCE DERMAN, Ph.D.

Who am I according to the culture in which I live involves credentials (Ph.D. in 1967 from University of Georgia); jobs (Staff Psychologist at Olive View Outpatient Clinic and private practice, Gestalt-Reichian Therapy Center) and biographical data (separated, 34 years old, and one child). On a deeper level I am committed to my own self-healing and bringing together my life-style and professional work into a community type structure. As part of my effort to integrate and develop myself as a therapist, I have created three new approaches: multiple personality therapy, nothing therapy, and the Gestalt-thematic approach. My overall therapeutic orientation could be basically described as Gestalt-Reichian. However, philosophically I feel most confluent with Baba Ram Dass and Joel Kramer. In essence my life consists of freeing myself from all that I think I am and facing my fears of living life as an empty cup from moment to moment.

JAMES E. DUBLIN, Ph.D.

Dr. Dublin is Clinical Director, Choice, Inc., a private practice operation in Bloomington, Indiana, which specializes in Gestalt, bioenergetics, Reichian, and transactional psychotherapy. He is a member of the Board of Directors, South Central Indiana Mental Health Center, and a Clinical Consultant to The Center for Human Growth, a Bloomington training facility affiliated with the Indiana University Department of Counseling and Guidance, and to Exodus, a Bloomington Growth Center. Currently, he is president-elect of the Midwestern Region of the American Academy of Psychotherapists. He has authored some 18 articles in psychiatric, psychological and philosophical journals, and presently is authoring a book, tentatively titled *Bioexistential Therapy*. He lives with his wife and professional colleague, Elvie Wilson Dublin, Ph.D., and David and Toni, four horses, and two dogs, at their 15-acre, hand-carved homestead, Tall Oaks, Bloomington, Indiana.

JOEN FAGAN, Ph.D.

Joen Fagan is Professor of Psychology at Georgia State University and Co-director of Pine River Center, Inc., Atlanta, Georgia, which offers professional therapists training in the Gestalt approach. Her training in Gestalt therapy included several workshops with Fritz Perls, and also with Jim Simkin, Walt Kempler, and Erv Polster. She has led training workshops in Gestalt therapy around the United States and in England, Greece, and Japan.

Dr. Fagan's academic training was at the Pennsylvania State University, with her Ph.D. awarded in 1958. Her professional memberships include Fellow status in the American Psychological Association, a number of offices held in the American Academy of Psychotherapists, and a clinical diplomate from A.B.P.P.

Dr. Fagan is well known for her writings in the area of Gestalt therapy, including co-editing with Irma Lee Shepherd *Gestalt Therapy Now* in 1970 and editing and contributing to the 1974 issue of *The Counseling Psychologist* devoted to Gestalt therapy. She is on the editorial boards of several publishers and professional journals, including Science and Behavior Books, *Voices*, *Journal of Contemporary Psychotherapy*, and *Psychotherapy: Theory, Research and Practice*.

CHARLES GAGARIN

Charles Gagarin is a graduate of Yale University, class of 1972. He has just finished his first novel, a mystical tale called the *Circles Crossed,* and lives in Newport, Rhode Island.

For nine months, from 1970 to 1971, Mr. Gagarin lived at the Stillpoint Foundation, Los Gatos, California, where he studied the I Ching, Tai Chi, shiatsu massage, and became familiar with Taoist Gestalt therapy. He has also been to the Esalen Institute at Big Sur, California.

GEORGE B. GREAVES, Ph.D.

George Burton Greaves has been a frequent contributor to psychology and psychiatry journals since receiving his doctorate in psychology from Georgia State University in 1970. Following a year's post-doctoral work in clinical psychology at the Ohio State University College of Medicine, Dr. Greaves has been the director of a number of major programs and clinics, and is currently director of a community mental health center in Ohio. He is also the first non-medical staff consulting scientist of the major Holzer Medical Center, Department of Internal Medicine, in Gallipolis, Ohio. In a teaching or research capacity, Dr. Greaves has been affiliated with a number of colleges and universities including Georgia State, the Ohio State University College of Medicine, and the University of California Medical Center in San Francisco. He is best known for his research contributions in drug dependency and for his clinical treatment of psychophysiological disorders. The present article is a reflection of his background as a philosophy professor and his interest in "applied philosophy."

ROBERT A. HALL, M.D.

Born: May 7, 1920
M.D.: Albany Medical College, 1945
Psychiatric and Psychoanalytic Training, 1948-1954
Hospitals: Bellevue (N.Y.), Rockland State (N.Y.), Agnews State (Cal.)
School: Columbia University (N.Y.), Psychoanalytic Clinic for Training and Research
Private Psychiatric Practice: San Jose, Los Gatos, Saratoga (Cal.), 1955-1974
Diplomate American Board of Neurology and Psychiatry, 1955
Fellow American Psychiatric Association, 1959

Research (neurophysiological) at the Institute for Medical Research of Santa Clara County, 1962-1974 (most recently on evoked brain potential correlates of emotion and hyperkinesis). (*Science, 170*, 998, 1970; *180*, 212, 1973. *Psychophysiology, 10*, 52, 1973).

Clinical Assistant Professor of Psychiatry, Stanford University School of Medicine, 1966-1974

Publications: 15 scientific articles

Gestalt Therapy Background, 1972-1974

Training (260 hours): with Jim Simkin, Ph.D., Erv Polster, Ph.D., Miriam Polster, Ph.D., Jerry Greenwald, Ph.D., Cindy Sheldon, M.S.W., Dick Price, Ph.D.

Experience: Gestalt individual, family, and group work in private practice; leading many open weekend workshops; leading several Gestalt training workshops for health care professionals; giving course titled "Introduction to Gestalt" at West Valley College, Saratoga, California; teaching Gestalt therapy at the California School of Professional Psychology.

YORAM KAUFMANN, Ph.D.

1966: B.A. in psychology from Bar-Ilan University, Ramat-Gan, Israel.

1972: Ph.D. in clinical psychology, New York University.

1972: Graduate of the C. G. Jung Training Center, New York.

1972 to present: private practice; faculty member of the C. G. Jung Training Center, New York.

1973: Author-contributor to *Current Psychotherapies*, R. Corsini (Ed.), Itasca: F. E. Peacock, 1973.

SHELDON B. KOPP, Ph.D.

Dr. Kopp is a practicing psychotherapist and teacher of psychotherapy in Washington, D.C. His writing about this pilgrimage includes three books published by Science and Behavior Books, Inc. (Palo Alto, California). They are titled: *Guru: Metaphors from a Psychotherapist* (1971), *If You Meet the Buddha on the Road, Kill Him!!!!* The Pilgrimage of Psychotherapy Patients (1972), and *The Hanged Man: Psychotherapy and the Forces of Darkness* (1974).

He can also be heard discussing his ideas, his feelings, and his experiences on several series of cassettes produced by Instructional Dynamics, Inc. (Chicago).

DONALD D. LATHROP, M.D.

Donald D. Lathrop is a Jungian psychotherapist who uses groups as a primary tool for education, supervision, and therapy. He is at home with psychoanalytic theory, Gestalt, transactional analysis, and other contemporary expressions of expanding consciousness. He lives on the Pacific Ocean in Los Angeles with his son, James. He is editor and publisher of *The Psychotherapy Newsletter*, a non-denominational medium for personal exchange.

ABRAHAM LEVITSKY, Ph.D.

Dr. Levitsky received his Ph.D. in Clinical Psychology from the University of Michigan in 1955. He has held teaching positions at Brooklyn College, University of Michigan, and Washington University. For some years his therapeutic orientation was an amalgam of psychoanalysis, rational-emotive therapy and hypnotherapy. He published a number of papers on clinical and experimental hypnosis. He then had an opportunity for extensive training in Gestalt therapy with Frederick Perls and co-authored with him a paper on "The Rules and Games of Gestalt Therapy." At present he is in private practice in Berkeley and on the faculty of the San Francisco Gestalt Institute. A strong current interest is in the integration of psychoanalysis and Gestalt therapy.

DENIS O'DONOVAN, Ph.D.

My first contact was reading *Gestalt Therapy* in 1952. I mostly accepted many invitations to forget it in my army and graduate work (Ph.D., University of Florida, 1960). The one exception was the training I received from Henry Wunderlich. In 1958 I began working with the philosopher Charles Morris. Only now am I beginning to bring together Charles' Maitreyan integration of feeling, thinking, and acting with Gestalt.

In 1967 I met Fritz Perls. He came to a party I gave, sat down and ordered a chicken salad sandwich. In 1968 I was looking for a men's room, accidently opened a door and there he was pontificating. I lay down on the rug and half-listened to his reading from the manuscript of *Garbage*. To me at that moment he was communicating just exactly what repelled me, and his awareness excited me. From that moment until his death I got whatever I could from him, and I changed my life.

Laura's power I experienced one day in Wurzburg, Germany. I owe further debts to others in this book, which I repay by leading my own good life.

The chapter here is one of my Gestalt fables, which I am looking to publish. I am also working on a manuscript called *The Road to Now*, which contains a fuller story of my adventures with Fritz, Laura, and others.

LAURA PERLS, D.Sc.

D.Sc. in Psychology, 1932 (Frankfurt/Main).

1928-33, psychoanalytic training at the Frankfurt, Berlin and Amsterdam Psychoanalytic Institutes.

Private Practice (1933-73)
Johannesburg, South Africa, 1933-47
New York, 1947-73

Co-developer of Gestalt therapy and Co-founder of the New York Institute for Gestalt Therapy

Training workshops for professionals in the helping professions in New York and other places in the States, Canada and Europe

Publications in professional journals and collections of Gestalt papers (*Gestalt Therapy Now* and *Recognitions in Gestalt Therapy*. Colophon Books, Harper and Row.)

President, New York Institute for Gestalt Therapy.

IRMA LEE SHEPHERD, Ph.D.

Irma Lee Shepherd received her doctorate in psychology from Pennsylvania State University in 1958. She is currently Professor of Psychology at Georgia State University and Chairman of the Graduate Psychology Committee. She holds the diploma in Clinical Psychology from the American Board of Professional Psychology and is currently President of the American Academy of Psychotherapists. She received her training in Gestalt therapy from Fritz Perls and Jim Simkin and has co-led workshops with each. She has led workshops throughout the United States and in London, Mexico, Greece and Japan. With Joen Fagan, she co-edited *Gestalt Therapy Now* and continues professional training of psychotherapists through the Pine River Center in Atlanta.

Her work and her life continue open-ended and unpredicted.

EDWARD W. L. SMITH, Ph.D.

Dr. Smith was born in South Bend, Indiana, in 1942, and grew up in Iowa. After completing a B.A. in Psychology at Drake University in 1963, he attended the University of Kentucky as an N.D.E.A. Fellow in experimental psychology. In 1966 he completed his M.S. degree and continued study at the University of Kentucky until 1969 when he received his Ph.D. in Clinical Psychology. During his doctoral study he obtained clinical experience at the United States Public Health Service Hospital in Lexington, completed a V.A. Traineeship in clinical psychology at the Lexington and Louisville V.A. Hospitals, and worked as a counselor at the University of Kentucky Counseling and Testing Center. Since 1969 he has been at Georgia State University, where he is now an associate professor of psychology and associate director of the Laboratory for Psychological Services. During his time at Georgia State Dr. Smith has obtained post-doctoral ongoing training in Gestalt therapy with Drs. Fagan and Shepherd and workshop training in Gestalt therapy, bioenergetics, and psychomotor therapy with various trainers, including Vivian Guze, Albert Pesso, and Drs. Laura Perls and James Simkin. Dr. Smith lives in Atlanta with his wife Lynda and their daughter and son. His non-therapy interests include Tai Chi Chuan, Yoga, travel and friends.

JAMES A. STALLONE, Ph.D.

James A. Stallone, Ph.D. has studied and practiced Zen Buddhism, Gestalt psychotherapy, and Transcendental Meditation, in that order, over the past few years. He has participated in workshops/courses conducted by Alan Watts, Roshi Philip Kapleau, Laura Perls, Jack Downing and Maharishi Mahesh Yogi. Among his publications are "Yoga and Counseling Psychology" in *Psychic*, August 1970, and "Zen Buddhism and Gestalt Psychotherapy in America" delivered at the *International Congress of Orientalists*, Paris, July 1973. Dr. Stallone, his wife and two children live in Pennsylvania where he currently teaches educational psychology and counseling at Slippery Rock State College.

CHARLTON S. STANLEY, Ph.D.

Some of my past life roles have included being a teacher, school counselor, and high school principal. For several years in the late 1960's I worked in the St. Louis inner city with programs aimed at assisting unemployed persons in learning social and vocational skills so that they might enter the world of work. I received my doctorate from the University of Mississippi with a dissertation based on a study of the effects of encounter groups on interpersonal communication. My interest in groups goes back over twelve years, but my exposure to the work of Fritz Perls in 1966 had a profound influence on my thinking. Subsequently, I changed my whole approach to include the philosophy and concepts of Gestalt therapy.

At present I am a staff psychologist with the Mississippi State Hospital at Whitfield. Other activities include consulting and lecturing at the University of Mississippi Jackson Branch, and the Jackson State University. I also have a part-time private practice consisting mostly of conducting weekend encounter groups. My present work as a therapist is based on my concepts of Gestalt therapy and existential philosophy within the framework of dynamic interpersonal communication.

EDWARD C. WHITMONT, M.D.

Edward Whitmont is a graduate of the Medical School of the University of Vienna and first practiced internal and psychosomatic medicine in New York in 1941. After training in Jungian Analytical Psychology he began using those methods circa 1950. He has been active in the formation of the C.G. Jung Foundation and Training Center of New York. He is a training and supervising analyst as well as a board member of the Training Center. He initiated group and Gestalt methods into the Jungian analytic process.

He is the author of *The Symbolic Quest*, Putnam, and contributed the chapter on Jung in the *Comprehensive Textbook of Psychiatry* and *Current Psychotherapies*, as well as publishing many papers dealing with the psychoanalytic process in relation to religion, the magic dimension, the group and the individual. He lectures, teaches and holds workshops. At present another book on analytical psychology and changing religious archetypes is in progress.

Index

Aboutism, 17
Acceptance and self-acceptance, 119, 120
Accommodation, 154-159
  types of, 156
Act psychology, 20, 21, 23
Adler, A., 4, 6
Aha, 167, 169, 170
American functionalism, 23
Anger, 104, 105
Angyal, A., 29-31
Anxiety, 29
Association psychology, 5
Atkinson, 27
Avenarius, 20
Avoidance responses, 129
Awareness, 17, 43, 128, 138, 172, 175, 186,
  202, 204, 207, 208, 214, 221, 225

Barker, 27
Basic needs, 31
Behaviorism, 23, 24
Being with, 131, 132
Beisser, A., 33, 119
Benussi, 21
Berenson, B., 175
Berne, E., 6, 10, 41, 146
Binet, A., 23
Binswanger, L., 17, 131, 135, 136, 148
Blake, W., 92, 94
Blofield, J., 183, 191
Bogen, J. E., 59, 63
Boss, M., 131, 148
Boundary function, 223, 224
Bretano, 20, 21, 23
Brien, L., 166, 167
Broca, 59
Buber, M., 15, 16, 64, 143
Buddha, 183, 184, 204

Cantril, 27
Carkhuff, R. R., 110, 161-165, 175
Cassirer, E., 19
Ch'an Buddhism, 184
Cohn, R., 11, 19
Concentration therapy, 18, 128
Concrete-abstract dimension, 28
Confluence, 15, 45, 224, 225
Confucianism, 184
Content psychology, 20, 21, 23
Cooker, P. G., xv, 110, 160-178, 227
Cooperation/competition, 61
Core conditions of communication, 161-
  165, 176, 177
Cornelius, 21
Covert behavior, 167
Creative indifference, 5

Dasein, 17, 134-136, 138, 140, 141
Dass Baba Ram, 185
Deficit-surplus, 53-55
Deikman, A. J., 61
Dembo, 27
Derman, B., xv, 109, 151-159, 227
Deutsch, H., 4
Differential thinking, 5, 33
DeRopp, R., 182
Descartes, R., 135
Dewey, J., 23
Dublin, J. E., vii, viii, xv, 109, 124-149, 228

Eastern Religion, 4, 32-35
Ebbinghaus, 20
Ehrenfels, 21, 24
Eidetic imagery, 22
Ego, 103, 125, 127, 135, 136
Elasticity, 223
Empty chair, 42, 46, 174

Enactment, 93-98, 101
Evaluative function, 105, 106
Existential-Gestalt, 131-141
Existential philosophy, 3, 5, 15-18, 51, 124
Extraverted, 104

Fagan, J., xiv, 37, 58-68, 124, 144, 145, 204, 228
Federn, 4
Feelings, 104
Feldenkrais, 49
Feng-Fu-Gia, 214, 215, 217
Fenichel, O., 4, 6, 13
Ferenzi, 64
Festinger, 27
Figure-ground relationship, 22, 26, 28, 32
Forem, J., 204
Frankl, 17, 133, 135
French functionalism, 23
Freud, S., 4-7, 10, 13, 33, 35, 40, 59, 63, 64, 93, 103, 104, 106, 107, 125-128, 135, 146, 148
Friedlander, 4, 5, 33, 125
Fromm, E., 181, 186
Functionalism, 23, 24

Gagarin, C., xv, 179, 212-217, 229
Galin, D., 58-60
Games-ego states, 41, 51, 171
Gazzaniga, M. S., 60
Gelb, 26, 28, 32
Gestalt
  analytical psychology, 87-102
  approach, 43, 44, 47-51, 106, 107, 112, 151, 152
  communication facilitation, 161-177. See Core conditions of communication
  definition, 3, 87, 89, 221-226
  dreams, 148
  ego analysis, 126-129
  existential vs Perls-ism, 17, 125-149
  existential therapies, 131-141, 148, 165, 166
  experiential, 43, 51, 65, 66, 128-130, 132, 221
  functional essence, 129-131
  Gestaltqualität, 21
  historical background, 1-35
  hypnosis, 111-123
  meditation, 62
  Perlsian, 145-149
  Perls-ism, 124-149
  psychology, 3, 5, 18-32

right lobe therapy, 58-68
  style, 222
  split brain research, 60-64
  tantric Buddhism, 181-200
  tantrism, 182, 185, 191, 198, 199. See Spirituality and Tantric methods
  taoism, 33-35, 184, 213-217
  thematic approach, 151-159. See Theme and Method
  transcendental meditation, 202-210
  wholeness, 87, 103-107
  Zen, 181-200, 202-210. See Ch'an Buddhism
Goldstein, K., 26, 28-32, 64
Greaves, G. B., xv, 179, 181-200, 229
Group therapy, 98-100
  dreams, 100, 101, 223
  directed fantasy, 101

Hall, R., xiv, 37, 53-57, 229, 230
Harnick, 4
Hegel, G., 4, 5, 135
Heidegger, 135, 136
Heider, 27
Helper-healer, 69-71, 77, 80
Herbart, 19
Here and now, 17, 172, 174, 175, 185, 186, 202, 204, 221
Hering, 20, 21
Hesse, H., 4
Hirschman, 4
Holistic organismic concept, 5, 31, 32
Homme, L. E., 167
Horney, K., 4, 6, 7, 186
Hot seat, 58, 69, 138, 145, 174, 175, 209, 215
Hull, 25
Humanistic psychology, 31
Humphreys, C., 204
Hunger instinct, 5, 6
Husserl, E., 4, 20, 23, 134-136
Huxley, A., 4
Hypnosis
  fantasy production, 123
  hypnosis with Gestalt, 111-123
  hypnotic state, 46
  integration of, 111, 112
  should-ism, 120
  stay with it, 122

I-it, 16, 17, 132
I-thou, 16, 17
Infantile instinctual conflict, 8
Illusion of fusion, 13, 14

Insight learning, 25
Intraceptive, 116
Introjection, 15, 127-130, 138
Introverted, 104
Intuition, 105, 106

Jackson, 59
Jaensch, 22, 23
James, W., 23, 181, 184, 186, 187
Janov, 216
Jaspers, 135
Jones, W., 4
Judeo-Christian influence, 92, 93
Jung, C., xiv, 4, 6, 30, 40, 50, 64, 85-90,
    97-99, 103-107, 148, 186
Jungians, 50, 51, 86, 98
    unconscious objective, 87, 88, 91, 103,
        106, 107

Kaiser, H., 13, 14
Kant, I., 4, 18-20, 23
Kapleau, P., 183, 190, 204
Katz, 22, 23, 27
Karsten, 27
Kaufmann, Y., xiv, 86-102, 230
Kempler, W., 58
Kepner, E., 166, 167
Kierkegaard, S., 17, 134, 135, 149
Koans, 183, 188-190, 192-197, 205, 209
Koffka, K., 24, 26, 28
Kohler, W., 18, 24-26, 28, 32
Kopp, S., xiv, 37, 69-81, 104, 182, 230
Korzibski, 136
Kounin, J., 27
Kulpe, 20, 21, 24

Laing, R., 144
Landanner, 4
Lathrop, D. D., xiv, 86, 103-107, 231
Law of closure, 25
Law of effect, 25
Law of Pragnanz, 26
Lecky, P., 29-31
Levitsky, A., xv, 17, 109, 111-123, 231
Lewin, K., 18, 26-28, 30, 32
Linear psychology, 5
Lipps, 21
Lived-body, language, awareness, 135-137
Logotherapy, 17

Mach, 20, 21
Mantras-mandalas, 191, 198, 209

Marcel, 135, 136
Marx, K., 4, 5
Maslow, A., 29-31, 170, 176, 186
Ma-tsu, 184
May, R., 131, 132
Meares, A., 113
Meinong, 21
Merleau-Ponty, M., 135-137
Messer, 20, 21
Metaneeds, 31
Metaphysical deduction, 19
Method, 154-159
Mind-body dichotomy, 8
Mini-Satori, 167, 169, 170
Minkowski, E., 131, 135
Miura, I., 204
Mondo, 190, 192, 196, 197
Mood, 105
Moreno, 130
Morita, 182
Mudras, 191, 199
Muller, 20
Myers, 59

Naranjo, C., 17, 18, 58
Natorp, P., 19
Nebes, R. D., 60
Neurosis, 89, 90, 168-170, 186
New experience, 40. *See* Here and now
Nietzsche, F., 17
Norm, 88, 89, 223
Now, 39, 117, 127, 128, 138, 153, 163

O'Donovan, D., xiv, 37, 83, 84, 231, 232
Open-endedness, 39, 41, 51, 52
Organismic assimilation, 127
    theory, 28, 31
        equalization process, 29
        self-actualization, 29, 32
Organismic flow, 53-57
    impasse, 53, 56, 57
    schema, 54
    stages, 53-57
Ornstein, R. E., 58-60, 62
Ovsiankina, 28, 32

Paradox, 33, 34
Patterns, 104
Patterson, C. H., 161
Penfield, 59
Perceived motion, 24
Perceptual function, 105, 106

Perls, F., xi, xiv, xv, 1, 3-18, 28, 29, 31-35, 39-47, 49-51, 55-58, 64-66, 69, 85, 86, 97, 103, 105-107, 109, 111, 112, 117, 118, 121, 122, 124-131, 133, 135, 136, 138, 141-149, 151, 160, 161, 165, 168-170, 174, 176, 179, 187, 196, 203, 204, 207, 212-214, 222, 223
Perls, L., xv, 18, 64, 203, 219, 221-226, 232
Perls-ism, 124-149
Persona, 99
Personality study, 26, 27
Pesso, A., 46, 109, 154
Phenomenology, 20, 134, 135, 137, 138, 166, 167, 169
Phi phenomenon, 24
Polanyi, M., 192
Polster, M., xi, xiii-xvi
Progoff, I., 50
Projection, 15, 16, 127-130, 138, 166, 171, 226
Psychoanalysis, 3-6
Psychosomatic language, 8, 9
Psychomotor, 109

Rank, O., 6, 64
Rational emotive therapy, 50
Recreation, 146
Reich, W., 4, 6-13, 49, 64, 75, 128, 129, 136, 223
Reichian approach, 49
  character analysis, 3, 7-15
  content, 75
  theory of ego, 126
Relationships and applications, 170-177
Resistance, 120, 121
Resnick, R. W., 144
Response ability, 15
Resting state, 53, 54
Retroflection, 8, 15
Rickert, 20
Ricoeur, 136
Robeach, 27
Rogers, C. 6, 110, 160, 172, 173, 176, 186
Rolf, I., 42
Rolfing, 49, 222
Ross, N. W., 183
Rubin, 22, 23

Sanders, J. R., 58, 59
Sartre, J. P., 135, 141
Sasaki, R. F., 204
Satori, 35, 189, 190, 199, 204-207, 209
Scheler, 15

Schilder, 4
Schlosberg, H., 22, 23
Sears, 27
Secondary narcissism, 10
Sekiguchi, S., 204
Self-consistency, 30
Self-expansion, 30
  autonomy, 30
  homonomy, 30
Self-interference, 223
Self-realization, 85
Self-responsibility, 112
Self-suggestion, 115
Selver, C., 41, 49
Sensation, 105, 106
Sensory approach, 49
Sensory body processes, 93
Sensory input, 47
Sensory state, 46
Separateness, 44, 224, 225
Sex instinct, 5
Shadow, 99, 100
Shepherd, I. L., xiv, 12, 37, 39-52, 124, 144, 145, 204, 232
Shouldism, 17
Signs, 96, 97
Sinikin, J., 47
Skinner, B. F., 25
Smith, E. W. L., vii, viii-xiv, 1-35, 233
Smuts, J., 31, 32
Sperry, 59
Spirituality, 186, 187
Spitzer, R., 35
Stallone, J. A., xv, 179, 202-211, 233
Stanley, C. S., xv, 110, 160-178, 233, 234
Stevens, J., 144
Stone, A., 124, 145, 146
Straus, 135
Structuralism, 23, 24
Stumpf, 20, 21, 24
Sturm und Drang, 48
Sullivan, 6
Superordination, 21
Suzuki, D. T., 189, 190, 193, 204
Symbolic experiencing, 96-98
Symbols, 96, 97

Tantric methods, 188-199
Tao, 212, 214, 215
Theme, 152-154
Theory of resistances, 6-9
Thorndike, E. L., 25
Tillich, P., 15

Titchener, 20
Tobin, S., 14
Top-dog, 41, 56
Toxic. *See* Introjection
Transactional analysis, 50, 51, 98, 123
Transcendental meditation, 202-210
Transference, 91, 100, 106, 107, 131
Transposibility, 21
Trial-and-error, 25
Trickster, 71, 72, 77, 78, 80
Truax, C. B., 110
Tsu, C., 212, 213
Tubbs, W., 142
Twain, M., 4
Tzu, L., 73, 76, 212, 213

Under-dog, 91, 106, 127, 146, 168, 176, 188
Universal ambiguity, 30
Universal triad, 13, 14

Vaihinger, 4
Vernon, 22
Vogel, 59
Von Franz, M. L., 103, 105

Watson, 23, 24
Watts, A., 41, 183, 204
Watzlawick, P., 62, 63
Weil, A., 61, 62
Wertheimer, 18, 24, 26, 28, 32
What is, 17
Whitaker, C., 76, 223
Whitmont, E. C., xiv, 86, 87-102, 234
Windelband, 19, 20, 23
Witasek, 21
Wolberg, L., 113
Woodworth, R., 22, 23
Wulf, 26
Wundt, 20, 23

Yogi, Mahesh, Maharishi, 203-205
Yuan, Chang, Chung, 183, 188, 189

Zazen, 184, 190, 198, 207
Zeigarnik, 27, 28, 32
Zeigarnik effect, 27, 28
Zen, 33-35, 41, 43, 53, 62, 70, 76, 181-200, 202-210